THE GLOBALIZED GOVERNANCE OF FINANCE

Big banks are capable of wreaking havoc on the global economy, and governments have often felt powerless to stop them. Regulators have responded by developing coordinated programs to handle banks, insurers, broker dealers, shadow banks, and other businesses that can blow up in a crisis. This program began informally and undemocratically, and has developed into something much more organized, formalized and predictable, even though it has never been legally enforceable. David Zaring examines the realities of the current international financial system and concludes that in fact this is a well-ordered and functioning regulatory environment: the international financial system enjoys a substantial degree of compliance, and operates predictably and harmoniously. As a result, perhaps this could serve as a paradigm for future global governance. Zaring explores three aspects of international financial regulation that can inform global governance: harmonization through rules, cooperation on enforcement, and agreement on fundamental principles.

David Zaring is Professor in the Department of Legal Studies and Business Ethics at the Wharton School of the University of Pennsylvania. He writes at the intersection of financial regulation, international law, and domestic administration. He has written over fifty articles, including publications in the *Chicago*, *Cornell*, *Michigan*, *NYU*, and *Virginia* law reviews, and a number of international law journals.

The Globalized Governance of Finance

DAVID ZARING
University of Pennsylvania

CAMBRIDGE
UNIVERSITY PRESS

CAMBRIDGE
UNIVERSITY PRESS

University Printing House, Cambridge CB2 8BS, United Kingdom

One Liberty Plaza, 20th Floor, New York, NY 10006, USA

477 Williamstown Road, Port Melbourne, VIC 3207, Australia

314–321, 3rd Floor, Plot 3, Splendor Forum, Jasola District Centre, New Delhi – 110025, India

79 Anson Road, #06–04/06, Singapore 079906

Cambridge University Press is part of the University of Cambridge.

It furthers the University's mission by disseminating knowledge in the pursuit of education, learning, and research at the highest international levels of excellence.

www.cambridge.org
Information on this title: www.cambridge.org/9781108475518
DOI: 10.1017/9781108594295

First published 2020

A catalogue record for this publication is available from the British Library.

Library of Congress Cataloging-in-Publication Data
NAMES: Zaring, David, author.
TITLE: The globalized governance of finance / David Zaring, University of Pennsylvania.
DESCRIPTION: Cambridge, United Kingdom ; New York, NY : Cambridge University Press, 2019. | Includes bibliographical references and index.
IDENTIFIERS: LCCN 2019019732 | ISBN 9781108475518 (hardback : alk. paper)
SUBJECTS: LCSH: International finance – Government policy. | Financial institutions, International.
CLASSIFICATION: LCC HG3881 .Z37 2019 | DDC 332/.042–dc23
LC record available at https://lccn.loc.gov/2019019732

ISBN 978-1-108-47551-8 Hardback
ISBN 978-1-108-46859-6 Paperback

For Jacoba, Elias, and Phoebe

Contents

Acknowledgments *page* viii

1 A Transformative Forty Years 1

2 The Structure and Rules of the Globalized Governance of Finance 13

3 Banking, Global Oversight's Ne Plus Ultra 46

4 Securities Regulation: Cooperation Instead of Harmonization 62

5 Cooperation in Insurance: a Slow Start, but a Fast Present 83

6 The Other Networks of Financial Regulation 99

7 International Financial Regulation and International Law 122

8 International Financial Regulation and China 142

9 The Next Financial Crisis 151

Index 162

Acknowledgments

Writing a book takes a lot of support, and I have been lucky enough to get it from many people. I'm grateful to Michael Carnevale, Ipek Guney, Jenny Lin, Robert Teitelman, Lani Matsumiya, Elana Stern, Jane Trueper, Jayme Wiebold, and Sophia Yan for their assistance, to Chris Brummer, Stavros Gadinis, Abe Newman, Eliot Posner, and Pierre Verdier for their insights on various portions of the manuscript, and to Anne-Marie Slaughter for her support, pathbreaking scholarship, and vision. I'd also like to thank my family for their patience with me.

1

A Transformative Forty Years

We don't like publicity. We prefer, I might say, our hidden secret world of the supervisory continent.[1]

—Basel Committee on Banking Supervision Chairman Huib J. Muller (1993)

International bodies derive legitimacy, however, only from their membership. They have no ability to promulgate regulations with the force of law.[2]

—Securities and Exchange Commissioner Kathleen Casey (2010)

One of the great achievements of international relations in the past forty years has been the transformation of the regulation of financial institutions. Not so very long ago, there was no way for regulators or investors to know what financial institutions were doing when they started doing business across borders. Today an international process sets the most important rules under which any financial institution of any size operates. It is a story about a new form of global governance – the regulatory network – that has provided detailed, organized, and binding oversight over the wild and woolly financial markets without adhering to almost any of the traditional mechanisms of international or domestic governance. To create the institutions of international financial regulation, no treaties have been signed. There is no bureaucratic code overseeing things.

And yet banks, shadow banks, insurers, and investment companies are now governed globally. This global oversight enjoys respect, compliance, and an increasing degree of order at a time when nations like the United States have turned away from their free trade commitments and worked to reverse international efforts to police war criminals or stop climate change.

Not every effort to come up with standard rules for the oversight of our financial markets has proceeded at the same pace or enjoyed the same kind of success, but the contributions and changes are undeniable. Regulators have gotten together and agreed to do things in the same way, and they have figured out a way to make those agreements stick. The result is a new model of international governance, one that makes policy on the global level and that implements that policy locally.

Because of this governance, banks have to finance themselves more by selling shares to investors, and less by borrowing money from depositors. They can take on risk through leverage, but the global regime has limited the amount of permissible leverage. Insurance companies also face an internationally consistent set of capital requirements. Capital markets regulators have agreed on a program of mutual assistance that is designed to allow them to ferret out fraud, no matter in which part of the world it starts. The global anti-money laundering and counterterrorism finance regime has supersized compliance departments in financial firms across the world. The big lenders to the developing world – the World Bank and International Monetary Fund – have insisted that their client countries adopt common approaches to deposit insurance, derivatives regulation, the handling of bankrupt financial firms, and a host of other financial policies on which regulators have agreed to agree.

This book tells the story of a successful international cooperation, realized through consistent interaction by regulators with other regulators. It is an account of technocratic governance, but one that has matured into a form of supervision that follows a consistent process, that entertains feedback from the public, that stands for some bedrock values, and that has started to open itself up to input from poor nations as well as wealthy ones.

One might think that this story of progress would be threatened by the new economic and international policies of less globally minded elected leaders. America's current presidential administration has withdrawn from numerous formal and informal international commitments. It has evinced skepticism of trade deals, and upped the scrutiny of foreign investment in the United States for national security reasons.

But instead of reducing regulatory cooperation with foreign bureaucracies, even policymakers inclined to focus on American first have continued to embrace international financial coordination.

President Donald Trump's choice for the chairmanship of the Federal Reserve Board, Jerome Powell, has describe international regulatory cooperation as "essential."[3] Randal Quarles, Trump's choice for the Federal Reserve Board's vice chairman for financial supervision, has observed that "America's active participation in the Financial Stability Board," the network to which all of the other networks belong, "is important to our nation."[4] He has been so enamored of the organization that he successfully campaigned to be appointed as its chair.

The administration's Treasury Department has stated that it "generally supports efforts to finalize remaining elements of the international reforms at the Basel Committee," the global banking regulatory network.[5] The Treasury Secretary in 2017 issued a statement of support for the coordination of shareholder financing requirements for banks.[6] The chair of the government's commodities and derivatives regulator, Christopher Giancarlo, has urged his European counterparts to "realize the dreams of cross border regulatory coordination and make it a reality."[7]

Regulatory cooperation, as it turns out, is "sticky." Perhaps because it works, and perhaps because four decades of active regulatory cooperation has created momentum, the development of common standards for the financial markets has proven to be a hard habit to break. The regular consultation and promulgation of rules in consultation with foreign regulators has proven to be a stabilizer of policy across administrations in the United States, and between different countries with varying leaderships across the world.

This general support for international financial regulation may suggest that the process has managed to convince even relatively deregulatory financial supervisors of its value, or that these regulators recognize that the globalization of finance has left them with no choice but to participate in a global effort to oversee it. At a minimum, it appears that regulators have developed a taste for international financial regulation that is relatively stable across administrations.

The global governance of finance is not perfect. It has not always been transparent, and it has been developed by rich countries acting in concert, without much representation from anyone else. It is technocratic in a good sense, but also has been made at a far remove from the observation or participation by the man in the street.

Whatever its faults, it serves as an example of governance without law. The big multilateral treaties of the twentieth century – the United Nations charter, the Global Agreement on Tariffs and Trade, the World Trade Organization – look impossible to duplicate in the twenty-first century. If cross-border cooperation is to be sustained, it will have to be sustained in a different way. The global governance of financial regulation suggests a path forward to those who would deal with the increasingly global problems in a multinational way. This book shows how that process has developed and offers some lessons, both salutary and cautionary, for how it might be developed elsewhere in the future.

***

In 1974, the world had many internationally active financial firms but no set of international rules and no global regulator to police how they should operate outside of their home countries. A German bank could enter into foreign-exchange swaps with foreign institutions, receiving Deutschmarks in the morning in Frankfurt in exchange for the promise to pay dollars that it would deliver later that same day in New York, perhaps six hours later, without worrying about violating some international convention on foreign exchange. An Italian banker could finance the purchase of an American bank by borrowing from Italian banks he controlled, then paying back the loans with capital siphoned from the US bank, secure in the knowledge that there was no money-laundering treaty to hinder him, and no international organization to track the transactions and prosecute him.

Bank regulators in that year could not always see proliferating international connections, and events underscored the consequences of this lack of transparency. In 1973 and 1974, a mid-tier Cologne bank, Herstatt Bank, did engage in foreign-exchange trading, and suffered significant losses in volatile markets, particularly for the dollar, which had recently been freed to float on international markets. On June 26, 1974, German regulators swooped in at the end of the German business day and forced Herstatt into liquidation – before it could deliver dollars in New York in exchange for the Deutschmarks it had received before its seizure. The broken foreign exchange trades in New York were a consequence not just of the failure of the bank but also of the way German regulators took it over. The result was a systemic failure that rippled through the global economy, grinding foreign exchange markets all over the world to a halt. The perilous situation generated a term that describes the possibility that a trade may not settle that is still taught in finance classes, "Herstatt risk."

In 1972, Long Island-based Franklin National Bank, another medium-sized bank, was taken over by a shadowy Italian banker named Michele Sindona, who had ties to the Vatican Bank and Italian organized crime. Sindona too played in the forex markets, losing large sums. To pay for these losses, Sindona drained Franklin's capital, triggering a run by depositors in mid-1974 and forcing the bank to borrow from the Federal Reserve and, subsequently, from the Federal Deposit Insurance Corporation (FDIC) – at the time, an unprecedented step. US regulators, unable to see how the bank's foreign owner was deploying its assets, felt forced to take. Sindona was eventually convicted in the United States of fraud and extradited to Italy, where he died of cyanide poisoning in prison.

The dramatic collapse of these two banks forced regulators to address the accelerating globalization of finance. The effort that resulted has been so consequential that even the largest banks in the world have felt its effects, often in painful ways. In 2010, Jamie Dimon, the chief executive officer of JPMorgan Chase & Co., one of America's largest banks, characterized the work that began after the collapses of Herstatt and Franklin as "blatantly anti-American."[8] In 2016, Xavier Musca, the Deputy CEO of the major French bank Credit Agricole, protested, "We need to stop this process."[9]

However, others insist that the internationalization of financial oversight has been a boon to prosperity. Jean-Claude Trichet, the former head of the European Central Bank and a former governor of the Bank of France, contended that through regulatory internationalization, "we eliminate uncertainty in a large area, which is a major contribution in consolidating the global economy."[10]

This book tells the story of how we moved from a world in which there was no way for regulators or investors to grasp the risks that rogue financial institutions were taking abroad to one in which international processes govern the most important rules under which financial institutions of any size operate. It is a tale about the creation and evolution of a new form of global governance –

the regulatory network – that has provided detailed, organized, and binding governance without adhering to the traditional mechanisms of international or administrative law. The centrality of the regulatory network in setting policy for today's global financial sector raises a question: Is this a form of governance that could or should be pursued elsewhere, instead of more traditional steps such as concluding treaties between nations and establishing tribunals? The rise of the regulatory network poses a traditional problem for lawmakers of legitimacy and accountability that is exacerbated by regulators' informal and technocratic approaches to dealing with problems that cross borders.

Much of what has taken place in international financial regulation began as an effort to solve problems of coordination that appeared to be intractable under international law. In 1947, with the world still recovering from World War II, twenty-three largely Western countries entered into the first multilateral trade deal, the General Agreement on Tariffs and Trade, and created the first two global international financial institutions, the World Bank and the International Monetary Fund. But these nations found it impossible to make progress on the creation of an international financial organization, and abandoned a modest effort to do so.

There is still no international financial organization or broad multilateral treaty that outlines how financial firms should be treated when they do business abroad. But there is a great deal of international financial regulation. Today, the networked institutions of international financial regulation continue to promulgate a dizzying array of standards, agreements, best practices, principles, and rules. Intertwined with these substantive efforts to coordinate the global regulation of finance has been the attempt to improve procedures followed by the coordinators. As this regulatory network has become established as the principal mechanism for coordinating global financial regulation, it has imposed procedural regularity and political oversight on a process that previously had neither.

The evolution, both procedural and substantive, of this regulatory network makes for a compelling story about the growth of a global regulatory enterprise with few peers. Traditional efforts to deal with cross-border externalities of finance, which were limited in their ambitions and range, have been cast aside. In their place, a new order has emerged over more than half a century that is hierarchical, procedurally regular, and politically supervised.

The emergence of this "legalish" system of global financial oversight is shaping up to be one of the principal accomplishments of modern international governance – one that has developed through regulation and regulatory cooperation rather than through more traditional mechanisms of public international law. But while regulatory cooperation involves a negotiated sort of informality that lawyers might easily dismiss as insufficiently law-like, the way cooperation has evolved, as this book chronicles, suggests something quite different.

Political supervision, increasingly regularized output, and bureaucratic order are familiar phenomena to students of the modern state. They are the fundaments of regulatory practice. International financial regulation works like an administrative agency stretched onto a global multilateral context.

This "agencification" of international financial regulation offers an alternative to traditional public international law. It creates a two-step process for legal obligation. The international context of financial regulation – the networks of regulators where policy is made – is the first step. It creates no binding obligations; those obligations come, if at all, after the international process has ended and financial regulators have returned to their home countries to complete the second step, which is making domestic administrative rules into binding law.

This hardly makes the first, international part of international financial regulation superfluous. In fact, the first step in international financial regulation is the most interesting. It is the source of the principles of international financial regulation. It is growing and developing in its own right. And it has added hierarchy, structure, and distributional consequence since the financial crisis of 2008.

Post-crisis financial regulation has resulted in institutionalization along hierarchical lines, with a political overseer, a regulatory supervisor, and a group of task-specific but increasingly coordinated regulatory networks making the rules for banks, capital markets participants, insurers, and other financial intermediaries. What those regulators do, moreover, is both procedurally regular and increasingly based on a few organizing principles that mimic fundamental principles espoused by hard-law international organizations, such as the standard that foreign businesses should be treated in the same way that domestic businesses are treated.

The transformation of international financial regulation has not only entailed the imposition of procedural regularity, bureaucratization, and a degree of political oversight. It has also created an increasingly tractable and definable enterprise, at least if defined through a legal lens.

In conjunction with these post-crisis reforms, there is emerging an identifiable commitment to a variety of legal principles that undergird particular decisions made by international financial regulators. At least six principles can be identified in the organization and institutionalization of the post-crisis financial regulatory settlement. Although many of these principles are rooted in the cooperation that existed before the financial crisis, the flurry of activity after the crisis accentuated them.

The legal principles include a commitment to *national treatment*, meaning that domestic and foreign financial intermediaries should be subject to roughly similar rules, and a *most-favored nation* (MFN) principle identifiable through the consensus practices of regulatory organizations that govern the myriad forms of finance. These principles are institutionalized through *rulemaking*, rather than adjudication – international financial regulation sets its standards in advance, without the assistance of a tribunal. Those standards are administered with adherence to a principle of *subsidiarity*, whereby each agency engaged in the global financial regulatory architecture is charged with implementing the rules and standards agreed to internationally in its own domestic jurisdiction, without international direction. That subsidiarity is paired with a *peer-review* process meant to check implementation decisions of member agencies in lieu of a third-party dispute resolution, such as that offered by an international tribunal.

All of this evinces an approach that prefers the commitment of the institutional form of the *network* over all others – a final, discernible legal principle that governs and characterizes international financial regulation. Anne-Marie Slaughter has said that networks are "really any collection of people or things that are linked together on an ongoing basis."[11] In financial regulation, networks are comprised of agencies, are not disciplined or authorized by governmental treaties, and meet informally and regularly to handle problems posed by globalization in their task-specific issue areas. But they are not creatures of formal public international law. Any effort to create a more formal treaty-based organization to ensure that financial regulation is accomplished globally and consistently has so far been eschewed in favor of an increasingly elaborate network. Global financial regulation, while idiosyncratic, has become a form of the rule of law. The problem for lawyers – and this is a problem that has long characterized all sorts of international law – is that the rule of law embodied by global financial regulation has few of the formal characteristics of the rule of domestic law, ranging from promulgation to enforcement.

In other ways, of course, the bedrock principles espoused by the increasingly global outlook of agencies involved in international financial regulation are unique. It is useful to think of the transformation of financial regulation from something domestic to something international; from something devised by supervisors and central bankers of individual countries in isolation to something designed in coordination through a multinational and institutionalized process of network regulation; from something created by backroom deals to something created in the way that law is created, through the orderly promulgation of rules through a recognized process. Moreover, this soft law may be more effective than many hard-law instruments, making it particularly interesting to compare it to formal international law.

Some analysts – certain sorts of realists, for example, or those persuaded that international law is rooted exclusively in state interaction sanctioned by treaty or custom – may question the utility of this soft law. These skeptics compare global financial regulation to trade law, another central form of economic regulation on the global stage, and find it wanting. After all, trade law features a treaty, a court, the offices of foreign and trade ministries, and it is undoubtedly as binding as international law gets. More to the point, it appears to enjoy a substantial degree of compliance. By offering a process of dispute resolution, the broad principles of trade law (principles that are not unfamiliar to financial regulators, as we shall see) can be applied to specific contexts, such as whether Japan or Korea can tax shochu differently than vodka or gin without violating the national-treatment principle, or whether a Canadian automobile production and import agreement that privileged incumbent car manufacturers discriminated in favor of those manufacturers' countries of origin in violation of trade's MFN principle.

Global financial regulation is largely incapable of rendering such fine-grained legal pronouncements, though occasionally it does get quite detailed. Moreover, soft law is not international law as Section 38 of the statute creating the International Court of Justice (ICJ) – the paradigmatic definition of public international law – defines it.[12]

It is, however, a form of law that occupies many lawyers' time and attention – perhaps there are even more international banking lawyers than there are lawyers who practice "hard" trade law – and financial regulation exemplifies this sort of soft law. It would not surprise some of the thousands of lawyers engaged in global financial regulation that the work they are doing has something to do with their professional qualifications. Those lawyers include private-sector luminaries such as Rodgin Cohen, the former chairman of white-shoe law firm Sullivan & Cromwell, who has weighed in on Basel's international capital adequacy rules in the pages of *Bloomberg Businessweek* and CNBC, as well as on behalf of his clients. As for public-sector lawyers, Christopher Cox, when he chaired the Securities and Exchange Commission, said that international work "easily comprises over half of my time and responsibilities."[13]

All of this amounts to soft law that nonetheless meets a standard definition of what international economic law is supposed to do. The Restatement (Third) of International Law provides that:

> The law of international economic relations in its broadest sense includes all the international law and international agreements governing economic transactions that cross state boundaries or that otherwise have implication for more than one state, such as those involving the movement of . . . funds.[14]

International financial regulation, with no assistance from treaties, has provided the rules for the movement of funds that have implications for more than one state. It is a crucial variant of the "law of international economic relations" of which the Restatement speaks, without being the sort of law that the other parts of the Restatement are supposed to define and govern.

That apparent contradiction lies in this fact: international financial regulation makes no pretense to be law. As Peter Cooke, the regulator perhaps most responsible for the work of the committee has said, rather representatively, "[T]he Committee does not possess any formal supranational supervisory authority. Its conclusions do not have, and were never intended to have, legal force."[15]

Some have observed that the sort of network, soft-law governance offered by international financial regulation might present international lawmakers with a choice to regulate informally or to pursue a legal regime governed by the formal strictures.[16] The legal scholar Kal Raustiala has predicted that this alternative might present a challenge to public international law that could "reduce relative importance or 'share' of cooperative activity governed by treaties."[17] Others have agreed.[18]

But sometimes alternatives, at least in legal regulation, are not as different as they might otherwise seem. We can learn from the similarities between putatively different international financial regulation and public international law. In three distinctive ways – in its reliance on debate and negotiation for principles, in its purpose as a coordinative exercise, and in its reliance on domestic institutions for legal enforcement – international financial regulation shows how cross-border legal systems can work.

Reflecting on these points of comparison also offers some insights about international financial regulation. Much scholarship on international financial regulation, and on the networks that are part of it, has correctly focused on differences posed by the phenomenon. Georgetown's Chris Brummer characterizes international financial regulation as a return to, and even a triumph of soft law and coincidence of interest.[19] Raustiala, as we have observed, thought the network-style governance epitomized by finance would pose an alternative to traditional legal rules.[20] Those differences are critical; it is those, in many ways, that make the subject worth studying. But the distinctions should not obscure the ways international financial regulation works like the governance system perceived to be its alternative. Instead, international financial regulation shows that international governance, because of its horizontality, its tastes for consensus and decentralization, and other reasons, can look much the same whether it is conducted through treaty, custom, or other, less formal, mechanisms.

This book investigates the questions posed by the transformation of international financial regulation. Chapter 2 focuses on the emerging architecture of international financial regulation. What we have seen in financial regulation is an effort to place a political institution at the top of the regulatory pyramid, a managerial institution in the middle, and use those institutions as organizers of various networks of regulators that provide content and perform rulemaking and policymaking at the bottom. The chapter explores the nuances of this process, and provides the evidence to support the claim about the way the process works.

Chapters 3 through 6 analyze a variety of the networks that comprise the fundamental policymaking institutions of international financial regulation. Chapter 3 focuses on the Basel Committee on Banking Supervision and shows how this network, the most important of the financial regulators, has managed to implement a series of very specific rules on bank capital around the world. Chapter 4 analyzes the International Organization of Securities Commissions (IOSC), placing its efforts to enhance the enforcement capacity of its members into perspective and analyzing its signature achievement, its Multilateral Memorandum of Understanding on enforcement cooperation. Chapter 5 tackles the International Association of Insurance Supervisors (IAIS). It examines this least developed of the regulatory networks and the way it has changed in the wake of the financial crisis. In particular, the network has attempted to develop solvency rules for insurers that mark an international effort on an issue that has never been thought of as an important component of global financial stability by domestic regulators. The financial crisis changed that calculus.

Although the three networks concerned with banking, securities, and insurance regulation are often thought to be the most important in international financial regulation, it is fascinating to see how institutionalized this form of policymaking has become. Chapter 6 accordingly looks at the other financial regulatory networks, the often-overlooked deposit insurers, counterterrorism finance regulators, and others, that also play a role in efforts to institutionalize governance on this subject area.

Chapter 7 considers lessons that can be learned from the evolution and transformation of international financial regulation for international law. It argues that there are similarities between the two sorts of governance, which suggests that international law is not so different from the international arrangements that are the subject of this book. As it turns out, informal arrangements require policing by expert lawyers and regulators in the same way that more formal treaty organizations do. Sometimes international lawyers argue that what they are doing is different from other international arrangements. But really, any sort of international institution, even one formed without a treaty, can attain the sort of formality that international law often claims. By the same token, international law frequently depends on the sort of cooperation offered by domestic regulators that characterizes regulatory cooperation in global finance.

Chapter 8 considers what this increasingly elaborated global regime means for one of the countries who did not get a chance to participate in its founding. China is now very much part of the regime of international financial regulation, and is an important, if young, player in global finance. But it has come to financial regulation late – and yet it has embraced the prescriptions, at least in word, and partly in deed. It will be considered as an example of how the developing world might think through the adoption of the requirements of the developed world.

Chapter 9 concludes by considering the implications for the next financial crisis of the currently constituted system of international financial regulation.

International financial regulation features a set of institutions that increasingly perform all the functions of legal systems, even while declaiming legal authority. This makes their development important, not just to international policymakers, but to anyone interested in the often-fuzzy border between a legal system and less obviously enforceable norms and obligations. International financial regulation is essentially a nonlegal institution with bedrock principles that resemble legal principles and enforcement mechanisms that succeed in actually enforcing. In that sense, the account here differs from those of scholars who have questioned the extent to which regulatory networks have managed to achieve their ends, and the nature of the legal obligations created by the institutions. The law-like account undertaken in this volume differs from those that emphasize the importance of politics and that are more skeptical of the promise of international cooperation more generally, which, as it turns out, constitutes most of the scholarly literature.

Notes

1 Huib J. Muller, Address to International Conference of Bank Supervisors (May 16, 1988), *quoted in* Tony Porter, States, Markets, and Regimes in Global Finance 66 (1993).

2 www.sec.gov/news/speech/2010/spch061210klc.htm.

3 Michelle Price & Pete Schroeder, *Top U.S. Regulators Confident Watchdogs Can Ease Volcker Rule*, Reuters, Oct. 3, 2017, www.reuters.com/article/us-summit-regulation-volcker/top-u-s-regulators-confident-watchdogs-can-ease-volcker-rule-idUSKCN1C81M1.

4 Randal K. Quarles, Speech, *America's Vital Interest in Global Efforts to Promote Financial Stability*, Utah Bankers Association June 27, 2018, https://home.treasury.gov/news/press-releases/sm0232.

5 Treasury Dep't, *A Financial System That Creates Economic Opportunities*, June, 2017, www.treasury.gov/press-center/press-releases/Documents/A%20Financial%20System.pdf at 16.

6 Quarles, *supra* note 4.

7 J. Christopher Giancarlo, Speech, *Remarks*, Eurofi Financial Forum, Sep. 6, 2018 http://business.cch.com/srd/RemarksbyChairmanJChristopherGiancarloattheEurofiFinancialForum.pdf.

8 *JPMorgan CEO Says Bank Rules "Anti-American,"* Reuters, Sep. 12, 2011 www.reuters.com/article/us-banks-basel-jpmorgan-idUSTRE78A3Z420110912.

9 *Enough Is Enough, Basel Committee Told*, Fin. Trib., Sep. 16, 2016, https://financialtribune.com/articles/world-economy/49918/enough-is-enough-basel-committee-told.

10 *Trichet Says Basel III Won't Hurt World Economy*, Reuters, Sep. 13, 2010, www.reuters.com/article/us-basel-trichet/trichet-says-basel-iii-wont-hurt-world-economy-idUSTRE68C2BJ20100913.

11 www.slate.com/articles/news_and_politics/interrogation/2017/04/anne_marie_slaughter_on_her_new_book_about_networks.html.

12 Article 38(1) of the Statute of the International Court of Justice (ICJ) provides,

> 1. The Court, whose function is to decide in accordance with international law such disputes as are submitted to it, shall apply:
>   a. international conventions, whether general or particular, establishing rules expressly recognized by the contesting states;
>   b. international custom, as evidence of a general practice accepted as law;
>   c. the general principles of law recognized by civilized nations;
>   d. subject to the provisions of Article 59, judicial decisions and the teachings of the most highly qualified publicists of the various nations, as subsidiary means for the determination of rules of law.

Statute of the International Court of Justice, art. 38(1), 1947 I.C.J. Acts & Docs, available at http://tinyurl.com/npvuez. The article is often taken as a statement of the usual sources of international law. For a discussion of how Article 38(1) interacts with one variant of international economic law, see David Palmeter & Petros C. Mavroidis, *The WTO Legal System: Sources of Law*, 92 AM. J. INT'L L. 398, 398–401 (1998).

13 Christopher Cox, Chairman, U.S. Sec. & Exch. Comm'n, Address to the American Institute of Certified Public Accountants' International Issues Conference: International Business – An SEC Perspective (Jan. 10, 2008), *available at* http://tinyurl.com/740mldd.

14 RESTATEMENT (THIRD) OF FOREIGN RELATIONS LAW OF THE UNITED STATES Part VIII, intro. note (1987).

15 Peter Cooke, Chair of the Basel Committee, *quoted in* JOSEPH JUDE NORTON, DEVISING INTERNATIONAL BANK SUPERVISORY STANDARDS 177 (1995).

16 *See, e.g.*, Andrew T. Guzman, *The Design of International Agreements*, 16 EUR. J. INT'L L. 579, 612 (2005) (nothing that "the choice of form (i.e., treaty v. soft law) can be traded off against the substance of an agreement").

17 Kal Raustiala, *The Architecture of International Cooperation: Transgovernmental Networks and the Future of International Law*, 43 VA. J. INT'L L. 1, 88 (2002).

18 *See, e.g.*, Kenneth W. Abbott & Duncan Snidal, *Hard and Soft Law in International Governance*, 54 INT'L ORG. 421, 434–50 (2000); Richard L. Williamson, Jr., *Hard Law, Soft Law, and Non-Law in Multilateral Arms Control: Some Compliance Hypotheses*, 4 CHI. J. OF INT'L L. 59, 63 (2003). For a further discussion, see Gary E. Marchant et al., *International Governance of Autonomous Military Robots*, 12 COLUM. SCI. & TECH. L. REV. 272, 315 (2011).

19 CHRIS BRUMMER, SOFT LAW AND THE GLOBAL FINANCIAL SYSTEM: RULE MAKING IN THE 21ST CENTURY (2011).

20 Kal Raustiala, *Rethinking the Sovereignty Debate in International Economic Law*, 6 J. INT'L. ECON. L. 841 (2003).

2

The Structure and Rules of the Globalized Governance of Finance

2.1 THE INSTITUTIONS OF FINANCIAL GOVERNANCE

Before the 2008–09 financial crisis, financial regulation was a task-specific matter pursued by aggregations of domestic regulators, with very little political oversight and a degree of siloing that limited the amount of comprehensive international policymaking that could be done. Before 1974, international regulators almost never cooperated, with central bankers being a principal exception. Even central bank cooperation was largely limited to monetary policy, although there were some cross-border efforts, both public and private, to stem the bank runs and financial panics that regularly afflicted nineteenth and early twentieth century banks.[1] Triggered by international crises that started, much to the surprise of domestic overseers, by failures of Bank Herstatt and the Franklin National Bank, two modestly sized banks, German and American, financial regulation engaged in progressively more cross-border coordination, albeit along relatively narrow lines. Domestic bank regulators began to talk more to their foreign counterparts, as did capital-markets regulators, and eventually insurance regulators.

But banking, insurance, and securities regulators spent little time talking to one another. Perhaps as a result of task-specific siloing, the outcomes of international interactions, loosely formalized in networks of regulators who met regularly and tried to develop metrics of cooperation and common approaches to oversight, varied depending on the industry. International bank regulation proceeded at a relatively quick pace, international regulation of capital markets at a more moderate pace, and international regulation of insurers at a very slow pace indeed. After the financial crisis, there was an effort, roughly parallel to the United States' 2010 Dodd-Frank Wall Street Reform Act's insistence on coordinated supervision, to coordinate efforts of previously siloed networks of regulators, and to monitor them with more politically accountable actors such as the G20.[2]

Before the financial crisis, siloing remained the standard practice of these task- and issue-specific regulators. Each network proceeded at its own pace and usually with only a limited amount of interaction with its counterparts, which contributed to the variance in the constraints they managed to impose on the global financial system. A particularly undeveloped example of this sort of pre-crisis coordination can be found in insurance. Insurance regulatory harmonization taking place under the auspices of the IAIS has proceeded at least until recently, very slowly; it essentially ceased after promulgation of the core principles designed to ensure a rough band of regulatory coordination among members of the network and a memorandum on enforcement cooperation, until after the financial crisis.

Despite the varying speeds of network-rule harmonization, the world's financial institutions and markets in which they operate have continued to integrate, whatever the state of their regulatory compatibility. Financial intermediaries operate across borders all the time, and cross-border conflicts created by financial failures have attested to problems of local supervision of what have quite clearly become global enterprises. Georgetown's Chris Brummer has described the ensuing dynamic as nothing less than a global market for financial law.[3]

As international coordination began, it relied on market leaders and individual networks to solve globalization problems that confronted bank supervisors, capital markets overseers, insurance supervisors, and other traditional financial regulators on a problem-driven schedule. That is, specific cross-border problems or crises would present themselves, and the regulators responsible for the area would gather with their foreign counterparts, and try to solve it.

For example, after the 1974 bank failures, the first project of the Basel Committee on Banking Supervision was to figure out a way that regulators could divide supervisory responsibilities over banks doing business in multiple jurisdictions. The SEC in the USA pushed the International Organization of Securities Commissions (IOSCO) to agree to cooperate on cross-border enforcement when it realized that many of its most significant securities fraud matters included an international component. The process was technocratically, rather than politically, driven and, as a matter of international law, there was no effort to codify the efforts through a treaty, and no doubt that whatever came out of the networks was "soft" law that derived its legitimacy from domestic enforcement processes and implementation by member regulators.

These aspects of regulatory networks have changed in the wake of the financial crisis. In the aftermath of that signature event, the various and divergent efforts of regulators have been coordinated much more carefully. The siloed and task-specific approach has been transformed into a still-disaggregated, and still-networked, but more deeply interlinked regulatory system.

For banks, and for financial regulators, there are three critical players. First, the G20 has begun to provide a degree of political oversight to the process.[4] Second, the Financial Stability Board (FSB) has been created by the G20 as a "network of networks," which coordinates and encourages the work of the networks under it, takes a global approach to financial sector regulation, and is meant to serve as an early warning system for financial instability. Third, reinvigorated, remodeled, and expanded task-specific networks – exemplified by the Basel Committee on Banking Supervision – have been charged with promulgating the most significant and onerous reforms of the financial system in the wake of the crisis. The Basel Committee is the preeminent example of a formerly siloed regulatory network; its relationship with its new overseers, and its redoubled efforts, demonstrates how those other networks, including IOSCO, IAIS, and the other financial regulatory networks have been given new marching orders.

The interlocking parts of regulatory governance amount to a form of administration. It represents the "agencification" of a previously informal and diverse regulatory process, replete with a degree of political oversight, a bureaucratic middle, and a bottom that has adopted many of the trappings of administrative law to get the work done.

These organizations – the G20, the FSB, and networks like Basel, IOSCO, and IAIS – all play different roles in the post-crisis global regulatory architecture, but they are each sources of policy that domestic regulators are meant to apply to their own financial institutions. They offer only some of the procedural safeguards that constrain domestic policymaking; indeed, it is fair to say that each institution was created with almost no attention to the regulatory process at all. As these fora have evolved to embrace more regulatory responsibilities in the wake of the financial crisis, some procedural safeguards have followed, if only as a voluntary, and in some cases warily embraced, phenomenon.

A second common, if not universal, theme, which runs from leader (the G20) to supervisor (the FSB) to policymaker (the Basel Committee), is exclusivity. Networks like IOSCO and IAIS are less exclusive, but put policymaking responsibility on special committees of regulators from well-heeled jurisdictions. Basel and many of the lesser-known financial regulatory networks are staffed with citizens of the wealthiest countries, with some allowance made for representatives from the developing world, but not too many of them. In addition to the BRIC (Brazil, Russia, India, and China) countries, South Africa, Saudi Arabia, Indonesia, Turkey, Argentina, and Mexico regularly send representatives to the organization.

The G20. The G20 plays its role in the new financial regulatory architecture through regular meetings of heads of state and financial ministers of the twenty invited members. G20 member nations include the world's most important economies and some large additional ones. At the conclusion of these meetings, communiqués are issued and ways forward are mooted. The G20 has grown out of the smaller, and still extant, Western head-of-state meetings that began in the 1970s, the G6, and G7. These organizations developed a reputation as talking shops, and indeed, were founded in part as get-to-know-you affairs for important anti-communist world leaders.

The G20 was created to respond to financial crises; its first meeting in 1999 was designed to address a series of debt crises in Latin America and Asia. After the turn of the century, however, it focused on growth and development best practices, rather than on crisis policymaking. In the midst of the financial crisis, however, the G20 provided much of the leadership for the global response, such as it was. At head-of-state summits in Pittsburgh and London in 2009, the G20 agreed that it would make a priority of the international regulatory coordinative process.

In those meetings, the G20 mandated the creation of the FSB, a network of networks designed to coordinate international financial regulation. It also set an agenda for the board and the underlying networks regarding reform of the financial regulatory system. The G20 directed financial regulators to increase capital requirements for banks, to create a more centralized process for derivatives trading, to explore ways to "resolve" (that is, quickly fail and recapitalize) insolvent banks, and to look into ways that executive compensation at these institutions incentivized risk.

Because of these directives, the G20 appears to have taken on an important role in setting the agenda for post-crisis financial regulation, although, since its summits are purely political and somewhat secretive events, some of that can only be gleaned through surmise. Nonetheless, what the institution does say is instructive. The G20 has followed up on the progress made on the agenda it has set by commenting on progress reports from financial regulators at subsequent meetings. Indeed, financial regulatory reforms, in addition to macroeconomic surveillance, global warming, and anger over offshore tax havens have comprised the bulk of the G20's stated agenda.

The result is that financial regulation has a political overseer, and, as the top of the increasingly elaborate post-crisis pyramid of international regulation, it is a unique example of political oversight in international governance. Created without any bow to legal legitimacy, the G20 is perhaps best described as a modern day Concert of Europe – a congress of the important nations. It includes, as the old Concert of Europe did, not only democratically elected leaders, but representatives from important, though hardly free countries, such as Russia, Saudi Arabia, and China. Other international legal organizations, born from treaties and subject to intensive organization, do not resemble it. The political inputs provided by the G20 are not cabined or authorized by an authoritative international agreement, and although it adds an element of democratic (or, at least, head of state/political) legitimacy to financial regulation, its exclusivity calls that legitimacy into question in other ways.

The G20 does not make its internal deliberations known. It does, however, issue regular communiqués after meetings, which make for some pretty dry reading. Affidavits declaring that the politicians are still on the case and interested in financial regulation projects would be, if taken too seriously, a somewhat naïve exercise in the commitment to disclosure of high level economic diplomats. Moreover, it is often not possible to know whether the communiqués reflect real agreement within the political meetings, or some more palliative exercises in modest hopefulness. For example, the 2018 communiqué issued after the finance ministerial in Argentina welcomed the "finalisation of Basel III['s]" capital accords, an endorsement. It also indicated that the G20 "look[ed] forward to the FSB-led evaluation of the reforms, including their effects on the financing of infrastructure investment and on incentives for central clearing of over-the-counter derivatives" – the latter an assignment. But it also included a commitment "to the full, timely and consistent implementation and finalisation of the reforms and their evaluation to help identify and address any material unintended consequences and ensure that the reforms accomplish their objectives," a platitude.[5]

Nonetheless, as a process matter, the G20 is evolving. Although the areas of potential international coordination contain multitudes, the G20 has focused on a few issue areas in particular. In its post-crisis meetings, the G20 has regularly considered risks to the financial system, and has focused on global growth, with at least lip service towards making that growth inclusive (in particular, including countries that are not members of the G20). The organization has consistently decried tax havens and mused about improving the international monetary system. Increasingly, like the networks it directs, the G20 spends time on what it calls "assessment," that is, determining whether its policy prescriptions have in fact been implemented, and, if so, whether they have had a desired effect. These policies are, once again, communicated through its end-of-summit communiqués.

Those communiqués are negotiated documents, coordinated by the "troika" of leaders hosting the current, the prior, and the following summits. The summit host serves as the president of the G20, which essentially means that it takes on the administrative tasks of the organization for the year; there is no G20 secretariat. The president, with the assistance of the troika, sets the agenda for the G20 meeting.

Although heads of state and finance ministers observe their many protocols, the G20 is meant to operate informally. Its decisions are made by consensus. The content of its communiqués, as well as the blueprints and white papers presented at its meetings, and sometimes endorsed by the group, are devised through a process of negotiation that begins well before any summit takes place and that includes bureaucrats from each of the member countries. In particular, so-called Sherpa meetings, involving chief economic advisers of the member countries, precede and follow each summit. The G20 also has set up ministerial meetings that gather the heads of the agencies overseeing finance, trade, energy, labor, agriculture, and tourism. Then there are all the meetings of G20 working and study groups, which consist largely of bureaucrats taking on specific issues of cross-border communication, which will either result in the release of a paper designed to encourage coordination around particular best practices, or could lead to endorsement through one of the end-of-summit communiques. Because of its origins as a response to financial crisis, the group divides its work product into two; it designates some matters as appropriately handled through a finance stream, including macroeconomic and monetary as well as financial regulatory issues.

Running through the communiqués and the regular meetings is a theme: the G20 remains engaged with what the regulatory networks are doing about financial systemic stability. It expects regular updates on progress made to help ensure systemic stability, and it has received many of them, ranging in topic from capital adequacy to starting a derivatives clearinghouse to the hot-button issue of executive compensation at financial intermediaries.

It is fair to say that in the wake of the financial crisis, the G20 is providing new political direction constituting a new sort of supervision over what used to be a technocratic, exclusively bureaucratic exercise.

The FSB. The second innovation that came out of the financial crisis is a new network of networks, the Financial Stability Board, which the G20 created by transforming a relatively quiet institution, the Financial Stability Forum, into a vigorous regulatory middle manager that has become the G20's coordinator and conduit.[6] The FSB is comprised of all of the principal financial regulatory networks, principally the Basel Committee, IOSCO, and IAIS. The G20 also added two important treaty-based international organizations to the FSB's membership – the World Bank and the International Monetary Fund. These institutions were not included to augment the legitimacy or legality of the FSB, however (or at least not only for that reason), but rather to make it a more threatening enforcer of international financial regulatory norms, and a more far-seeing lookout for future financial crises. As an intermediate policer of financial regulatory networks, and as an international institution designated to take the gestalt perspective on global finance, it is fair to say that there is nothing quite like the FSB. More than any other post-crisis financial initiative, the FSB exemplifies the desire of states and their regulators to create a new, not-entirely-legal international system with checks, balances, and a coherent organizational chart.

And so its contribution to post-crisis international financial regulation is above all the provision of bureaucratic order, the likes of which are mimicked by domestic regulatory agencies, to a formerly disaggregated international process. The contribution, and the institutionalization that it represents, may be exemplified by the goals to which the FSB is pledged, and by the way it is organized.

The FSB's objectives are threefold, and involve some of its own policymaking, a great deal of monitoring of networks and member agencies, and a nascent financial market surveillance function. The FSB has declared that it will first "promote financial stability by developing strong regulatory, supervisory, and other policies."[7] This is its *strong regulation* goal, if you like. The FSB, however, is also dedicated to "fostering a level playing field through coherent policy implementation across sectors and jurisdictions."[8] This is its *harmonization* goal. Competitive equality among regulators, of course, has nothing to do with the actual quality of the regulation, and so the goals of strong regulation and harmonized regulation are entirely capable of diverging. Finally, the FSB has been charged with monitoring the stability of the global financial system for signs of weakness – to be, in effect, an *early warning system* for the G20.

As it is, although the FSB has weighed in on a very wide-ranging sort of initiatives in its first decade, from efforts to scrutinize compensation of financial executives to policies designed to fail (or "resolve") insolvent banks quickly and with a minimum of disruption, it is probably most accurate to say that the organization is playing more of an oversight than a policymaking role, pursuing strong regulation through its networks, rather than through itself. Its capacity to operate as the early warning system for the world's financial regulators, attuned to the potential of a future crisis, is, as yet, a work in progress.

The FSB is not a carefully delineated institution, but its structure, as a network of networks, looks like those of its members. To the extent that it has any staff at all, it is comprised of regulators seconded from agencies that participate in its member networks; its secretariat shares space with the Basel Committee at BIS headquarters. The FSB's charter is only ten pages – long enough to outline its objectives, some organizational guidelines, and membership rules. The charter has little to say about FSB processes other than to announce a commitment to consultation, and to specify, as is the case with most classic international organizations (often to the detriment of their ability to act), that it will operate through consensus.[9]

The FSB has tried to pursue its monitoring function through cajoling and peer review, bolstered by the institutionalized financial sector reviews performed by the IMF, which, like the World Bank, is a member. Once its members pass rules that the FSB, or the networks under it, have adopted, presumably for their prospect of promoting financial stability, the FSB conducts regular reviews of both the membership, on a country-by-country basis, and on particular issues for all its members at once. Peer review requires members to report on their implementation progress to the FSB. Its mandate also provides for the ability to review "the policy development work of the international standard-setting bodies to ensure that their work is timely coordinated, focused on priorities and addressing gaps," and while it rides herd over the standard-setting bodies, it is also charged with "assess[ing] vulnerabilities affecting the global financial system" that requires it to review the work of its member states.[10] But the Board has suggested that it may, on occasion, pursue those goals by promulgating its own rules, which it has done on occasion.

As for organization, the FSB's plenary body is "the decision-making body of the FSB" and requires consensus before action.[11] The plenary allows in new members, appoints the chair of the FSB, makes amendments to the charter, and "decides on any other matter governing the business and affairs of the FSB."[12] Members attend plenary sessions, but to do so, they must show up with a gaudy cast of regulatory characters – nothing less than a central bank governor, head or deputy of the main supervisory agency, and deputy finance minister. There, priorities are set, and votes are allocated according to the size of the national economy and financial markets, meaning that large countries get more seats than do medium or smaller G20 members.[13]

The plenaries occur twice a year; they serve, inter alia, as the place for the appointment of a chair and steering committee to govern the FSB. At them, there may also be the establishment of working groups and ad hoc committees. The chair is appointed for a three-year term, renewable once, and must have "recogni[z]ed expertise and standing in the international financial policy arena."[14]

Like other networks, the FSB explicitly eschews any legal power contained within it. Indeed, its charter provides that it is "not intended to create any legal rights or obligations."[15]

Members of the FSB. If the G20 and the FSB constitute innovations that served to restructure financial regulation after the financial crisis, the lowest regulatory level of the new paradigm has changed less. Before the crisis, issue and task-specific regulators handled the siloed areas of financial regulation with varying degrees of specificity and intrusiveness. That has continued in the post-crisis paradigm; there has been an effort to coordinate what these networks do from above, but there have been no mergers or major restructurings. What has changed, however, is the inclination of the networks to come up with a more ambitious regulatory agenda designed to forestall the next crisis, and, paired with that renewed substantive vigor, an increasingly elaborate attention to process.

The financial regulatory networks that make up the FSB's membership have all adopted a relatively standardized set of commitments to transparency. They make information available on their websites, they hold annual meetings and invite the public to attend portions of them, and they promulgate major initiatives only after relatively standardized processes of notice and comment rulemaking. This commitment to procedural regularity is, in many ways, one of the things that binds the varied networks together.

But those networks remain nothing if not varied. The oldest and most prominent network is the Basel Committee on Banking Supervision, which was founded in 1974, just before a predecessor organization to IOSCO was launched to serve as a mechanism for coordination among securities regulators. The network for insurance supervision followed these two. Still, the twenty-first century has seen a real flowering of the task-specific financial regulatory network. For instance, the Financial Action Task Force handles money laundering and counterterrorism finance. As we will see, other networks have developed common principles for deposit insurance, payments processing, accounting-standards harmonization, and so on. The network is the form privileged by financial regulators seeking to solve cross-border problems.

There is, of course, much more to be said about the substantive achievements of networks, and much more that will be said about each of them in the rest of this book, but in this chapter, they will be considered mostly as a somewhat interchangeable – if task-specific – set of ground-level regulators, who promulgate rules and observe procedural formalities in a relatively consistent way upon the direction of the G20 and the FSB. Later, we will investigate in detail how exactly these varied networks got their start, how their histories and accomplishments unfolded, and how they are currently organized. For the purpose of this chapter, however, they may be considered as a particular sort of organization that, although subdivided into an array of issue areas, exhibits a consistent set of characteristics and features.

2.2 THE NEW RULES OF FINANCE

While international financial regulation has changed institutionally, it has also, perhaps because its new institutions have embraced process and bureaucratic regularity, become increasingly amenable to legal description. You can characterize the structure undergirding the new international regulatory regime through six legal and organizational principles. These principles identify the direction in which the elaborate procedural armature of the financial regulator is evolving, despite being nonbinding as a matter of public international law. They mount a challenge to the traditional international law paradigm, while adopting principles recognizably within the traditional legal regime. Let's take a look at these six principles.

2.2.1 *National Treatment*

National treatment is the term used to denote a non-discriminatory principle adopted by the European Union and the World Trade Organization (WTO). Article III of the General Agreement on Tariffs and Trade (GATT) articulates the best-known legal version of this principle. It requires GATT's "contracting parties [to] recognize that ... regulations and requirements affecting the internal sale ... products ... should not be applied to imported or domestic products so as to afford protection to domestic production."[16] The goal is to ensure that regulators do not discriminate in favor of domestic businesses at the cost of foreign ones.

International financial regulation, in addition to being driven by the extensive interconnectedness of financial intermediaries, is also shaped by an interest in subjecting those intermediaries to a variant of the national-treatment principle. The point of developing a single set of accounting principles for capital markets participants, for instance, is to make idiosyncratic local rules more globally consistent. The goal is partly driven by an interest in efficiency that will be familiar to trade negotiators. Common regulatory standards make it easier for businesses to operate across borders. But they are also antidiscriminatory. Under national treatment, regulators are not permitted to make life harder for foreign firms they regulate within their countries than they do for domestic competitors.

This commitment to national treatment is most commonly expressed through a commitment to the often-declared goal of creating a "level playing field." The general manager of the BIS had indicated that the organizations housed in his building – the Basel Committee and the FSB – are trying to implement reforms in an "internationally consistent and non-discriminatory" manner.[17] IOSCO has insisted that its Principles for Financial Market Infrastructures will ensure, among other things, a "global regulatory level playing field."[18] The G20's leaders emphasized the importance of the level playing field in a statement at the conclusion of its 2009 meeting in Pittsburgh, and the Basel Committee has accordingly monitored the progress of implementation of its Basel III capital-adequacy accord in part on regulatory consistency, to ensure, again in its words, a "level playing field."[19] The British central banker and economist Charles Goodhart has characterized the goals of the capital accord as twofold: to ensure that banks had higher levels of capital requirements, and that there be a "level playing field."[20] The insurance supervisory network, for its part, promised to create capital standards on a "level playing field."[21]

The interest in a level playing field for exporters of financial services particularly motivates wealthy countries that dominate financial regulatory policymaking. Most of them feature at least one (and sometimes only one) large incumbent interested in encouraging domestic regulators to make arrangements to ensure foreign access, while offering a threat to incumbent institutions of other countries that would like to operate overseas. The level playing field motivates firms to support regulators trying to devise common standards, because internationally active firms want the protections national treatment provides.

In this way, national treatment underscores the rapid globalization of finance, and the efforts of financial regulation to catch up. It would be an unnecessary principle if banks from one country did not attempt to expand operations to other countries; because all countries that participate in the global financial regulatory architecture have banks that do so, national treatment is one of the basic ways that regulators can champion their industry's interests to one another. Securities, insurance, and other financial industries have similar incentives. National treatment is the most trade-oriented of the basic principles of financial regulation.

To be sure, financial regulation's national-treatment principle is not a simple copy of the GATT model. In finance, the national-treatment goals not only attempt to harmonize standards, but to raise them across jurisdictions, rather than to minimize barriers against foreign competition, which has been the goal of the GATT. But is the attention to the level playing field underscores how important national treatment is to both financial regulation and trade law.

As with any legal rule, the application of national treatment in any particular case can be uneven; the home banks of any regulator that has signed on to the system will always hope they can convince a regulator to look on them more favorably than it will on foreign competitors. American regulators, for example, have been accused of unfairly burdening foreign banks by insisting on a version of "ring-fencing" that makes it difficult for them to realize the benefits of a global market. The most recent version of ring-fencing requires banks with US subsidiaries to allocate capital to subsidiaries that meet the capital adequacy standards of domestic banks. That means that many foreign banks need to keep capital in the US if they want to meet these standards, and there is suspicion that the same requirement does not apply to US multinational institutions. The European Union and China have already begun to make moves to require similar ring-fencing by US banks operating abroad.

This sort of dispute is endemic to any legal regime, where the question as to whether rules are being applied evenly surfaces with great persistence. National treatment is a rule designed to require this sort of fair application, but its observation, like any rule, requires monitoring; international financial regulation has developed unique ways to do this sort of monitoring, as we shall see.

2.2.2 *Most-Favored Nation*

Many believe that the WTO's most-favored nation (MFN) principle prevents countries from discriminating among their trading partners, for geopolitical advantage or for any other reason. The MFN provides that if one WTO member is granted a special favor, such as a lower customs duty rate for a specific export, all WTO members are entitled to the same benefit. In the GATT, the MFN principle is expressed as follows:

> [A]ny advantage, favour, privilege or immunity granted by any contracting party to any product originating in or destined for any other country shall be accorded immediately and unconditionally to the like product originating in or destined for the territories of all other contracting parties.[22]

The MFN principle in trade is designed to reduce the complexity of rule navigation among the various jurisdictions to which an exporter might want to send its goods, as well as to drive the tariff-reduction process through the various rounds. MFN has thus made lowering of trade barriers a global, rather than a bilateral or regional effort.

International financial regulation has embraced a similar, if not identical, commitment to making sure that every nation has the same approach to foreign financial intermediaries. It evinces its MFN predilection most obviously with its taste for consensus. "The FSB's consistent ability to forge consensus has led to common ownership and, in most cases, timely and comprehensive implementation of reforms at the national level," said Mark Carney, the chair of the FSB and the head of the Bank of England.[23] The Basel Committee, IOSCO, and IAIS all operate on a consensus basis, or something close to it. So does the G20 and the FSB.

Each of these institutions has tried to stop its members from negotiating side deals favoring particular foreign regulators or banks, partly through their peer-review processes, partly through tradition. Indeed, the Basel Committee owed its first capital-adequacy accord to concerns that two of its members – banking regulators in the USA and Britain – were contemplating issuing their own capital standards, potentially excluding foreign banks that did not meet the requirements.

The G20 speaks with one voice, for example on its so-called "Seoul Development Consensus," but also through communiqués transmitted without dissents or glosses at the conclusion of summits. The consensus requirement in international financial regulation is a way of ensuring that a deal available to one member of the international financial regulatory architecture is open to all, and, at the same time, that commitments made by members to improve their regulatory performances within their own jurisdictions will be matched by their counterparties. MFN policies simplify the complexities of managing regulatory requirements that exist in different countries by promoting uniformity around the best deal on offer to an outside country.

In some ways, the principle works slightly differently in financial regulation than it does in trade, where it is thought to drive deregulation. MFN in financial regulation partly exists as a developmental goal, with regulatory agencies from every country, no matter their size or sophistication, adopting the same core approaches, as revealed by principles adopted by the networks and endorsed by the FSB. This developmental goal is meant to elevate the practices of many regulators, as well as preclude side deals with foreign counterparts.

For example, IOSCO's multilateral memorandum of understanding on enforcement cooperation (the MOU) is designed to improve securities-law enforcement by enabling securities regulators to seek cooperation from counterparts abroad in investigating violations of the law, many of which cross borders. The network has now all but required its members to sign the MOU; 117 of them have. As for those who have not, IOSCO in 2018 reported that, "Most of the 13 members on the IOSCO List of Non-signatories have taken concrete steps to address through legislative amendments the issues preventing them from complying." This is an effort to establish consensus on cooperation (which is admittedly different than substantive consensus on actual regulatory standards, say, on preoffering quiet periods or insider trading).[24]

2.2.3 *Rulemaking*

If national treatment and MFN principles undergird the substance of global financial regulation, the phenomenon also evinces a number of procedural principles that mirror fundamental processes of the modern administrative state. Most importantly, the system of global financial regulation has chosen to regulate through rules, rather than adjudicate by tribunal. It has eschewed efforts to devise a dispute-settlement system, which characterizes the WTO, the EU, and other prominent formally constituted international organizations. There is no court overseeing the implementation of Basel III (which involves securities, insurance, payments, and the like) or dictates of the FSB, and no hint that such a mechanism is in the offing.

This has made international financial regulation more difficult to study. Scholars reflexively look for tribunals to articulate the substance of legal principles. Some international lawyers, such as John Jackson and proponents of the International Criminal Court, have argued that a tribunal is a critical component of a meaningful regime; without a relatively independent court, they contend, international obligations tend to go unenforced.[25]

But a preference for rulemaking does not mean that the system has abandoned legal precision. American academics familiar with that country's administrative law principles tend to present the choice between adjudication and rulemaking as one with procedural implications, but not one that either dooms an agency to obsolescence or guarantees its effectiveness. It is instead a regulatory taste – in some cases, regulation will be pursued by rule, in others by adjudication.

There are differences, of course. Adjudication allows broader regulation through precedent via the common-law accumulation of prior standards, which can then be applied more broadly by lawyers and regulators involved with the regulated industry. Some US agencies regulate by adjudication exclusively.[26] The National Labor Relations Board (NLRB) and the Board of Immigration Appeals (BIA) are two significant agencies known for this practice, though they have been criticized for doing so.

Other institutions regulate through rulemaking, which is the regulatory version of legislation, in that it is forward-looking and applies, at least ordinarily, to a class of regulated institutions rather than to a particular legal dispute. It therefore is a form of law devised *ex ante* a set of facts, rather than *ex post*. The result is a prospective form of lawmaking, one that features an opportunity to comment before promulgation as the most accessible form of public participation in the governance process (as opposed to the right to litigate after the fact), and one that applies more broadly to swaths of regulated industry rather than narrowly to particular parties to a dispute.

All of the international financial regulatory bodies operate through rulemaking, rather than adjudication. In addition to Basel III and the FSB, IOSCO, IAIS and IASB all hew to rulemaking over adjudication (the only important exception involves the FSB's development of lists of systemically important financial institutions, the thirty banks and seven insurers marked for greater regulatory scrutiny and stronger capital standards because of their size and interconnectedness, as I discuss below).[27] The rulemaking process has become standardized, as well. The Basel Committee's website, for example, features publications, press releases, working papers, and newsletters all aimed at explaining and promoting its rulemaking efforts. These institutions propose rules and then take public comment on them; those comments are available on the network website as well. Most of the regulatory networks at the bottom of the pyramid of international financial regulation work in precisely the same way.

Rulemaking affords regime builders flexibility and control over the regulatory process, but when done internationally often lacks the sort of procedural formality that administrative lawyers expect of domestic regulatory initiatives. International rulemakers proceed in three ways: through "hard" rules, harmonization principles, and best-practices style guidance. The hard rules are generally not as hard as in domestic rulemaking; the harmonization principles are general approaches to regulation; and best practices, while capable of being quite specific, rely on their superiority and make no claim to adoption by all members of the network.

When international rulemakers promulgate hard rules, they adopt specific requirements that their members must implement, and increasingly commonly tend to accompany those requirements with some of the procedural safeguards that we see in domestic rulemaking. The still-developing but potentially far-reaching effort to harmonize accounting standards – a slow process that has also been marked by comment periods and notice – is an example of a hard international rule. The developing insurance capital standard has similar characteristics.

While only some global regulators attempt to promulgate detailed rules governing every aspect of an international regulatory scheme, soft, principles-based regulation is indeed an almost universal first step for financial regulatory organizations. The process adopted for these forms of rulemaking is oriented towards international consent by public agencies, sometimes supported by external review by interested parties. The idea is that every regulator must agree on a set of standards and principles before an organization will adopt it. Principles-based rulemaking offers regulators the flexibility of setting their own compliance schedules and more vague commitments open to interpretation.

A final prominent form of international regulatory rulemaking is explicitly non-binding and particularly popular. It takes the form of recommendations by the international version of blue-ribbon panels, white papers issued by multilateral committees on effective regulatory techniques, and the endorsement of best practices by international regulatory bodies.

Best practices, a term popular in business management, which has made its way into the public sector, is a method of regulation that works through horizontal modeling rather than through a hierarchical organization. In a classic best-practices scheme, international regulatory bodies select and publicize certain approaches to either regulation or regulation compliance as "best," but do not mandate adoption of the practices. The idea is that the wisdom of the practices will become clear and be adopted. Best practices-style rulemaking exemplifies what would seem to be particular problems in international rulemaking: the rules it produces are unenforceable and promulgated unaccompanied by any procedural safeguards.

As such, best practices are tailor-made for the rather small secretariats and non-binding nature of international regulation. They are aimed at coordination by regulators, or advice to regulated industry. For instance, IOSCO has issued a flurry of white papers designed to provide these best practices to securities regulators and the capital markets. In February 2017, the organization issued

"Technical Guidance on Harmonisation of the Unique Transaction Identifier," a set of recommendations on payments processing, "Findings of the Survey on Loan Funds," and a "Research Report on Financial Technologies (Fintech)," in addition to a more formal statement and a report on the completion of a peer review.

Best practices are well suited for a decentralized world, and their flexibility is less likely to result in the difficulties, procedural barriers, and "ossification" of domestic administrative rulemaking. But offering regulators an attractive combination of casualness and detail is not without cost. There are the usual transparency problems posed by volume – it is difficult for observers to keep up. The processes of adoption – of selecting what areas are suitable for best practices, and what are more appropriately regulated by more formal rules – can also be opaque. And, of course, enforcement of rules promulgated through a global soft-law process poses all the usual challenges of international law enforcement with an added fillip of avowed nonbindingness.

But the point here is not to argue that the preference for rulemaking – broadly applicable, *ex ante* guidance – is unambiguously good, rather it is to suggest that rulemaking is how regulators choose to express their views on policy.

To be sure, there have been some actions by international financial regulators that have not followed the rulemaking-only paradigm. The FSB creates its annual list of the world's financial institutions that are "too big to fail," and which it deems "systemically important financial institutions." The creation of this list of 30 banks and seven insurance companies means that their regulators are charged with imposing extra capital surcharges on them designed to reduce the likelihood that they will ever need to be bailed out. Eight US banks made the list, including Bank of America, Bank of New York Mellon, Citigroup, Goldman Sachs, JPMorgan Chase, Morgan Stanley, State Street, and Wells Fargo. These banks must hold more capital than ordinary banks. Three American insurance companies – Prudential, AIG, and MetLife – have appeared on the list of global systemically important insurers. These firms are also subject to extra supervision.

This development shows how international supervision continues to evolve. It used to be that networks came up with the rules and left implementation to their members. Now one such network is making an individualized determination about how risky a bank is, and what actions it must take to mitigate its riskiness. Lawyers would call that determination an adjudication; it is one, however, that only reaches a relatively small number of financial institutions. Most of the world's financial companies experience international financial regulation as a set of rules enforced by their domestic regulators. Most of the international policymaking that affects even the large systemically important financial institutions (SIFI) comes not from their designation, but from capital rules that apply to all the financial institutions in their network. It is unlikely, given the small size and limited capacity of the networks themselves, that it will be different any time soon.

2.2.4 *Subsidiarity*

If international financial regulation is devised through rules without the benefit of a tribunal to enforce them, then the question of rule application and enforcement becomes somewhat fraught. Many observers believe that tribunals are the epitome of effective vindication of international legal rights, and some of the push to transform the GATT into the WTO was driven by the desire to ensure that a more powerful court could ensure compliance with trade agreements.

The emerging regime of international financial regulation relies solely on its members to enforce its edicts in their own jurisdictions in their own manner. The decision to place the responsibility for enforcement and implementation at the domestic level, rather than the international one, suggests that international financial regulation is peculiarly attached to a principle familiar to European Union observers: the principle of subsidiarity, with its attendant preference for action by smaller units of government wherever possible. Article 5(3) of the Treaty of the European Union provides:

> Under the principle of subsidiarity, in areas which do not fall within its exclusive competence, the Union shall act only if and insofar as the objectives of the proposed action cannot be sufficiently achieved by the Member States, either at central level or at regional and local level.[28]

The subsidiarity here is subsidiarity of enforcement, not policymaking. While decisions about the content of global rules are meant to be made at the network level, enforcement is delegated to national agencies that are members of the network. And of course, matters for which global uniformity is not necessary are meant to be left to local authorities.

Subsidiarity is an essential feature of the soft law institutions of international financial regulation. Because these institutions cannot hope to mandate global standards – an occupational hazard for entities unwilling to go through the formal process of institutionalization through a treaty and so ever-willing to claim that they are not lawmakers – they can only agree on them, and rely on their members to do the hard work of enforcement and implementation. That dependence on local implementation is, in some ways, an unambitious aspect of the emerging financial regulatory regime. But, given the attention paid to the regime by heads of state and domestic regulators, it does not appear to negate the importance of international policymaking efforts.

To be sure, subsidiarity could mean that international financial regulation amounts to nothing more than a purely optional exercise for domestic regulators who join the international institutions that propound it. After all, it is entirely up to the members of the Basel Committee and FSB as to whether and how they enforce rules devised through the international process. There is also no court if other regulators think that a member agency is failing to meet its promised obligations.

But subsidiarity has not meant that international financial regulation is just a matter of local option and international talking shops. It has instead enjoyed a generally high degree of compliance, and, in a testament to the substantiveness of the international regulatory enterprise, it has received a great deal of attention from lawyers engaged in managing the regulatory burdens on international banks. Delegation on implementation to domestic agencies is a thread that runs through all of financial regulation, but not apparently yet to the detriment of its international institutionalization.

2.2.5 *Peer Review*

International financial regulation has sought to solve the compliance problem created by its strict observance of subsidiarity in implementation, through an increasingly standardized process of peer review. Peer review as practiced by the financial regulatory networks involves some invited visitation, the perusal of reports prepared by countries that have joined the organization, and some free riding on the Financial Sector Assessment Program (FSAP) analyses conducted by the IMF and World Bank.

It is through peer review – and the subsequent shaming of a member institution out of compliance – that international financial regulation seeks to bind its constituents. Peer review is, of course, no panacea. It would be inaccurate to say that international financial regulation has always successfully ensured that its rules are implemented, as the Basel Committee can attest given the late and partial implementation of the Basel II Capital Adequacy Accord by the USA.

But peer review is an innovation that even domestic regulators have found promising; it has a cherished place in academia, and is an increasingly utilized management tool. International financial regulation's embrace of peer review as an enforcement mechanism in lieu of lawsuits before an international tribunal is not unprecedented, and may even be appropriate in an international order increasingly lacking in a hegemon that can police compliance by countries through a variety of other sanctions.

In 2010, the G20 announced its plan for financial reform that includes four guiding principles, one of which is a commitment to peer review. The leaders of the G20 have declared that they will "aim[to improve assessment of risk by relying on the IMF and World Bank Financial Sector Assessment Program and FSB peer reviews."[29] The FSB, in turn, has performed peer reviews in both individual member countries and for general issue areas. According to the press release announcing the FSB's completion of South Africa's peer review, "FSB member jurisdictions have committed to undergo an FSAP assessment every five years and, to complement that cycle, an FSB peer review two to three years following an FSAP."[30] The extensions of FSAPs to G20 members was an appropriation of a review process that had only been applied to the developing world. Because countries like the USA, the UK, and Japan did not seek assistance from the IMF or World Bank, they were not required to undergo FSAPs as a condition of that acceptance.

The IAIS, for its part, has recently begun its self-assessment and peer review on Insurance Core Principles 4, 5, 7, and 8. Other examples are not difficult to find. IAIS has also promulgated a Multilateral Memorandum of Understanding (MMoU), which is a "global framework for cooperation and information exchange between insurance supervisors."[31] The MMoU goes a long way toward ensuring national treatment of insurance supervisors, both by dictating "minimum standards to which signatories must adhere," and by "subject[ing] [all applicants] to review and approval by an independent team of IAIS members."[32] The Basel Committee, for its part, implemented a Regulatory Consistency Assessment Program (RCAP) in 2011, which involves the creation of an assessment team that evaluates the amount of domestic adoption of the Basel III rules by all the Basel committee members.

Horizontal enforcement and its difficulties have long been a characteristic challenge for international governance mechanisms. But peer review has not been a particularly institutionalized method to approach the problem. Assigning a third party to monitor compliance, creating a tribunal, or relying on secretariats to do so, has been more characteristic of international organizations in the past. In financial regulation, the agencies themselves are meant to do the job, which in some ways recasts the role of participant in international governance. The agencies at the base of the regulatory pyramid are responsible for implementing rules of the network both at home and among their peers. Asa result, peer review gives them an international role – and perhaps an international mindset to play that role.

It is possible that this peer-review process could evolve into an entity that looks like a tribunal, which would mean that the current taste for rulemaking would be supplemented. But international financial regulation is some distance from this point today. The idea would be that the peer-review process would be formalized into something that looked more like an adjudication. The GATT panel process, for instance, began as expert reviews of a country's conduct to see if it was complying with its trade obligations, then evolved into a more formal dispute-settlement body, and was finally transformed into the full-fledged tribunals, followed by appeals, authorized by the WTO. Currently, peer reviews in financial regulation are not driven by a complaint process, as the GATT was, and differ in many other ways from adjudication, too. But it is worth remembering that the principle of peer review, like some of the other principles, is not immutable, incapable of being changed. It is the way financial regulatory agreements are enforced now, not necessarily forever.

Peer review is often directed at a global rule, which is then assessed by the context of the regulators who have implemented it, and the way they have done so. But because it is also committed on a country-by-country basis, it is an opportunity for foreign regulators to make their noncompliance case to a particular domestic regulator. This sort of individualized treatment may make the peer-review process look like an adjudication – is Japan complying with its financial regulatory commitments? – but it is not. Instead it's an opportunity for a regulator's peers to take a hard look, and then make their complaint about policy consistency if necessary. In this sense, it is an individualized complement to the rulemaking process, designed to enforce those rules.

2.2.6 *Networks*

The vehicle for international financial regulation has overwhelmingly been – indeed, uniformly been – the network. As Anne-Marie Slaughter, the former Princeton University dean and current CEO of think tank New America, has put it, networks exhibit "patterns of regular and progressive movement among like government units working across the borders that divide countries from one another and that demarcate the domestic from the international sphere."[33] Networks are unique innovations in international financial regulation and they have been the mechanisms chosen by regulators to conduct their business.

Post-crisis financial regulation is essentially *only* done through networks, with some assistance from the World Bank and IMF. There is no other institutional approach, even though the alternatives to networks are easy to find in other areas of international law. For financial regulation, the precision and possibly enhanced compliance pull of a treaty or a tribunal has been no match for the flexibility of the confederations of regulators acting on agendas provided by political leaders meeting in concert.

As networks, the Basel Committee, IOSCO, and IAIS share common characteristics, despite different origins, achievements, and ages. Their members are not states, but agencies. The members explicitly view themselves as representatives of their bureaucratic employer, rather than their national governments.

Networks are created informally. The idiosyncrasy of their founding documents is striking. IAIS's was launched with a certificate of incorporation as a nonprofit organization in Illinois. IOSCO began via a private bill in the Quebec Assembly. The Basel Committee, unlike IOSCO, IAIS, and the other financial regulatory networks, does not even have a legal existence on the national level. Its existence was first marked by a press release issued through the BIS, and the Concordat that defines its approach to banking supervision and lays down no requirements or framework for the organization itself.

Finally, networks have flexible internal organization. Both IAIS and IOSCO have promulgated bylaws, but those rules are permissive and open-ended, rather than restrictive and definitive; IAIS's are eight pages long, IOSCO's are longer, but not by much. IAIS's bylaws permit its executive committee to take "all decisions necessary to achieve the objectives of the organization,"[34] while its modestly sized secretariat, headed by the secretary, "executes all other functions that are assigned" to it.[35]

The enabling tenor of the bylaws of both organizations, comparable to bylaws a business might pass for itself, suggests that they should be viewed as conduits for ongoing and flexible relationships. And indeed, networks are, in some senses, forums for jawboning and outlets through which regulators can contact other entities, both within and outside of the membership. By contrast, other international organizations have much more formal rules of order. The United Nations General Assembly, for example, has promulgated an elaborate procedural code governing its deliberations and the practice of its bureaucracy. The unencumbering bylaws of the networks make their goals and means flexible and less dependent on the status envisioned for the organizations at their founding.

Networks are also characterized by decentralized organizations and action. They have small bureaucracies, limiting the amount of centralization each organization can hope to attain. For example, IAIS's secretariat was originally delegated to a member organization, which in turn tasked a single employee to keep the records and answers requests. Secretariats have grown since then, but they hardly resemble those at formal international organizations such as the WTO, let alone the UN or European Union. Network secretariats in the financial regulatory environment do not enjoy headcounts that exceed double digits.

Finally, the legal authority in any network announcement is, if you believe the network, nonexistent. They make no claim to be promulgating laws or expounding on treaties. Regulators have claimed, again and again, that nothing they do in the organizations is legally binding. "We can't bind the United States," observed one SEC regulator who has participated in IOSCO,[36] which means that there are no formal legal consequences that attach to the SEC's participation in the organization. The general counsel of the Basel Committee has made a similar caveat about his organization's lawmaking powers; such declamations are, if anything, *de rigeur*. None of this means that the pronouncements of networks will never be legally binding; although their promulgations lack formal international legal authority when implemented at the domestic level, they gain local legal legitimacy.

A final characteristic of networks is that they spend a lot of time networking. Basel, IOSCO, and IAIS assiduously maintain connections with one another and have created an interlocking web of financial regulators, one formalized with the growing importance of that network of networks, the FSB. IOSCO and IAIS have also cultivated ties with regional securities and insurance regulators. IOSCO also works closely with private groups of self-regulatory organizations.

2.2.7 *Contextualizing the Six Principles*

Some of these six principles are comparable to the legal pillars supporting prominent organizations like the EU and the WTO, both of which espouse MFN and national treatment. The EU is also a prominent proponent and practitioner of subsidiarity, though that practice operates differently there than in financial regulation. Other principles, like the use of rulemaking, are comparable to domestic regulation. Peer review, while practiced in other contexts by FSB members the IMF and World Bank, and the network model are relatively distinctive, however, to international financial regulation.

Despite the recognizably legal nature of the paradigmatic principles of international financial regulation, the networks do not mimic classic international legal organizations in every way. For example, one of the hoary old tropes of public international law, sovereign equality, is not a fixture of international financial regulation. While treaties like the UN Charter provide that "[t]he Organization is based on the principle of the sovereign equality of all its Members,"[37] and the reporters to the Restatement (Third) of Foreign Relations Law cite, with approval, a declaration that "solemnly proclaims" the importance of the principle of sovereign equality of states, international financial regulation operates differently.[38]

Membership in the networks is not open to all sovereigns or agencies, most notably at the Basel Committee and the FSB, which limit themselves to regulators from twenty-eight and twenty large markets, respectively. The major countries of Europe, the USA, Japan, and, increasingly, China play outsize roles in these organizations, despite consensus rules that are commonly required for action by the selective membership. In this way, financial regulatory networks have followed the lead of more formal international financial institutions, such as the World Bank and the IMF, which favor larger contributors to the organization over smaller ones, and which divide their top jobs on regional loyalty bases that have little to do with sovereign equality. Moreover, when the financial networks have made gestures to consensus-based action, that consensus has sometimes been deemed by observers to be quite forced.

If global financial regulation does not resemble hard public international law in every way, it is certainly not a rejection or dismissal of the importance of legal rules either. Prior enthusiasts for international financial regulation and structures like it sometimes have propounded a somewhat mystical process of unorganized, disaggregated coordination. The mid-century historian and political theorist David Mitrany and political scientist Charles Sabel, for example, posit that the mere act of interaction can take on momentum that results in coordinated outcomes, even though the coordination itself is hard to institutionalize, define, or predict. Mitrany described this as a process of enmeshment, where some transnational coordination might lead to more.[39] Sabel, with Michael Dorf, characterized it in the domestic sphere as democratic experimentalism, whereby disaggregated groups try a number of different approaches to regulatory problems, the best of which would be used as benchmarks offered to everyone and then replaced by a new effort to exceed the benchmarks.[40] In their view, the design of the institution of cooperation does not matter much. What matters is the fact of cooperation, which can construct virtuous circles leading to more and more of cooperation, courtesy of some hard-to-grasp intangibles.

These insights are plausible, but there is more to be said about the capabilities and organization of global financial regulation, which is increasingly less shrouded in mystery and more explicable as a principled legal order founded on instruments of soft cooperation. Networks can solve problems and build momentum in Sabellian ways, but that momentum has taken – at least in financial regulation – a form with recognizably legal characteristics.

2.3 COMPARING FINANCE WITH ITS PEERS

The world's two most successful economic unions are the EU and the WTO. How does financial regulation compare to these two treaty-based, tribunal-featuring legal bodies? Although, as a matter of international law, international financial regulation has few of the classic characteristics shared by the EU and the WTO, the three institutions appear to be evolving along similar lines.

The historical evolution of the economic unions is an instructive guide to the state of the global financial regulatory institutions, especially when filtered through stylized stories told about the EU and WTO in seminal and related articles by New York University's Joseph Weiler and Joost Pauwelyn of the Graduate Institute in Geneva. Weiler and Pauwelyn were both seeking to explain the most impactful international economic law arrangements of the postwar era. Weiler came first, explaining the transformation of Europe from a balkanized system of states devastated by World War II to a relatively coherent, and increasingly political, union that has created the world's largest single market. Pauwelyn applied Weiler's legalistic account of the transformation of Europe to the transformation of the multilateral trade regime from the GATT to the WTO.

Where do financial regulatory networks stand on the institutional evolution spectrum first explored by Weiler, and later adapted by Pauwelyn?[41] There is no teleological requirement that international financial regulation's evolution follow along lines of either the EU or the WTO. But both the EU and the WTO serve as standards of international economic regulation against which all other efforts must be measured. The Weilerian approach is useful not only because of its own analytical power, but because it ultimately invites some caution about presupposing that the progress of international financial regulation will lead to a fully realized institution comparable to the EU and WTO in every way. If one upshot of the developing legal describability of international financial regulation is that it is becoming a body of international law (albeit of the soft variety, but no less principled than other institutions of international law), running the rule over international financial regulation as Weiler did with the EU, and Pauwelyn did with the WTO, also shows the limits of this development.

For Weiler and Pauwelyn, the initial and critical step in the legalization of the trade unions was the closure of "selective exit." Selective exit is Weiler's gloss on the sort of exit described in Albert O. Hirschman's trichotomy of voice, exit, and loyalty as fundamentals of any communitarian organization.[42] Weiler interpreted the critical mechanisms of the trichotomy in the following way:

> Exit is the mechanism of organizational abandonment in the face of unsatisfactory performance. Voice is the mechanism of intraorganizational correction and recuperation. Apart from identifying these two basic types of reaction to malperformance, Hirschman's basic insight is to identify a kind of zero-sum game between the two. Crudely put, a stronger "outlet" for Voice reduces pressure on the Exit option and can lead to more sophisticated processes of self-correction. By contrast, the closure of Exit leads to demands for enhanced Voice.[43]

As legal integration grew, it became clear during the foundational periods of both organizations that it would be increasingly unrealistic for members of either the European Community (the EU's precursor) or the GATT (the WTO's precursor) to abandon their institutional commitments, or to take those obligations on slower or faster tracks than other treaty signatories – and this marked the end of selective exit. As Weiler put it for Europe, "the closure of Selective Exit was just that: the process by which Community norms and policy hardened into binding law with effective legal remedies."[44]

To join either of the economic unions, then, was essentially a commitment to each and every one of the legal principles enforced by the legal institutions empowered by them; the foundational period for both made this clear. The cataclysmic predictions of the pain that would accompany Greece's possible exit from the EU (or the eurozone) underscores the point, which the difficulties of the UK's exit from the common market amplifies. The story is one where institutions evolved to insist on the observance of their basic propositions, in rough entirety. This occurred not through some public announcement of agreement by members, but rather through an evolutionary absorption of the fact that picking and choosing which rules to observe and which to ignore would not be countenanced. By the same token, partial, or two-speed, adoption of rules would not be permitted.

Under Hirschman's paradigm, the counter to the end of the realistic availability of exit was the invigoration of voice. Weiler and Pauwelyn explained that this led (in the late 1960s and early 1970s in Europe, and in the 1980s in trade) to a political reassertion of voice, in keeping with Hirschman's view that exit and voice ordinarily have a zero-sum relationship, and that exit and voice are often traded for one another. The reassertion of voice by countries that joined the EU and GATT halted the foundational period's process of rapid integration.

While the countries of Europe and members of the GATT claimed integration back from the legal institutions that drove it during the foundational period, the reclamation of voice was not the end of the integration story.

In Weiler and Paulwelyn's view, both the EU and the WTO experienced "quiet integration" after the foundational period. As Pauwelyn put it with regard to the GATT, "[d]eparting from an early balance between low discipline and low participation, as soon as GATT became operational, the original equilibrium gradually shifted toward more discipline and harder law, including less exit, and more participation or politics, including more demands for voice. This occurred piecemeal and over time, hence the reference to GATT's quiet mutation."[45]

During the quiet integration period, the EU established principles of jurisdiction between the EC and its member states, and developed the ability to mutate some obligations so that community jurisdictional limitations would be interpreted flexibly – occasionally at the cost of the privileges of member states, suggesting that the assertion of voice to halt willy-nilly integration had not ended the evolutionary process entirely, though it certainly slowed it.[46] The GATT's parallel quiet-integration period unfolded in a similar fashion. The assertion of voice, after rapid integration by GATT dispute-resolution panels, created a deadlock between the USA and the EU. The USA, on the one hand, tried to self-enforce some GATT norms against recalcitrant member countries, while the EU, on the other, blocked the dispute-resolution process on a number of controversial occasions. Still, during this period, trade rounds continued to be concluded, and general tariff reductions consolidated.

After this period of quiet integration, there were elaborate attempts to end the political checkmate that appeared to be the fate of both the EU and WTO. For the EU, this supposedly ultimate arrangement was embodied in its 1992 Treaty on European Union concluded at Maastricht. For the GATT, it was the WTO treaty of 1994. Both Weiler and Pauwelyn have been skeptical that these "final" institutional settlements were meant to or would result in the settlement and balance of voice and exit norms and could engender a loyalty and increasing economic integration among the member states. The current efforts of the UK to extricate itself from the European Union – the process popularly known as Brexit – has suggested that exit from these broad trade unions may not, in fact, be impossible. But it is certainly the case that decades of membership in a trade-barrier reduction enterprise makes exit from that enterprise politically difficult, economically painful, and bureaucratically complex.

Global financial regulation has not moved as far as this era of "final" settlement. Instead, it lies somewhere between the foundational period and the period of quiet integration.

First, the foundations of the regulatory regime are now solid, legally describable, and represent a remarkable evolution from the modest cooperation contemplated at the creation of the first international financial regulatory networks in 1974. By the time of Basel II, banking regulators had committed themselves to minimum capital requirements – that is, to treat every bank on its most important profit-making question in the same way. Insurance regulators are in the midst of adopting something similar, and all of the networks have adopted their core principles, which the relatively new FSB has imposed on its own members. To Weiler and Pauwelyn, this foundational period marks the foreclosure of selective exit from the institution.

Did financial regulation go through the same process? In theory, it is possible to selectively exit financial integration obligations, but, as the most recent financial crisis made clear, it is increasingly unrealistic to do so. The principles that regulatory networks have devised have been adopted widely, and the hard rules – on occasion including rules such as those adopted by the Basel Committee through the Basel Accords – may be implemented slowly, as the USA has done, but simply cannot be ignored. Rather than abandoning international financial regulation, the world's regulators have doubled down on its development.

Moreover, as selective exit has grown increasingly untenable, there has been a growth in voice and an assertion of political control, just as there was for the WTO and EU. During the financial crisis, the G20 took the reins of financial integration and added its imprimatur to the regulatory cooperation taking place on all sorts of financial fronts. With exit limited and voice asserted, one might expect to see stasis, but as Weiler and Pauwelyn saw earlier before, further quiet integration has occurred, and a consistent articulation of what belongs to international financial regulators – policymaking and peer review – and what belongs to domestic financial regulators – policy implementation.

Financial jurisdiction has mutated to handle issues like cross-border resolution, which would seek to coordinate the special bankruptcy process that countries must employ for multinational banks, increasingly elaborate money laundering cooperative schemes, and more and more general enforcement cooperation commitments. IOSCO processes over 3,000 requests for foreign enforcement assistance annually, a rapidly growing number.[47] The internationalization of enforcement and the addition of regularity to the interaction have formed the basis of these developments, which are impressive in their own right.

These networks are also continuing to quietly integrate their policymaking and enforcement arms.

Suggesting that international financial regulation has reached the integrative standards of the WTO and the EU, however, is asking it to shoulder a greater burden than a soft-law regulatory body can reasonably do. Nonetheless, as it becomes increasingly possible to talk about a set of principles that look like institutional arrangements and substantive rules for international financial law, the ability to compare the institutional enterprise to its more formal predecessors is both possible and an intriguing statement about the ever-advancing development of financial regulatory cooperation.

Weiler and Pauwelyn are not the only measurers of the quality of international economic institutions. Both in law and in political science, a number of academics have considered the phenomenon of international financial regulation and the regulatory networks that make it. In both disciplines, two camps arise – one that sees in these networks durable institutions that can shape international conduct in ways we might expect to see in legal systems, and one more skeptical that regulatory networks can overcome persistent state self-interest.

In the institutionalist legal camp, we can see, above all, the influence of Anne-Marie Slaughter. Her work on regulatory networks includes a chapter on the financial regulators studied here; she thought that the promise of these informal, intra-state networks could solve international problems in a way that was increasingly beyond the powers of the formal international legal system. She deemed them, at least potentially, a "new world order." Raustiala also argued that the networks could play an important role in international governance, not necessarily by replacing treaties, but by existing as alternatives to them, increasing their efficacy, or serving as prologues to treaty-based settlements.

Other observers have been more skeptical about the legal effectiveness of financial regulators, to varying degrees. Legal scholars who take this tack might be described as legal realists influenced by suspicions about binding powers of international law that political science realists have often shared. Georgetown's Chris Brummer, for example, believes that regulatory networks have contributed to an international financial regulatory regime, but that their contribution has been bolstered by interests and market incentives that regulators face today. In Brummer's account, regulators comply with non-binding regulations to signal that they have the sort of high-quality laws investors and other market participants want. However, this global market for law is imperfect for a variety of reasons, including the costs incurred in switching to a set of new regulatory standards, complacency with old standards, and so on. For these reasons, Brummer argues that many of the core principles of international financial regulation have not been implemented uniformly across the world's jurisdictions, and that we should only expect widespread coordination when realpolitik, regulatory interest, and investor-provided discipline align to encourage regulators, financial firms, and other institutional players to converge around a common, multinational set of standards. The University of California at Berkeley's Stavros Gadinis also views networks as more political than legal arrangements. He has argued that regulatory efforts with more political appointees and fewer bureaucrats are more likely to do well in a context when political deals, rather than adherence to law, is the coin of the realm.[48]

Even more skeptical, although also rooted in a legal and institutional analysis, is the University of Virginia School of Law's Pierre-Hugues Verdier, who argues that although financial regulation has some achievements to celebrate, its lack of a formal enforcement mechanism means that its effectiveness will, in many cases, be observed in the breach. Verdier does not particularly credit the legal achievements of regulatory networks, but views them as largely a political deal that is subject to domestic political pressures that limit the potential for agreement. For example, persuading offshore financial centers to comply with the best practices promulgated by networks is, he believes, unlikely to be availing. Verdier observes that deals reached through regulatory networks are likely to have distributional winners and losers, which in turn can destabilize the regime as a whole. The reason: addressing such disparities is not easy for regulators to do.

A general skepticism about the success of any regulatory regime has inclined Yale Law School's Roberta Romano to conclude that efforts of international financial regulation to create one set of standards is unlikely to avoid crises.[49] Regulation regularly fails to prevent financial crises, she observes, and uniform regulation, whatever its efficiency advantages, will create worldwide, rather than countrywide, blind spots, and prevent experimentation with different solutions to regulatory problems.

Political scientists also split up into institutionalists and realists. The institutionalists, beginning with Princeton's Robert Keohane, have been impressed with international institutions like the Basel Committee on Banking Supervision, but the impression is also quite nuanced. They are quite attentive to distributional consequences, the winners and losers of regulatory cooperation. Nonetheless, they are likely to find regulatory networks to be important drivers of global norms. Harvard Business School's Michael Porter, for example, has argued that the institutions of regulatory interaction are likely to develop shared understandings about what regulations require and how they should be implemented, reducing the importance of power politics in establishing global norms.

Case Western Reserve's Elliot Posner and Georgetown's Abraham Newman, for example, have argued that the best way to understand progress being made in some areas of financial regulatory cooperation and less in others is to see whether there are adverse distributional consequences to any participant in the process, who then will be likely to drag their feet. MIT's David Singer believes that regulators are constrained by their tastes for avoiding legislative intervention, meaning that international financial regulation is most likely to proceed when legislative involvement is unlikely and the regulatory need for participation is strong. These scholars take these regulatory network institutions seriously, but are disinclined to discount rational self-interest in figuring out how they work, particularly the rational self-interest of regulators who comprise them.

Other political scientists, reaching back to Hans Morgenthau, are even more skeptical of the stability of informal, international arrangements (let alone, in his case, formal ones). These realists have real doubts about the legal efficacy of networks. They believe they are driven by power, and will be ignored when powerful countries deem it within their best interests to do so. As Morgenthau observed, "There can be no more primitive and no weaker system of law enforcement than [international law]; for it delivers the enforcement of the law to the vicissitudes of the distribution of power between the violator of the law and the victim of the violation." Daniel Drezner, at Tufts' Fletcher School, for example, argues that network outputs can basically be understood with reference to power politics in the interstate political context. This means, in his view, that the preferences of the USA and the EU are the most important – perhaps the only important – inputs in trying to understand what the output of international financial regulation will be.

The Morgenthau view has largely been supplanted in the last thirty years with the recognition that institutions mattered in international relations, and that informal institutions like regulatory networks could matter just as much as formal ones. The legal approach to understanding international financial regulation adopted here builds particularly on the work of Anne-Marie Slaughter. She argued that regulatory networks offered an alternative to traditional forms of international law with promise that arose from their informal origins. She largely named and identified regulatory networks as important, and much of the work in the field of financial regulation builds on her pathbreaking insights.

Finally, there are observers who argue that international financial regulation can be understood with reference to traditional mechanisms of formal international law. An example of this sort of analysis can be found in Tulane University Law School's Adam Feibelman's work on the IMF, a venerable international financial institution duly created by a treaty, staffed by officials who enjoy diplomatic immunity, and so on. If it is the case that the IMF and the World Bank, which rather than serving mostly as enforcers of the rules created by the regulatory architecture outlined in this book, are also primary designers of that architecture, then perhaps traditional international legal institutions are still playing important roles. Feibelman lays out the case that because of a wide-ranging surveillance responsibility, "the Fund plays a direct regulatory role in the international financial system, both *ex ante* (at the time of policy design) and *ex post* (in assessing the macroperformance of its members' policies and enforcing their obligations)."[50]

To be sure, there is little doubt that the IMF and World Bank really do matter for lower-income countries, where their surveillance and financing makes them so heavily intertwined in policymaking that it is difficult to characterize them as only transmitters of rules developed elsewhere. In fact, their endorsement of those rules has significantly accelerated the take-up of the rules of international financial regulation in the developing world.

Still, it is possible to overstate the importance of the World Bank and IMF. International financial regulation has created, as far as content, rules that do not depend on input from treaty-based organizations like the international financial institutions, though enforcement by those institutions has helped the regulatory process. The IMF and World Bank are not full members of the Basel Committee. And yet, we see compliance with World Bank and IMF mandates by the wealthy member-countries despite the fact that the pair have very little leverage over them. Neither institution really matters to the USA, the wealthiest countries in the EU, Japan, or China, none of which depends on them for borrowing.

If these institutions play a limited role in setting the terms of international financial regulation, other formal tools are of even less moment. Without a treaty, without the participation of heads of state or foreign ministers, the standard tropes of international law and diplomacy have been upended by the practice of international financial regulation. The remainder of this book shows exactly how.

Notes

1 *See* LIAQUAT AHAMED, THE LORDS OF FINANCE (2009).

2 To be sure, before the financial crisis there was some coordination in the international financial network space. Apart from banking, securities, and insurance, payment systems were also given a financial network. Finance and law enforcement officials collaborated on a Financial Action Task Force (FATF), designed to address money laundering, and, after 9/11, terrorism finance. And other financial regulatory networks developed as well.

3 Chris Brummer, *Stock Exchanges and the New Markets for Securities Laws*, 75 U. CHI. L. REV. 1435, 1473 (2008).

4 Sungjoon Cho & Claire R. Kelly, *Promises and Perils of New Global Governance: A Case of the G20*, 12 CHI. J. INT'L L. 491, 516 (2012).

5 G20 Finance Communique (March, 2018), http://www.g20.utoronto.ca/2018/2018-03-30-g20_finance_communique-en.html

6 As Chris Brummer has explained, the FSB has evolved into one of the fulcrums of post-crisis financial oversight and "given a mandate to monitor global financial stability and promote medium-term reform." Chris Brummer, *Post-American Securities Regulation*, 98 CAL. L. REV. 327, 359–60 (2010).

7 CHARTER OF THE FINANCIAL STABILITY BOARD pmbl. (amended and restated June 19, 2012), *available at* www.financialstabilityboard.org/publications/r_120809.pdf.

8 *Id.*

9 Specifically the charter provides that "In the development of the FSB's medium and long-term strategic plans, principles, standards and guidance, the FSB should consult widely amongst its Members and with other stakeholders, including private sector and non-member authorities. This process shall include … an outreach to countries not included in the Regional Consultative Groups." *Id.* at art. 3.

10 CHARTER OF THE FINANCIAL STABILITY BOARD art. 2 (amended and restated June 19, 2012), *available at* www.financialstabilityboard.org/publications/r_120809.pdf.

11 José Viñals and Sean Hagan, IMF Membership in the Financial Stability Board art. 7 (Aug. 10, 2010), *available at* www.imf.org/external/np/pp/eng/2010/081010.pdf.

12 *Id.*

13 Michael S. Barr, *Who's in Charge of Global Finance?*, 45 Geo. J. Int'l L. 971, 1017 (2014).

14 *Id.*

15 *Id.*

16 General Agreement on Tariffs and Trade, art. III(1), Oct. 30, 1947, 61 Stat. A-11, 55 U.N.T.S. 194, *available at* http://tinyurl.com/7y374yh.

17 Communiqué, G20, Meeting of Finance Ministers and Central Bank Governors (Feb. 26, 2012), *available at* www.g20.org/sites/default/files/g20_resources/library/250212_Finance_Ministers_and_Central_Bank_Governors.doc.

18 Bank for Int'l Settlements & Int'l Org. of Secs. Comm'ns, Implementation Monitoring of PFMIs – Level 1 Assessment Report 1 n.2 (2013), *available at* www.bis.org/publ/cpss111.htm.

19 Communique, G20, (Sep. 25, 2009), http://www.g20.utoronto.ca/2009/2009communique0925.html ("We are committed to take action at the national and international level to raise standards together so that our national authorities implement global standards consistently in a way that ensures a level playing field and avoids fragmentation of markets, protectionism, and regulatory arbitrage.").

20 Charles Goodhart, The Basel Committee on Banking Supervision: A History of the Early Years (2011).

21 IAIS, *The IAIS Risk-Based Global Insurance Capital Standard (ICS): Ultimate and Interim Goals, Principles for Development and Delivery Process* (July 2016), www.iaisweb.org/. . ./ics-goals-principles-and-delivery-process-updated-19-july.

22 Art. 1, General Agreement on Trade and Tariffs, www.wto.org/English/res_e/booksp_e/analytic_index_e/gatt1994_01_e.htm#article1.

23 Mark Carney, *Ten Years On: Fixing the Fault Lines of the Global Financial Crisis*, Apr. 2017. Fin. Stability Rev., www.fsb.org/wp-content/uploads/BdF-Financial-Stability-Review.pdf.

24 IOSCO, *Fact Sheet*, www.iosco.org/about/pdf/IOSCO-Fact-Sheet.pdf at 7 (Feb. 2018).

25 John Jackson, The Jurisprudence of GATT and the WTO 122–23 (2000).

26 Katie R. Eyer, *Administrative Adjudication and the Rule of Law*, 60 Admin. L. Rev. 647, 648 (2008), *available at* http://ssrn.com/abstract=1267988; Michael J. Hayes, *After "Hiding the Ball" Is Over: How the NLRB Must Change Its Approach to Decision-Making*, 33 Rutgers L.J. 523, 565 (2001).

27 *See Basel Committee on Banking Supervision*, Bank for Int'l Settlements, www.bis.org/bcbs/index.htm; *Cases & Decisions*, Nat'l Labor Relations Bd., www.nlrb.gov/cases-decisions; *BIA Precedent Decisions*, Bd. of Immigration Affairs, www.justice.gov/eoir/vll/intdec/lib_indecitnet.html.

28 Article 5 of the Treaty of the European Union may be found at www.lisbon-treaty.org/wcm/the-lisbon-treaty/treaty-on-european-union-and-comments/title-1-common-provisions/9-article-5.html.

29 Arie C. Eernisse, *Banking on Cooperation: The Role of the G-20 in Improving the International Financial Architecture*, 22 DUKE J. COMP. & INT'L L. 239, 249 (2012).

30 Press Release, Fin. Stability Bd., FSB Completes Peer Review of the United Kingdom (Sept. 10, 2013), *available at* www.financialstabilityboard.org/press/pr_130910.pdf.

31 *IAIS Multilateral Memorandum of Understanding (MMoU)*, INT'L ASSOC. OF INS. SUPERVISORS, www.iaisweb.org/MMoU-381.

32 Press Release, Int'l Assoc. of Ins. Supervisors, Mauritius Joins International Information Exchange Agreement (Jan. 13, 2014), *available at* www.iaisweb.org/view/element_href.cfm?src=1/20848.pdf.

33 ANNE-MARIE SLAUGHTER, A NEW WORLD ORDER (2004).

34 IAIS Bylaws at art. 15.

35 IAIS Bylaws at art. 33.

36 Telephone Interview with Paul Leder, Deputy Director, Office for International Affairs, SEC (Jan. 11, 1996).

37 U.N. Charter ch. I, art. 2, para. 1. This, of course, is an oversimplification. The existence of the Security Council illustrates the incompleteness of this guarantee.

38 Declaration on Principles of International Law Concerning Friendly Relations and Co-operation Among States in Accordance with the Charter of the United Nations, G.A. Res. 2625, U.N. GAOR, 25th Sess. Supp. No. 28, U.N. Doc. A/8028, at 121, (1970), *reprinted in* 65 AM. J. INT'L L. 243 (1971); RESTATEMENT (THIRD) OF FOREIGN RELATIONS LAW § 712 (1987). Meanwhile, hornbooks like the MAX PLANCK INSTITUTE'S ENCYCLOPEDIA OF INTERNATIONAL LAW also celebrate the concept of sovereign equality. According to Julianne Kokott, "Sovereign equality is a fundamental axiomatic premise of the international legal order. It is the source of other most important principles such as the ban on the use of force and the prohibition of intervention." Julianne Kokott, *States, Sovereign Equality*, MAX PLANCK INSTITUTE'S ENCYCLOPEDIA OF INTERNATIONAL LAW (Rüdiger Wolfrum & Frauke Lachenmann, eds., art. updated Apr. 2011), *available at* http://tinyurl.com/d7pfqwz.

39 *See* DAVID MITRANY, A WORKING PEACE SYSTEM (1966). To Mitrany, functional cooperation was a matter of creating specialized agencies on the international level that pursued similar goals to those pursued by the New Deal agencies. In his view, "[t]he growth of specific administrative agencies and laws is the foundation of modern government." *Id.* at 113. The most promising international organizations were therefore those that pursued specific and technical goals. "Internationally . . . while a body of law grew slowly and insecurely through rules and convention, many common activities were developed effectively by means

of functional organs." *See* David Zaring, *International Law by Other Means: The Twilight Existence of International Financial Regulatory Organizations*, 33 TEX. INT'L L.J. 281, 292–97 (1998), and Michael C. Dorf & Charles F. Sabel, *A Constitution of Democratic Experimentalism*, 98 COLUM. L. REV. 267 (1998) for a discussion.

40 Dorf & Sabel, *supra* note 39, at 287–88 ("The model requires linked systems of local and inter-local or federal pooling of information, each applying in its sphere the principles of benchmarking, simultaneous engineering, and error correction, so that actors scrutinize their initial understandings of problems and feasible solutions. These principles enable the actors to learn from one another's successes and failures while reducing the vulnerability created by the decentralized search for solutions."); *see also* ALBERT HIRSCHMAN, EXIT, VOICE, AND LOYALTY: RESPONSES TO DECLINE IN FIRMS, ORGANIZATIONS, AND STATES 77 (1970). As the following analysis will underscore, utilizers of Hirschman's trichotomy tend to ignore loyalty, which even Hirschman himself failed to find as fruitful as the tradeoff between exit and voice. *See* Lyman Johnson, *After Enron: Remembering Loyalty Discourse in Corporate Law*, 28 DEL. J. CORP. L. 27, 73 (2003), for a discussion of Hirschman with particular attention to the hazy concept of loyalty.

41 Pauwelyn has explained the intellectual debts in the following terms: his article "borrows from the theoretical framework of exit and voice, introduced in 1970 by the economist Albert Hirschman and later brilliantly applied by Joseph Weiler to the transformation of the European Community." Joost Pauwelyn, *The Transformation of World Trade*, 104 MICH. L. REV. 1, 4 (2005).

42 J.H.H. Weiler, *The Transformation of Europe*, 100 YALE L.J. 2403, 2409 (1991).

43 *See id.* at 2411.

44 See *id.* at 2427.

45 Pauwelyn, *supra* note 41, at 18.

46 Weiler, *supra* note 42, at 2431–40 ("Constitutionally, no core of sovereign state powers was left beyond the reach of the Community. Put differently, if the constitutional revolution was celebrated in the 1960's albeit 'in limited fields,' the 1970's saw the erosion of these limits.").

47 Henry Klehm III et. al., *Securities Enforcement Has Crossed the Border: Regulatory Authorities Respond to the Financial Crisis with a Call for Greater International Cooperation, but Where Will That Lead?*, 13 U. PA. J. BUS. L. 927, 935 (2011) ("In 2009, IOSCO saw 1261 information requests made by its members to fellow regulators via the MMoU, an increase from 867 in 2008, a figure that was itself an increase of eighteen percent from 2006.").

48 Stavros Gadinis, *The Financial Stability Board: The New Politics of International Financial Regulation*, 48 TEX. INT'L L.J. 157 (2013).

49 Roberta Romano, *For Diversity in the International Regulation of Financial Institutions: Critiquing and Recalibrating the Basel Architecture*, 31 YALE J. ON REG. (2014), *available at* http://digitalcommons.law.yale.edu/yjreg/vol31/iss1/2.
50 Adam Feibelman, *Law in the Global Order: The IMF and Financial Regulation*, 49 N.Y.U. J. INT'L L. & POL. 687, 738 (2017).

3

Banking, Global Oversight's Ne Plus Ultra

On June 26, 1974, when Bank Herstatt collapsed, capital markets the world over were roiled and banks scrambled to fund – or in some cases stop – outgoing payments as they waited for dollars to arrive in exchange for Deutschmarks provided to Herstatt. Eurodollar market interest rates rose, and smaller banks, which looked a lot like Herstatt, found it difficult to borrow in that market at all. The wide-ranging effects of the collapse of the regional German bank, and the cross-border implications presented by that collapse, spurred national regulators into international action, as did the impact of other bank failures, including that of the Italian-controlled Franklin National Bank in New York.

The result was the creation of the Basel Committee on Banking Supervision. Today, the Basel Committee is the quintessential regulatory network. It has accomplished much through its specific and rigorous rules on capital adequacy, and yet those rules are nothing more than soft law, as Basel's principals reiterate. Indeed, the Basel Committee might be considered to be nothing more than a collection of efforts by bank supervisors, bound loosely by an organization that declaims legal substance and one that used to act entirely without the sorts of procedures expected from formally constituted regulators.

Nonetheless, its capital adequacy accords, which have gone through three iterations, have always looked a lot like a "hard rule" in domestic law, with clarity and specificity about bank requirements – requirements that deeply affect the profitability of those institutions. Over the course of those iterations, the committee has adopted new procedures. And, in addition to the rule, it has authored a blizzard of other documents: white papers, best practices, and principles in this or that narrow area of banking supervision. The Basel Committee resembles a global agency with regard to its promulgations, and yet it holds to the network model – a small central body, relying on its members for enforcement and peer review, dedicated to leveling playing fields, and promulgating rules through consensus. It enjoys a strong, if not perfect, record of observance of its dictates, and yet has all of the horizontal and informal characteristics of an agency-to-agency relationship.

Nonetheless, much of the change over time that has characterized the way the Basel Committee acts reflects an evolution towards bureaucratic governance, rather than the development of a unique and different form of cross-border governmental oversight. As regulatory networks evolved, they have often adopted the trappings of traditional domestic administrative law. Like domestic regulators, international networks that began – perhaps in a Swiss bar, as one origin story of the Basel Committee would have it – among financial and other regulators of like mind but with little attentiveness to procedure have evolved into something that increasingly requires notice, comment, and opportunity to respond before taking any steps. A remarkable example of this change lies in the contrast between the first Basel Accord on Capital Adequacy, which was concluded in secret by the Basel Committee in 1988 and released in a twelve-page document, and the second ("Basel II"), which was put through nearly a decade's worth of comment by hundreds of interested individuals and institutions and resulted in a correspondingly long and detailed regulatory product. The third accord ("Basel III"), initially proposed in 2010 and slowly taking effect over the better part of a decade starting in 2013, was also the subject of a great deal of good administrative practice, at least if by "good" one means conventional notice and comment. That accord was released in a series of rulemakings, some of which were hundreds of pages long.

In adopting these new procedures, the committee has embraced bedrock principles of international financial regulation. Its consensus approach and commitment to a level playing field – indeed, the latter value is one of those that drove the development of the Basel Committee – demonstrate how it values national treatment and most-favored nation principles. It is the quintessential cross-border rulemaker and it enforces through peer review, conducted by the committee itself, by its members, and increasingly by the Financial Stability Board, in which it plays a central role (the first two chairs of the board, and only two as of this writing, have been central bankers).[1] It relies on its members for implementation of its dictates, and has largely enjoyed success in ensuring that they do so.

The embrace of the committee's pronouncements by American regulators marks the willingness of those regulators to turn abroad even as the other institutions of the US government – the Senate, in its treaty-ratifying role, for example – regards the very concept of global governance with suspicion. In 2017, legislation in Congress was introduced that would have limited the ability of US financial regulators to negotiate with foreign counterparts in almost any context. Even some members of the Federal Reserve have been skeptical about Basel; one governor wrote a book about how much he disliked the second iteration of the Basel capital adequacy accord.[2] Despite this wariness, American regulators have been, in the end, Basel's strongest proponents. The current Fed Chairman Jerome Powell, has described international regulatory cooperation of the sort done by Basel as "essential," and the Treasury Department issued a report stating that it "generally supports efforts to finalize remaining elements of the international reforms at the Basel Committee."[2]

In the rest of this chapter, we will review the institutional details of the committee and how they have changed. Understanding the methods of institutionalization helps to make sense of what Basel really does, and so spend some time going through them, as we will the other regulatory networks. Because the Basel Committee has promulgated every variety of pronouncement that cross-border networks make – specific rules, broad principles, white papers, and other documents laying out best practices – we will also consider its representative achievements.

3.1 THE BASEL COMMITTEE'S INSTITUTIONAL FORM

Prompted by the failures of Franklin National Bank and Bank Herstatt, the central bank governors of the G10, Luxembourg, and Switzerland established the Basel Committee on Banking Supervision. The founding mandate of the committee lies in a press communiqué from the central bank governors issued through the Bank for International Settlements on February 12, 1975, in which the BIS "confirm[ed] that the central-bank Governors of the Group-of-Ten countries and of Switzerland have established a standing committee of experts on banking and foreign-exchange regulations and supervisory practices."[3] The organization has since promulgated no formal constitution or bylaws and has no staff or facilities. The BIS, which is headquartered in Basel and was created after World War I in part to process German reparations payments, is commonly thought of as a central bank for central bankers; it is owned by a set of relatively large central banks currently numbering over fifty. The BIS is not large by the standards of international financial institutions, and acts as the committee's secretariat, though, as Charles Freeland has explained, "there is no formal BIS participation in the committee."[4] The Basel Committee traditionally met at least four times per year at the BIS, while regulators among its members charged with representing their agencies before the committee stay in touch more regularly, through task-specific meetings, conference calls, reporting responsibilities to the Financial Stability Board or G20, and other ways. Until 2009, the Basel Committee was composed of the same twelve central bankers who founded it; it has since expanded its membership to take in different parts of the world, including the BRIC countries, and other developing markets in conjunction with the reinvigoration of the G20 in the wake of the financial crisis. In 2014, it expanded its memberships again, meaning that it now has forty-five members from twenty-eight jurisdictions, with extra members from jurisdictions with multiple banking supervisors, such as the USA, which sends representatives from the Fed, the New York Fed, the Office of the Comptroller of the Currency (OCC), and the Federal Deposit Insurance Corp. (FDIC) to Basel. The committee also has nine observers including central banks, supervisory groups, and international organizations like the IMF. Moreover, although the Basel Committee has taken some real steps towards transparency, it still meets in secret.

In 1974, the members declared, via a press release, that the primary purpose of the committee would be to provide members with a regular forum for airing cooperative approaches to the supervision of multinational banks.[5] But it has gone beyond merely offering itself up as a place for institutionalized conversation. Since its founding, the committee, pursuant to this mandate, has served both as the venue for the exchange of information about supervisory practices and as the mechanism for the promulgation of hard standards to which all members of the committee must subscribe.

The use of a press release to announce an organization's purpose and activity is rather far removed from a conventional international legal treaty and accompanying annals of drafting, and it illustrates how different the Basel Committee is from a formally constituted international organization. *The Economist* magazine has characterized it as nothing more than an "international club for banking regulators."[6] The committee's secretariat is comprised of professional supervisors on temporary secondment from member banks to the BIS, technically a private bank mostly owned and operated by the central banks of thirty-one countries and mandated "to promote the co-operation of central banks and to provide additional facilities for international financial operations."[7]

As the committee's list of achievements has lengthened, and its importance in the policy formation of baseline rules of financial regulation grew, there was a sense that an originally rather technocratic effort needed some supervision by political appointees. To that end, the committee has been subjected to the oversight and direction of the Group of Governors and Heads of Supervision (GHOS), a governing committee comprised of central bank governors and supervisory heads of Basel's member agencies, though it is not an organization with much institutional presence, or, one suspects, much independent purpose outside of its supposed Basel-supervising role. These regulators meet regularly, particularly before G20 meetings, and play roles in the oversight of organizations that, in turn, oversee the Basel Committee, such as the Financial Stability Board. Functionally, however, the supervisory role is clearly delineated. Basel proceeds under the general direction provided by the governing body and all major initiatives require GHOS endorsement. The committee also relies on GHOS to "(a) approve the BCBS Charter and any amendments to [the charter]; (b) provide general direction for the BCBS work programme; and (c) appoint the BCBS Chairman from among its members."[8]

The Basel Committee characterizes its "key objectives" as "strengthen[ing] international cooperation, improv[ing] the overall quality of banking supervision worldwide, and ensur[ing] that no foreign banking establishment escapes supervision."[9] The Committee has developed principles of "consolidated supervision" over the past decade and created a multinational framework for bank capital adequacy requirements, among other regulatory efforts. It describes itself as "a forum for ongoing cooperation between member countries on banking supervisory matters."[10]

It does not, however, make its forum open to the public. The Basel Committee operates in secret and has sought throughout its existence to maintain as low a profile as possible. As noted in the introduction, former committee chairman Huib J. Muller emphasized the value of this governing approach: "[W]e don't like publicity. We prefer, I might say, our hidden secret world of the supervisory continent."[11] Indeed, the Basel Committee's 1975 founding agreement was not released to the public for over five years after the central bankers adopted it.

Although it meets in secret, Basel has increasingly adopted some indicia of transparency, which has been accelerated by the vogue for publicity that came with the financial crisis. It has for some time circulated its proposed actions to the public for consultation. It has also maintained an increasingly elaborate web presence, notifying interested parties of its activities and agenda and publishing peer-review results. Speeches are reported on the site, conferences are announced, standards, sound practices, and guidelines are published. The committee has also publicized its work program, which is a broadly worded agenda of its immediate priorities.

The committee operates by consensus, and values an interactive and decentralized method of ensuring compliance. The committee has declared that "the development of close personal contacts between supervisors in different countries has greatly helped in the handling and resolution of problems affecting individual banks as they have arisen. This is an important, though necessarily unpublicized, element in the committee's regular work."[12] The committee pursues those contacts within its membership and has sought to develop others with outside banking regulators, including regional banking supervisory organizations such as the Nordic Supervisory Group and The Group of Banking Supervisors in Arab Countries. This quest for common ground is Basel's substitute for binding agreements.

The committee also uses peer review as a tool to measure progress. The committee compiles a semiannual checklist indicating the progress made towards implementation of its regulatory framework that surveys all of its members. It also does individual assessments of the consistency of domestic rules of member countries with those frameworks, and some reports on member compliance on particular areas of interest. In 2017, for example, the committee published a report on the "progress in adopting the principles for effective risk data aggregation and risk reporting," promulgated by the committee for the world's largest banks.[13]

Peter Cooke, a former chair of the Basel Committee, has observed that "[t]he committee does not possess any formal supranational supervisory authority; its conclusions do not have, and were never intended to have, legal force."[14] The committee has agreed that it possesses no such formal authority. Rather, it formulates broad supervisory standards, practices, and guidelines which individual authorities use to implement the detailed arrangements – statutory or otherwise – which are best suited to their own national systems. In fact, the committee enforces its rules through its members; each national financial regulator is expected to adopt and promulgate the standards to the various financial institutions. Basel operates under the assumption that each national regulator will incorporate its agreed-to provisions into their supervisory approaches – while its principles refer to financial networks and systems, its primary audience is government bodies that regulate on the national level. As the Committee's charter lays out, "standards [are] to be incorporated into local legal frameworks through each jurisdiction's rule-making process."[15] In this way, the committee encourages convergence toward common approaches and common standards without attempting detailed harmonization of member countries' supervisory techniques.

Through subtle cajoling and the inertia of widespread enactment, the informal agreement has become a non-legal measure that "now applies to virtually all financial institutions worldwide."[16] Basel supervisor Charles Freeland has claimed that "[w]ithout in any way approaching the legal status of a treaty . . . [an] agreement is considered to be binding on its members."[17] Moreover, its endorsement by the G20 and FSB has added to its compliance pull. American banking regulators have generally treated the Basel Committee's theoretically voluntary proposals as the basis for rapid domestic regulatory action, with one notable exception. They made portions of the second capital adequacy accord optional for most small- and mid-sized banks in the USA.

3.2 THE VARIED SUCCESSES OF THE BASEL COMMITTEE

The Basel Committee's accomplishments are led by its series of capital adequacy accords that its members have imposed on their banks.

Basel began the evolution of its capital adequacy program with rules on the allocation of supervisory responsibilities for multinational banks. In 1983, the committee issued its Principles for the Supervision of Banks' Foreign Establishments, which focused on the foreign branches problem – that is, whether they were safe and sound, and who was responsible for that, given that foreign branches could be overseen by the national regulator in the country of the bank's headquarters, or the regulator in the country where the branch bank was located. The committee also sought to allocate responsibilities for branches or subsidiaries (in banking, subsidiaries and branches are different because of their corporate form: branches are part of companies, subsidiaries are companies owned by the bank) between host and parent (or home) supervisory authorities. This document was a revised version of a paper originally issued in 1975, which came to be known as the Concordat. The text of the earlier paper was expanded and reformulated to take account of changes in the market and to incorporate the principle of consolidated supervision of international banking groups (which had been adopted in 1978). The Concordat was revised again, albeit modestly, in 1990, and 1992, showing that the committee's members believed that the delineation of supervisory responsibilities was important, and worth working on through this international process. By 1996, it was being applied to the banking supervisors of nonmember countries, and gradually evolved into a set of principles for effective supervision of international banks. The Core Principles For Effective Banking Supervision have been revised regularly since, and currently include twenty-nine broadly worded directions that the committee believes encompass the powers and responsibilities of effective bank supervisors.

The committee's most notable contributions to bank regulation are its thrice-issued capital accords.

The first accord, agreed to in 1988, laid down universal minimum capitalization standards (ultimately pegged at 8 percent of assets) for international banks under the regulatory aegis of the members' central banks. All the committee's members have imposed those minimums on their domestic banks.

The political-economy story told about the capital adequacy accord turns on increasing international competition by financial institutions, and a sense that a regulatory level playing field had to be created if some Western banks were to flourish in that competition. In particular, US banks were feeling the pinch of tight monetary policy and increasing regulatory scrutiny, driven in part by an understanding that its savings and loan sector was extraordinarily troubled, and that more cosmopolitan banks were exposed to troubled sovereign debt from Latin America. But while better regulation of the domestic financial markets might have been good domestic policy, it created problems for those banks when competing with foreign institutions that did not have to establish their capital levels so definitively. American bankers worried particularly that Japanese banks, with, they thought, no capital adequacy requirements, would be able to use their lower cost of capital to win financing business from US institutions.

Of course, American regulators could have abandoned their seriousness about capital rules if their top priority centered on the ability of their financial institutions to compete in world markets. Instead they tried to use Basel to persuade the rest of the world to increase their capital standards. There was opposition from both continental Europe and Asia to the push, but that opposition collapsed after the USA and UK concluded a bilateral capital adequacy agreement in 1987, leading to concerns that both countries might close their markets to undercapitalized foreign competitors. Faced with these American and British commitments, the rest of the members of the Basel Committee went along with the initial capital accord.

The agreement – running "little more than two dozen pages and … adopted within seven months after the committee's first (and only) consultative paper was published for comment," as one US regulator observed[18] – provided for implementation of a credit risk measurement framework for all banks. This implementation was impressively widespread. The 1988 capital adequacy standards were fully implemented by all the committee-member countries by 1992, to notable effect on the banks in those countries. The implementation required US banks to add $10 billion to $15 billion to their capital reserves in total; French banks, $13 billion; and Japanese banks, $26 billion to $50 billion. In fact, some observers have concluded that the implementation of the 1988 Basel Accord forced Japanese banks to raise so much capital that the country's domestic markets were flooded with assets that depressed prices and the value of collateral, thereby forcing more sales and creating a "vicious circle" that contributed to that country's recession in the 1990s.

Basel I was a relatively simply applied rule that focused on the balance sheets of regulated banks. It established a ratio between equity and risk-weighted assets, requiring that equity and some other forms of capital to amount to 8 percent of the value of the risk-weighted assets. Risk weighting meant that banks would not need to hold as much capital against assets that were deemed to be safe; the safest asset Basel I counted was the sovereign debt of Organisation for Economic Co-operation and Development countries. That, of course, was convenient for Basel members that depended on financial markets to issue and roll over their government debt. Banks that held cash or OECD government debt did not have to hold *any* capital against those assets, meaning that they were risk-weighted at 0 percent. Banks could risk weight debt from large private banks at 20 percent of their face value. They could discount the value of residential mortgages held by 50 percent, and could not discount the value of private sector debt at all.

Once assets held by banks had been placed in these four buckets – 0 percent, 20 percent, 50 percent, and 100 percent – and discounted accordingly, bankers and regulators could calculate the amount and kind of capital on the liabilities side of the bank balance sheet and see if that amounted to 8 percent of the value of the risk-weighted assets. Basel I was thus a balance-sheet exercise above all, and although bank balance sheets can be quite complicated (the first capital accord made provisions for – or basically ignored – off-balance-sheet assets, letters of credit, among others), the idea behind the capital rule was that all banks should only be permitted so much leverage, and that there ought to be a standard minimum relationship between the equity of the bank and its assets, accounting for their quality.

Getting every regulator of large banks the world over to agree on both the principle behind Basel I and on details like the risk weightings and the 8 percent number, was quite a feat. Moreover, Basel I created some distorting incentives for banks, as may be the case with any bright line rule applied to a complicated sector of the economy. It made it attractive for them to hold sovereign debt and mortgages, and less appealing to be owed money by corporations. Moreover, Basel I treated all OECD member debt equally, ranging from the USA, which has famously never missed a bond payment since the days of Alexander Hamilton, to Greece and Portugal, which have engaged in restructurings more recently.

After a decade of experience with the 1988 accord, the Basel Committee decided to try to improve it. In January 2001, it issued a proposal for a revised accord that would replace the 1988 agreement. The second iteration focused on: 1) new minimum capital requirements, with a more sophisticated weighting of the soundness of types of assets in assessing capital adequacy, 2) common standards of "supervisory review of an institution's capital adequacy and internal assessment process," and 3) "effective disclosure" that would, in theory, encourage "market discipline." The first of these goals marked the broadest change, as the committee turned from crude risk weights imposed by regulators to a form of risk weighting that relied in part on the internal models of the banks themselves.

In this sense, the second capital adequacy accord marked a form of deregulation, whereby regulators trusted certain banks to manage much of their credit risks themselves. But it also broadened the focus of the Basel Committee away from credit risk and asset quality and towards a view of the risks that banks faced, including operational and macroeconomic risks, even if Basel II did not require much of the banks with regard to these matters. The efforts to standardize supervisory review meant that Basel stood not just for a check of the balance sheet, but rather a second regulatory pair of eyes that would review every bank's capital calculations and would think about risks not captured by a focus on asset quality. By the same token, Basel II's disclosure requirements were designed to permit investors to also scrutinize banks and reward those engaged in prudent risk management. As for the more sensitive capital weightings, Basel II allowed many firms to take a so-called "standardized approach" to evaluating the quality of their assets. Instead of considering the four buckets of Basel I, Basel II allowed banks to risk-weight their assets with reference to external credit ratings provided by Moody's and Standard & Poor's, among others. In other cases, where banks could convince regulators that their internal estimates of losses given defaults were well founded, regulators would defer to the internal ratings-based approaches of banks. Basel II made bows at market risk and operational risk in the minimum capital requirements as well.

The second accord also looked very different than the first one. It ran for hundreds of pages, many times the size of its predecessor. The document resembled eye-glazing domestic regulations more than international treaties.

Basel II was created through a much more elaborate process than the first. The second has been opened to serial waves of comments, 250 of which were received on the first public draft, including comments from banks, self-regulatory organizations, and other regulators, and 200 on a consultative paper about the accord in 2003. Basel kept the public apprised of the evolution of its efforts to amend the accord on its website, as did is members: the Fed devoted an entire section on its own website to updating interested parties on developments in the revised accord.

One of the testaments to the effectiveness of the Basel Committee lies in the blame that was laid at the feet of its second capital accord after the financial crisis. The first financial institutions to fail during the crisis were, at least in the view of the SEC, adequately capitalized under Basel II up to the moment they collapsed. This was the case for both Bear Stearns, which failed in the spring of 2008, and Lehman Brothers, which went bankrupt that September. More generally, the favorable regulatory treatment of housing by the accord may have encouraged financial institutions to overweight those assets, since they did not have to hold as much capital against housing as against corporate or commercial loans, contributing to the creation of the housing bubble. By the same token, the favorable treatment of wealthy country sovereign debt was thought by many to incentivize the willingness of banks to continue to fund sovereign borrowing by countries, such as Greece, that qualified for favorable regulatory treatment as members of the European Union, but which had amassed enormous deficits and debt.

Unsurprisingly, the Basel Committee's principal effort since the financial crisis has been a third revision of capital standards, now known as the Basel III Accord.[19] While it has focused on revising and increasing capital standards, it has taken other steps to deal more directly with the rationale behind such standards – that is, to minimize systemic risk in global financial markets. Accordingly, while all the Basel accords increased the amount of core capital and common equity banks must keep on hand against loans (at least as compared to pre-Basel requirements in most countries), the committee has taken the opportunity with Basel III to go further. Systemically important financial institutions will receive more attention from regulators in the future under the accord.

Among other things, Basel III extends the requirements to hold capital against off-balance-sheet activities and derivatives trading. It has raised the minimum level of required capital, including an increase in the minimum common equity requirement from 2 percent to 4.5 percent, to which it has added a capital conservation buffer of 2.5 percent for some firms, meaning that, against their assets, banks must hold total common equity of approximately the traditional 8 percent, with some banks holding more. Basel III also devised some alternative measures of safety and soundness. It introduced an international harmonized leverage ratio to serve as an alternative to the risk-based capital measure, and also introduced a short-term liquidity coverage ratio and a longer-term structural net stable funding-ratio requirement. Last, the accord is designed to encourage banks to build up capital buffers in good times to resolve the problem of counter-cyclicality, which is when banks need money the most they are least able to raise it.

Basel III has also ventured into loss-given-default risk estimates, executive compensation strictures, and other tools of modern financial supervision, albeit more cautiously.[20] There is even a component of Basel III that urges supervisors to do a better job via guidelines designed to encourage steadfast monitoring and has made substantive changes in how bank riskiness is measured and limited.

Many of these standards are quite elaborate, and can substantially affect the bottom line of the banks subject to them. It is fair to say that while the post-crisis Basel Committee continues to engage in the pronouncement of principles and best practices that still mark all network regulatory enterprises, it has also gone substantially further.

The common capital adequacy standard for banks is meant to be "internationally consistent and non-discriminatory."[21] As we have seen, much of the impetus for international financial regulation was not only to forestall crises, but also to solve problems of competitive inequality created by regulatory differences across jurisdictions.

The desire to obtain national treatment protections has been a primary motivation for regulatory cooperation in finance, given that every country has a large incumbent (or in some cases, an oligopolistic) bank, that can both push their domestic regulator to cut a deal with recalcitrant foreign agencies, and that constitutes a threat to institutions that would like to parlay their trade internationally.[22]

We have already had occasion to mention the way the first version of the Basel accord was facilitated by a threat by American and British regulators to set up their own capital adequacy requirements, raising the prospect of potential discrimination against European and Asian non-participants in the process. The first accord avoided the prospect of regional moats by creating a common scheme meant to apply to all banks doing cross-border business.

National treatment is also a point of contention, with regulators often arguing that some domestic safety and soundness measures violate national-treatment principles; an example might be the inclination of US regulators to introduce a modest "ring-fencing" requirement for foreign banks (the EU looks set to duplicate the rule), requiring them to allocate capital to their American subsidiaries, rather than across global operations. Because ring-fencing rules applied to foreign banks treat them differently than US banks, the national-treatment implications have been serious enough to occasion controversy. British regulators have also indicated their interest in ring-fencing requirements; there too, there is a suspicion about the burden such a rule would impose on foreign entrants into the London market. All of this is the sort of thing that gets argued about in and through the Basel process.

In addition to implementing more stringent guidelines, the committee has also strengthened its peer-review procedure to ensure compliance. In mid-2012, all Basel members agreed to and adopted the Regulatory Consistency Assessment Program (RCAP) that reviews and reports on each member's implementation of the Basel III rules and principles. The assessment proceeds on three levels: to ensure timely adoption of Basel III, regulatory consistency with Basel III, and consistency of outcomes. The procedure includes both a self-assessment component – a questionnaire to be completed before the assessment, and updated regularly – and a peer-review component, in which technical experts from other member countries assess implementation progress. The findings are then published by the committee on its website. Like many other compliance assessment and reporting schemes, RCAP has a series of prescribed procedures for each step of the review, including those for follow-up monitoring of assessed jurisdictions. Basel does not stand alone in this enforcement venture. RCAP is intended to support the monitoring mechanisms that the FSB already has in place for G20/FSB financial reforms.

Almost as interesting as the content of Basel III is the manner of its promulgation. The revised accord was devised through a type of notice-and-comment process while responding to schedule and broad policy directives set by the G20. In the period between January 2008 and August 2011, the committee opened seventeen rulemaking proposals for comment and received 147 comments. Most of these comments came from individual banks and national banking associations, though on rare occasions an affected stock exchange or regulator has contributed a view, as has the occasional individual. Consequently, as a member of the committee suggested, "the supervisory community had to fight a fierce battle to require more capital and less leverage in the financial system in the face of significant resistance from some quarters of the banking industry," which suggests in turn that supervisors considered the views of regulated industry to be important, as is the usual case in traditional, domestic administrative procedure.[23]

The committee has embraced notice and comment, which establishes the basics of transparency, at least through a US lens. Basel's comments come from a variety of institutions and individuals, but they have a unifying theme; the vast majority come from domestic trade associations of the finance industry and large finance institutions of a global nature. Notably, regulators or stock exchanges (which often perform a quasi-regulatory function), have submitted few comments to the rulemaking process. By contrast, the most prolific commenters, weighing in on five of the committee's first seventeen proposals, were British and Japanese banking associations; the French, Canadian, and Australian associations offered four comments each to the same set of proposals. The banking associations of German, Canada, Italy, Hong Kong, and numerous other countries also weighed in. And large banks like Barclays, Nomura, BNY Mellon, and Credit Suisse participated on occasion. Financial institutions and associations of financial institutions, such as the industry organizations of those institutions in the various countries that are members of the Basel Committee, submitted the large majority of comments, with banks submitting fifty-two and bank associations fifty-seven of the total, some 75 percent of all comments.

Civil society has been less involved. One comment has been filed by an association of trade unions, and another by the University of Reading, while regulators outside the committee have filed a total of three. It is clear that the comment process is dominated by regulated industry. The commentary suggests that financial institutions take the Basel process seriously, and that, somewhat alarmingly, they comprise the majority of voices afforded to committee outsiders.

Perhaps as a result of the pressure, Basel III has been implemented slowly: internationally active banks were given until 2019 to transition to the new leverage and capital ratios required under Basel III. Nonetheless, the committee has vowed that it "intends to monitor and review the application of the framework in the period ahead with a view to achieving ever greater consistency."[24] It has, in the wake of the financial crisis, embraced peer review; its members are also subject to review of their implementation efforts through the FSB, though Basel has long modestly observed the practice. In 1995, the committee vowed that it "intends to monitor and review the application of the framework in the period ahead with a view to achieving ever greater consistency."[25] Since issuing Basel III, the committee has published progress reports twice per year on how the implementation process is going; the FSB also files an annual report on implementation with the G20.

In addition to calling the quality of Basel's capital rules into question, the crisis also illustrated the role of the regulatory network; it is, first and foremost, a rulemaking regulator, rather than a locus of crisis response. The crisis did not send every central banker and bank supervisor bolting to Switzerland for war room negotiations under Basel's auspices. It responded to the crisis with small beer, such as a speech by the committee chair during the depths of the problem on "The Importance of Banking Supervision in Financial Stability" and the promulgation of unspecific supervisory principles on liquidity risk. And the coordinated injections of funds into the monetary supply by central banks beginning in the fall of 2008, which was at least an example of regulatory cooperation, has no obvious links to the Basel Committee, even though the committee, with its regular meetings, seems a likely outlet for such coordination. Of course, the existence of Basel relationships may have bred some familiarity, which made this coordinated crisis response possible.

This familiarity may have been important, of course. During the financial crisis, central bankers smoothly extended loans and supplied stable currencies to one another. Such transactions are known as currency swaps, and the agreements to commit these currency swaps are called swap lines. "Swap lines became mechanisms to outsource the Federal Reserve's bedrock power – its lender of last resort role – to foreign central banks," Oklahoma's Colleen Baker has observed. During the financial crisis, the Fed extended swap lines to Brazil, Mexico, South Korea, Singapore, as well as the world's largest central banks, on the rationale that, as the Fed put it, "intensification of stresses in [these countries] could trigger unwelcome spillovers for both the US economy and the international economy more generally."[26] Swap lines were examples of central bank cooperation that were likely facilitated by the regular interactions provided by Basel, and the trust engendered through them.

The sort of work done by the Basel Committee in the wake of the financial crisis exemplifies the new commitment to the possibilities of international regulatory efforts. Basel has since extended its notion of cooperation and consensus to its work with other organizations. For example, the recent peer-review program under Basel III was structured as a supplement to the FSB monitoring program for its set of financial regulatory principles.

The Basel Committee has for decades served as the epitome of the governance through a network of regulators. The network has broadly affected the ways financial institutions operate while adopting increasingly elaborate forms of procedure. Basel's compliance mechanisms have evolved as well, relying on peer review, through which the committee has regularly checked in on the progress of implementation of its capital- adequacy accord. Its record of compliance is not perfect: the USA was a laggard in implementing Basel's second iteration for its smaller financial institutions. But no banker or financial lawyer thinks that the committee is a paper tiger, producing blue ribbon reports that regulators ignore.

Some of its effectiveness lies in the cosmopolitan nature of banking and banking supervision. Central bankers have been collaborating since the early twentieth century, and the financial institutions supervised by them or by supervisory agencies have been crossing borders for even longer. Banking supervision is a cosmopolitan enterprise in a way that has been less the case in the other areas of financial regulation, such as capital-markets regulation and insurance supervision. But if Basel's foundation has a cultural element, its effectiveness is quite law-like. The regulations adopted by the committee are meant to apply to all banks, with little variation permitted in the way supervisors implement the core capital-adequacy rules. It is a soft law institution that claims to have all the bite of the most binding sorts of international agreements.

Notes

1 It has also made use of the World Bank and IMF's financial section assessment program (FSAP) to monitor compliance.

2 DANIEL TARULLO, BANKING ON BASEL (2009) (expressing skepticism about Basel II in particular).

3 Bank for International Settlements, *Press Communique*, Feb. 12, 1975, www.bis.org/press/p19750212.pdf.

4 Charles Freeland, *The Work of the Basel Committee, in* 2 CURRENT LEGAL ISSUES AFFECTING CENTRAL BANKS 231, 232 (Robert C. Effros ed., 1994).

5 *See* BIS, Press Communiqué 1 (Feb. 12, 1975) ("The committee is designed to assist the Governors in their continuing work of surveillance and exchange of information."); Joseph J. Norton, *Trends in International Bank Supervision and the Basel Committee on Banking Supervision*, 48 CONSUMER FIN. L.Q. 415, 415 n.1 (1994) (stating that the founding mandate for the Committee is found in the Feb. 12, 1975 press release).

6 *Getting Closer?*, ECONOMIST 82 (May 25, 1996).

7 BIS, *Information Flows Between Banking Supervisory Authorities* (Apr. 1990), *available at* www.bis.org/publ/bcbsc313.pdf (Basel Concordat); Basel Comm. on Banking Supervision, *International Convergence of Capital Measurement and Capital Standards* (July 1988), *available at* www.bis.org/publ/bcbs04A.pdf (original Basel Accord); John D. Hawke, Jr., Comptroller of the Treasury, Basel II: A Brave New World for Financial Institutions?, Address at the American Academy in Berlin (Dec. 15, 2003), *available at* www.occ.gov/static/news-issuances/news-releases/2003/nr-occ-2003-99a.pdf.

8 BASEL COMM. ON BANKING SUPERVISION, CHARTER (Jan. 2013), *available at* www.bis.org/bcbs/charter.pdf.

9 BASEL COMM. ON BANKING SUPERVISION, A BRIEF HISTORY OF THE BASEL COMMITTEE 1 (July 2013), *available at* www.bis.org/bcbs/history.pdf.

10 *Id.*

11 Huib J. Muller, Address to the 5th International Conference of Bank Supervisors (May 16, 1988), *quoted in* TONY PORTER, STATES, MARKETS, AND REGIMES IN GLOBAL FINANCE 66 (1993).

12 BASEL COMM. ON BANKING SUPERVISION, HISTORY OF THE BASEL COMMITTEE AND ITS MEMBERSHIP 6 (Mar. 2001), *available at* www.bis.org/publ/bcbsc101.pdf.

13 Basel Committee on Banking Supervision, *Principles for Effective Risk Data Aggregation and Risk Reporting*, Jan. 2013, www.bis.org/bcbs/publ/d399.htm.

14 Peter Cooke, Chair of the Basel Committee, *quoted in* JOSEPH JUDE NORTON, DEVISING INTERNATIONAL BANK SUPERVISORY STANDARDS 177 (1995).

15 BASEL COMM. ON BANKING SUPERVISION, CHARTER, *supra* note 8, at 6.

16 Heath Price Tarbert, *Rethinking Capital Adequacy: The Basel Accord and the New Framework*, 56 BUS. LAW 767, 792 (2001), *quoting* Lawrence L.C. Lee, *The Basel Accords as Soft Law: Strengthening International Banking Supervision*, 39 VA. J. INT'L L. 1, 6 (1998).

17 Freeland, *supra* note 4, at 233. The General Accounting Office (GAO) has also concluded that "the committee must continue to rely on moral suasion rather than legal authority to encourage adoption of its standards and monitor their implementation." *See* GEN. ACCOUNTING OFFICE, INTERNATIONAL BANKING: STRENGTHENING THE FRAMEWORK FOR SUPERVISING INTERNATIONAL BANKS 37 (1994).

18 *See* John D. Hawke, Jr., *Remarks by John D. Hawke, Jr., Comptroller of the Currency Before the American Academy in Berlin, on Basel II, December 15, 2003: A Brave New World for Financial Institutions?*, 23 Q.J. 125 (Mar. 2004), *available at* www.occ.gov/static/Publications/qj/qj23-1/QJ23-1.pdf.

19 Kenneth W. Dam, *The Subprime Crisis and Financial Regulation: International and Comparative Perspectives*, 10 CHI. J. INT'L L. 581, 627–28 (2010) ("Since the subject is capital adequacy regulation, an amendment to the Basel agreements will be required.").

20 *Id. see also* Jeffery Atik, *Basel II: A Post-Crisis Post-Mortem*, 19 TRANSNAT'L L. & CONTEMP. PROBS. 758 (2011) ("Basel II is dead. Basel III will continue to impose capital adequacy standards, but these standards will be simplified, will be adjusted, and will call for improvement in their 'quality.' New requirements involving procyclicality buffers, leverage limitations, and liquidity maintenance requirements will augment capital adequacy.").

21 Or so he indicated in a speech on derivatives regulation. Jaime Caruana, General Manager of the BIS, at the annual Pierre Werner Lecture, Luxembourg (July 7, 2011) (transcript available at www.bis.org/speeches/sp110711.htm) (expressing his

sense that the reforms "are being implemented in an internationally consistent and non-discriminatory way.").

22 A study by the European Central Bank observed that "The original Basel Capital Accord has been discussed extensively in Japan and some observers saw it as a conspiracy of certain Western banks in order to halt the international expansion of the relatively undercapitalized Japanese banks." Adrian van Rixtel, Ioanna Alexopoulou & Kimie Harada, *The New Basel Capital Accord and Its Impact on Japanese Banking: A Qualitative Analysis*, *in* THE NEW BASEL CAPITAL ACCORD 371–429 (Benton E. Gup ed., 2004). The Bank for International Settlements tried to quantify the disparity of the impact of the Basel Capital Accord for global banks; the institution had particular sympathy for Japanese banks. *See* Patricia Jackson, et al., *Bank for Int'l Settlements, Capital Requirements and Bank Behavior: The Impact of the Basel Accord* (Basel Comm. on Banking Supervision, Working Papers, No. 1, 2000), *available at* www.bis.org/publ/bcbs_wp1.pdf. But the losers of the financial regulatory globalization process were not only located in East Asia. Belgian banks, for example, had to increase the amount of capital in their reserves by 1.7 percent international financial regulatory efforts, and other countries were affected even more. *Id.*

23 Hervé Hannoun, Deputy Gen. Manager, Bank for Int'l Settlements, Speech at BoJ-BIS High Level Seminar in Hong Kong (Nov. 22, 2010), *available at* www.bis.org/speeches/sp101125a.pdf (describing the "international rule-making process").

24 Basel Comm. on Banking Supervision, *International Convergence of Capital Measurements and Capital Standards* (1988) (amended 1995), reprinted in 1 Compendium of Documents Produced by the Basel Committee 58–82, at para. 6 (1997).

25 Basel Comm. on Banking Supervision, *International Convergence of Capital Measurements and Capital Standards* (1988) (amended 1995), reprinted in 1 Compendium of Documents Produced by the Basle Committee 58–82, at para. 1 (1997).

26 Nathan Sheets, Address at the Meeting of the Federal Open Market Committee (Oct. 28–29, 2008) (transcript available at www.federalreserve.gov/monetarypolicy/files/FOMC20081029meeting.pdf).

4

Securities Regulation: Cooperation Instead of Harmonization

The International Organization of Securities Commissions (IOSCO) exemplifies a more modest degree of cooperation than does the Basel Committee on Banking Supervision. IOSCO's crowning achievement is a memorandum on enforcement cooperation, and it has been sidelined on what is the most promising prospect of capital markets coordination: the harmonization of accounting standards.

The Ponzi scheme created by the American financier R. Allen Stanford in the 1990s exemplifies why regulators believe they need the enforcement cooperation that IOSCO has facilitated. Stanford created an offshore bank in the Caribbean that was particularly popular with Latin American investors, although it had its share of US clients as well. The bank offered very generous interest on its certificates of deposit, which it represented as backed by the American securities industry's version of deposit insurance. But rather than being funded by investment returns, the high interest rates were paid from investments from new customers; that is what made it a Ponzi scheme. The Securities and Exchange Commission (SEC) investigated Stanford's bank over the course of the decade, constantly concerned about whether it had jurisdiction over the banking and offshore aspects of the financial scheme.

In 2009, Stanford's bank collapsed after a series of raids, and the SEC brought a variety of claims against him and the businesses he controlled. The securities fraud case against Stanford International Bank was built with the collaboration of a number of Latin American regulators. The superintendent of banks in Panama and the Panamanian securities regulator seized and sold Stanford's subsidiaries to compensate his victims. The seizure and sale required these regulators to coordinate with US regulators and authorities in other jurisdictions, including Switzerland and the UK. To make a case against an Antiguan regulator who had been bribed by Stanford, the SEC gathered information in both Antigua and the USA. These cases both required the gathering of evidence abroad and the cooperation of overseas regulators.

The Stanford case exemplifies the need for an organization that can facilitate enforcement cooperation across borders. But IOSCO has had greater ambitions.

While capital markets around the world operate under different rules, using, at least when IOSCO began, different accounting standards, reporting requirements, and trading guidelines, the IOSCO network has evaluated and supported to a degree the coordination of capital markets oversight. That has made it a valued player in the sphere of financial oversight pursued by the Financial Stability Board, in which IOSCO and its member regulators participate actively. It has devised, as all networks do, some principles of regulation that its members are supposed to support – things like regulatory independence and the power to investigate misstatements and other wrongdoing in the capital markets. It has produced its share of white papers and technical guidance for capital market structure, the oversight of exchanges, and diverse other subjects.

Institutionally, the organization has welcomed all regulators who wish to join, rather than following the exclusive membership model adopted by the Basel Committee. But like the Basel Committee, IOSCO is committed to increasingly elaborate administrative procedures – it now uses notice and comment for almost everything substantive that it does – and to bedrock principles that underlie much of its activities. IOSCO is also committed to peer review, and has set reviewable benchmarks for its members to encourage adoption of its memorandum of understanding on enforcement cooperation. It has also stuck to its preference for consensus on the principles that it has promulgated. And while the MOU on enforcement permits a degree of "dissensus" – it facilitates the enforcement of domestic standards through the gathering of evidence from across borders, though it does not require that domestic standards be shared – it does suggest that securities watchdogs are likely enough to embrace common enough values that they are willing to assist one another in the observance of them. Moreover, IOSCO's core principles reflect the common ground, and search for a level playing field, that marks much of international financial regulation. And the turn to bureaucratic order and legal principle is observable in IOSCO, even though it has made only modest efforts to create a global model for securities regulation.

There can be an inertial quality to participation in regulatory harmonization efforts, one example of which concerns one of IOSCO's failures. The organization has had little to do with the creation of a uniform set of accounting standards applicable to every jurisdiction, largely because American members were unwilling to compromise on the requirement that foreign companies seeking access to US markets conform to American-created Generally Accepted Accounting Principles (GAAP). Instead, as we will see, those standards have been left to another network, at some cost to IOSCO's relevance.

4.1 IOSCO'S INSTITUTIONAL FORM

Like the Basel Committee, the evolution of IOSCO is an interesting story of growing elaboration and transparency, the latter achieved in important part through Internet publication. IOSCO and Basel are different, however, and the devil lies in the details. Basel is exclusive, and IOSCO is not; Basel's secretariat is built on the BIS, while IOSCO's stands alone. As with the Basel Committee, a deep dive into the intricacies of IOSCO's institutionalization is instructive.

IOSCO has an unorthodox origin story. It developed out of the Interamerican Association of Securities Commissions and Similar Agencies in 1983, when the members of that organization passed bylaws transforming it from a regional group founded a decade earlier to a global agglomeration of securities regulators.[1] IOSCO's members then agreed to

> cooperate together to promote high standards of regulation in order to maintain just, efficient and sound markets; to exchange information on their respective experiences in order to promote the development of domestic markets; to unite their efforts to establish standards and an effective surveillance of international securities transactions; to provide mutual assistance to promote the integrity of the markets by a rigorous application of the standards and by effective enforcement against offenses.[2]

IOSCO is a much less selective organization than the Basel Committee. It now claims approximately 200 members, overseeing almost all of the world's capital markets. These include over 100 "ordinary" members, most of whom are the primary national securities regulator, like the SEC; twelve associate members, consisting of other financial regulators, which includes the Commodities Futures and Trading Commission (CFTC); and approximately seventy affiliate members, most of which are stock and futures exchanges. By 2004, IOSCO could boast that its membership covered over 90 percent of the world's capital markets. Although the numbers have fluctuated over time, the organization now boasts a membership that regulates over 95 percent of the world's securities markets in more than 115 jurisdictions.

The organization's bylaws declare that "[a] securities commission or a similar governmental body that is not a member is eligible for ordinary membership of the Organization. If there is no governmental regulatory body in a country, a self-regulatory body, such as a stock exchange, from that country is eligible for ordinary membership of the Organization."[3] The willingness to tolerate private regulators and self-regulatory organizations is markedly different from the approach of the Basel Committee, which in addition to being exclusive, is exclusively comprised of central bankers and bank supervisors.

Thus far, the organization is doing much more than merely tolerating its more unconventional members; there is a dedicated Affiliate Members Consultative Group that includes self-regulatory parties and other interested parties and that actively participates to the organization's policymaking efforts.

However, in other matters of form, the two organizations are very similar. As with the Basel Committee, IOSCO combines an informal structure, an absence of claims that its pronouncements rise to the level of law, and a tradition that it is increasingly attempting to change of internal opacity. Much as *The Economist* said of the Basel Committee, the *Financial Times* has characterized IOSCO as the "international securities regulators club."[4]

If so, it is a club with some defined parameters. One way IOSCO differs from Basel is that although both institutions have begun to adopt the trappings of administrative procedure, the Basel Committee has remained relatively informal in its internal organization. IOSCO has taken a different approach. It has adopted, and revisited, a complicated organizational chart. IOSCO has rules that govern its organization, and traditionally, a committee and working group-heavy structure staffed with representatives of member agencies and organizations of the network, and overseen by a small headquarters. The detail should not be overstated; while domestic agencies are ordinarily created pursuant to lengthy statutes, IOSCO's bylaws are casual and short; its committee system is subject to change, and its institutional imprint is small.

One could nonetheless consider IOSCO's differences from Basel – a large membership, a possibly more elaborate and formal committee system – and indict the organization for achieving less with those two types of mores. Although IOSCO pursues the national treatment and most-favored nation values shared by other networks, although it operates by rule, consensus, and enforces through peer review and delegation to its members, it does not share the broad achievement of the Basel Committee represented by the capital adequacy accords. Compliance with its dictates is a smaller feature in the practices of lawyers for financial institutions than is compliance with the requirements promulgated by the Basel Committee.

IOSCO has no charter and was not formed by treaty; instead, it was incorporated by a private bill of the Quebec National Assembly, and began life in North America.[5] The organization has continued to amend and develop its bylaws and welcome new members. It has created and funded a permanent secretariat, originally based in Montreal, before moving to Madrid.[6]

IOSCO has structured itself into five components: a Presidents Committee, the board, a general secretariat, four regional committees, and a set of consultative committees. The organization's bylaws – its only governing document – are twenty pages long and consist of fourteen parts and a preamble.[7] The Presidents Committee is most comparable to the general assembly of more traditional international organizations, and is composed of presidents of all ordinary members or their agents. The bylaws grant the Presidents Committee "all the powers necessary or convenient to achieve the objectives of the Organization," including the power to sanction noncompliant members. The presidents operate secretly at IOSCO meetings – under its bylaws, "[o]bservers and special guests may not attend meetings of the Presidents Committee unless invited by the Chairman with the concurrence of a majority of the members." However, IOSCO "recognizes the importance of maintaining a close dialogue with" self-regulatory organizations and interest groups "that make up its affiliate membership and of allowing them to make a constructive input in the work of the Organization."[8]

The Presidents Committee selects the IOSCO board for two-year terms, and each newly constituted board selects a chairman and vice-chairmen for the two-year term. The board "takes all decisions and undertakes all actions necessary or convenient to achieve the objectives of the Organization."[9] Its responsibilities include recommending the admission of members to the Presidents Committee, preparing the annual budget, and recommending the imposition of sanctions upon members.[10] The duties of the board were until recently divided up into a technical committee that focused on the supervision of established markets and other committees focused on emerging markets. However, under an agreement reached in 2011, the new IOSCO board "subsumed the roles and activities of the executive committee, the technical committee, and the emerging markets committee advisory board."[11]

The general secretariat, IOSCO's third component, coordinates the organization's activities, and offers information and assistance to members and to the organization's committees.[12] The secretary-general, who is appointed by the IOSCO board, administers the general secretariat. Those officials tend to be assigned from member agencies. One recent IOSCO secretary-general, David Wright, served as a market expert at the European Commission in Brussels before joining IOSCO in March 2012. His predecessor as secretary-general, Greg Tanzer, became a commissioner at the Australian Securities and Investments Commission after leaving IOSCO. Wright's successor, Paul Andrews, had worked at two US regulators, the SEC and the self-regulatory organization, Financial Industry Regulatory Authority (FINRA).

IOSCO has a tiny budget, consistent with network practice, although it has grown over time. Membership dues finance the organization and IOSCO does not take kindly to delinquent payments. In 2002, the voting rights of Colombia and Paraguay, and the affiliate membership of Argentina's electronic trading market operator, were suspended until members paid their annual contributions, the single instance of the Presidents Committee exercising its sanctioning power. In 2011, the dues were €15,000 per member per year, but starting in 2012 IOSCO moved to a tiered structure with dues based on per capita income and gross domestic product. In 2016 IOSCO's revenues amounted to €5,009,926. The general secretariat staff has grown from three permanent staff members in 2000 to slightly more than twenty. By contrast, the World Trade Organization's 2016 budget was 197 million Swiss francs (approximately $198.5 million), supporting 642 staffers; the United Nation's annual budget is some $2.6 billion; and the SEC's annual budget has recently been reported at $1.32 billion.

The fourth component of IOSCO's structure consists of four regional committees (formerly regional standing committees): the African-Middle East Regional Committee, the Asia-Pacific Regional Committee, the European Regional Committee, and the Interamerican Regional Committee. These committees establish their own rules of procedure, and, with the exception of the European committee, are meant to play something of a developmental role, in that they are targeted at emerging markets.

Consultative committees, IOSCO's fifth component, are established by the IOSCO board to act "as a forum in which a group of members may discuss matters of common interest."[13] Like regional committees, consultative committees select a chairman and may determine their own rules and procedures. All of these parts of the organization function together in an effort to meet objectives set out by the secretary general and to promote cooperation in securities regulation. These forums are formally split among different aspects of financial markets. For example, there is one committee specifically dedicated to the regulation of secondary committees, while another focuses on credit-rating agencies.

Aside from the membership exclusivity that Basel enjoys and that IOSCO lacks, in other structural matters the two organizations are very similar. Like the Basel Committee, IOSCO operates an informal structure, its pronouncements do not rise to the level of law, and it has in the past practiced internal opacity. Also like the Basel Committee, IOSCO provides lots of material on its website and has opened itself up for comment. In 2012, for example, it issued thirty-two public documents, including reports on sound practices and statements of principles of supervision; in 2016, there were twenty-six. It also issues an annual report, sells recordings of some of the sessions of its annual conference, and catalogs press releases, memoranda of understanding, and IOSCO resolutions in its online library.

Observers have concluded that this flexibility has also enabled the most important financial regulators to play a central role. "The United States, European Union, and Japan control" IOSCO, notes Gary Klieman, a long time consultant and senior partner at Kleiman International.[14] And the scholar Tony Porter believes the SEC plays an overwhelmingly influential role in IOSCO.[15] The organization has tried to level the playing field for all members by maintaining a growth and emerging markets (GEM) committee that includes some of the world's rapidly developing economies such as Brazil and China. The recently renamed committee is intended to provide a voice to the majority of the organization's membership; the countries on the GEM committee amount to 75 percent of IOSCO's participants. The committee not only focuses on issues of special interest to growing markets, but also consults with the larger organization in formulating global policies and guidelines.

Like the Basel Committee, IOSCO's administrative procedures are ad hoc and flexible. IOSCO creates informal agreements on financial regulation and tells its members to implement them domestically.[16] It holds comment periods, but is not subject to open-meeting laws,[17] judicial review, or any other criteria such as those found in the Administrative Procedure Act (APA) in the USA. It takes comments, usually submitted by finance industry associations, large financial firms, and sometimes its affiliate membership.

Again, like the Basel Committee, IOSCO aspires to achieve its goals of regulatory harmonization through consensus. In the words of the SEC, "IOSCO is an organization that operates on the basis of consensus, rather than majority votes. Its resolutions are non-binding on its member organizations."[18] However, unlike the Basel Committee, and perhaps in order to achieve that consensus, IOSCO defines harmonization broadly. German Stock Exchange Federation Executive Vice President Ruediger von Rosen emphasized at one IOSCO meeting that whatever the merits of harmonization "value should be attached to the possibility of giving issuers and investors a choice between quite different rules and regulations."[19] Another securities regulator has said that "harmonization does not necessarily mean that regulations must be identical."[20] Thus, after IOSCO passes a resolution, the SEC has announced that "each IOSCO member would have to determine whether and how to consider adoption of these standards at a domestic level."[21] IOSCO's general principles candidly admit that "there is often no single correct approach to a regulatory issue."[22]

IOSCO also pursues its objectives through cooperation with a variety of other regulatory and private organizations. For example, it receives the advice of stock exchanges through its consultative committees. IOSCO has also established contacts with the Basel Committee, issued its report on over-the-counter derivatives in conjunction with the committee, and has in the past vowed to work closely with it. One Basel Committee member was "impressed by the fact that in a formal sense, through IOSCO and through the BIS, the banking regulators and the securities regulators are at least talking to each other, and talking to each other internationally; securities regulators are learning to deal with each other internationally ..."[23] IOSCO has also worked closely with the International Accounting Standards Committee (IASC) and originally intended to implement international accounting standards for the global listing of securities in conjunction with IASC. However, this process has been championed by another network, the IASB, to which IOSCO has ceded the field. IOSCO continues to "contribut[e] actively to the work of the IASB, through participation in various expert committees and responses to consultation,"[24] and "continue[s] to monitor the work of the IASB."[25] Lastly, IOSCO is an active participant in the FSB, and interacts with other regulatory networks through that coordinative institution.

4.2 IOSCO'S ACHIEVEMENTS: MUTUAL ASSISTANCE OVER HARMONIZATION

IOSCO did not achieve early regulatory success in implementing global standards for securities enterprises or exchanges. The organization's attempt to develop minimum capital requirements for securities firms failed in 1992 when SEC chairman William Breeden announced his opposition to the capital adequacy calculations promulgated by the Basel Committee and favored by European securities regulators.[26] Recognizing the unlikelihood of international consensus, IOSCO abandoned its efforts to reach a compromise. It also retreated from playing a leading role in the harmonization of accounting standards, again after opposition from the SEC.

Instead, the network's early activities largely centered around the preparation of reports on effective mechanisms that might be used to regulate the securities markets, and the creation of mechanisms for cooperation, with the idea that a crash in one capital market could create effects across borders, and that better supervision could make crashes less likely. In 1994 IOSCO's members resolved "to cooperate together to ensure better regulation on the domestic as well as on the international level," to exchange information and to provide mutual enforcement assistance, and "to unite their efforts to establish standards and an effective surveillance."[27] In practice, these harmonization efforts entail the examination of a number of technical regulations. Thus, IOSCO has evaluated access to markets, capital requirements, clearing and settlement rules, accounting standards, and more traditional securities and futures rules among its members and has debated which standards are the most amenable to common standard-setting within its committees. It has also discussed which standards are most effective on the domestic level.

The organization has a particular claim to success in mechanisms for cooperation. During the financial crisis, regulators from around the world agreed to briefly halt the short selling of stocks in an effort to help financial firms stabilize; the coordination of the ban was accomplished in an IOSOCO meeting. In 1986, IOSCO issued a Resolution Concerning Mutual Assistance that called upon all "securities authorities[,] to the extent permitted by law, to provide assistance on a reciprocal basis for obtaining information related to market oversight and protection of each nation's markets against fraudulent securities transactions."[28] Each signatory also designated a contact person who is responsible for the timely processing of all requests for assistance. Over sixty agencies have signed the declaration. IOSCO claimed that it was "nothing short of the ancestor to almost all the memoranda of understanding in place today."[29] In 1991, the organization approved a resolution outlining Principles for Memoranda of Understanding, which now proliferate among securities enforcement regulators.

IOSCO's principal achievement to date is its successor to these early resolutions, its Memorandum of Understanding on Enforcement, described as "the first global multilateral information-sharing arrangement among securities regulators" that "sets a new international benchmark for cooperation critical to combating violations of securities and derivatives laws."[30] Though not legally enforceable, the memorandum requires signatories to "make all reasonable efforts to provide, without prior request, the other Authorities with any information that it considers is likely to be of assistance to those other Authorities in securing compliance with Laws and Regulations applicable in their jurisdiction."[31]

In 2005, IOSCO resolved "to require all members to become signatories to the IOSCO MOU, or to commit to doing so, by Jan. 1, 2010,"[32] and has continually worked towards this goal[33] because "the MOU is critically important."[34] Of IOSCO's 118 ordinary members, ninety-seven have become signatories to the MOU on enforcement, thus accepting a mandate to share information when it is requested for enforcement purposes. Twenty-eight members have yet to sign the MOU and only twenty-three have expressed "their commitment to seek the legislative and administrative changes" required for compliance.[35] Accompanying a published list of yet-to-sign members is a set of graduated sanctions for non-signatory members. The punishments start at a nomination bar and increase to suspension of voting rights for members who have not signed by the end of September 2014. And perhaps the harshest punishment of all is that IOSCO has encouraged signatory members to take greater precautions in transacting with non-signatory parties, making the club-like benefits of membership in the network apparent. In more positive encouragement, IOSCO has pledged to render technical assistance and political support to any non-signatory members that may require it.

The MOU's success to date can be measured not only by the number of signatories but also by the quantity of requests for information from foreign counterparties subject to the MOU. In 2003, roughly fifty requests were made under the MOU. This number grew steadily to over 1,200 by the end of 2009; 3,330 requests for assistance were made in 2016. Former SEC officials have described the extent to which they rely on international assistance for their enforcement efforts as deep and essential.

Other resolutions passed by IOSCO are not necessarily formally implemented on the domestic level. Only about half of the members have ratified the organization's 1992 resolution on money laundering – a high level compared to other IOSCO resolutions. IOSCO has thus been less able than the Basel Committee to persuade members to abide by agreements forged under its auspices, with the exception of the MOU.

In order to promote inclusion and common values, IOSCO has tried to foster engagement without requiring formal commitment from its members. IOSCO promulgated a number of pronouncements in response to the financial crisis beginning in 2007, taking the expected pledge-like and flexible form. It has spoken on issues such as capital adequacy, commodity derivatives markets, and hedge fund oversight, and in 2017 revised its Objectives and Principles of Securities Regulation, as well as its method for assessing compliance with those principles. Assessment is increasingly important to the network; the organization has also been working towards a formal assessment process with peer review on securitization and money market funds, and provides assessments of compliance with IOSCO principles on a jurisdiction-by-jurisdiction basis.

It has also issued joint reports with Basel and the IAIS on issues related to the crisis such as regulatory differences, supervision and regulation of financial groups, hedge funds, mortgage insurance and origination, credit-risk transfer products, and recommendations for improvement in transparency and reduction of product complexity.

This does not constitute an unbroken record of success. The organization has failed to promulgate or even facilitate global accounting standards, although it did make efforts along those lines in the 1990s. Ultimately, the job for developing international accounting rules was left to the International Accounting Standards Board, which developed International Financial Reporting Standards (IFRS), with IOSCO playing only an observer role in the process. Nor has IOSCO promulgated capitalization requirements for broker dealers that might have kept Bear Stearns and Lehman Brothers afloat. Especially in light of the passage of Sarbanes-Oxley in the USA in 2002, it is fair to say that the United States and Europe have failed to harmonize their securities regimes. In fact, large differences between listing requirements in US and European, particularly UK, markets remain. These differences have led to an increasing amount of forum shopping by market participants, as Georgetown's Chris Brummer has demonstrated.[36]

IOSCO essentially ceased pursuing Basel-style harmonization after the promulgation of a set of "objectives and principles" that every capital markets regulator is meant to follow (such broad principles, which come in numbers of twenty-one, twenty-eight, or occasionally as many as forty, are one of the first acts of every financial regulatory network; IOSCO came up with thirty-eight of them[37]). Despite its dedicated focus on many different areas, with a number of committees and working groups, each dedicated to a distinct subset of a global problem, IOSCO has not moved beyond norm production.

Some of this is surely due to regulatory geopolitics. American securities regulators, convinced of the preeminence of their capital markets (at least until recently), and the quality and uniqueness of their relatively intensive markets oversight, have been more dubious about cross-border cooperation than banking regulators. Another reason for this reticence might lie in IOSCO's structure, which embraces a large membership, but then divided tasks to be taken on by the organization somewhat inconsistently along a developed-developing axis. The technical committee, once in charge of key documents and pronouncements and now nonexistent, included only top regulators from mature markets, and gave emerging regulators only consulting roles, perhaps limiting their interest in the promotion of more rules.[38] Nonetheless, the technical committee was to be the place that developed world regulators hashed out their differences, and it never managed to live up to its mandate. Exclusivity did not stop the Basel Committee from passing the Basel Accord, but the more half-hearted approach by IOSCO – membership for all, vague gestures of exclusivity to some – may have posed more problems for the organization. And its diverse membership may have simply made passage of rules more difficult.

For an example of IOSCO's legislative caution, consider its core principles, which are introduced through "some examples of *current practices*." IOSCO also has issued a flurry of white papers designed to provide, but not mandate, best practices. For example, the technical committee issued reports on "Collective Investment Schemes as Shareholders: Responsibilities and Disclosure,"[39] and "Investment Management Risk Assessment: Marketing and Selling Practices."[40] In the summer of 2013, the organization published on topics that covered everything from financial benchmarking to cybercrime in securities markets. The year 2018 saw interest in behavioral insights into investor decision-making and best practices for commodities storage and delivery, and so on. Such standards have ranged from general pronouncements to less detailed prescriptions. In its attempts to achieve consensus and provide for the disparate concerns of members, IOSCO may have fallen victim to its diverse membership. The varied maturity levels and financial structures of its member markets make formulation of a robust guiding framework nearly impossible because its members have different interests and concerns. Some may even have an incentive not to cooperate with others.[41]

These days, IOSCO is likely to play a role as a policy shop in dealing with the highest-profile issues of the moment, and to collaborate with other networks in developing a standard approach for oversight of rapidly developing parts of the market. For example, it has issued rules, preceded by notice, on the process for the regulation of central clearing of derivatives that reference currency exchange rates (or "currency swaps"). It has also issued white papers and reviews on a high-profile effort by banks to fix a benchmark interest rate, the London Interbank Offered Rate (Libor), used to set rates on a variety of loans, after charges of manipulation by traders at participating banks. It has weighed in on high-frequency trading and currency pools; the specifics of the issues are perhaps less important than the salience of them. Increasingly, IOSCO appears to feel that if securities and futures regulators are confronted by an issue with a high enough profile to create press coverage and other forms of visibility, then it should weigh in with a considered view as to how to best approach the problem.

The network's modesty does not mean that it is irrelevant to the US securities practice. Both the SEC and the CFTC have played a role in the organization's membership since its inception, and both have clearly acted pursuant to those IOSCO resolutions that have required compliance from them. For example, the revisions to the SEC's treatment of auditor independence were occasioned by the passage of US domestic legislation, Sarbanes-Oxley, but also as the agency acknowledged, "with the Principles of Auditor Independence and the Role of Corporate Governance in Monitoring an Auditor's Independence issued by … IOSCO … in October 2002 in mind."[42] More recently, the SEC adopted a new rule establishing minimum risk-management requirements for registered clearing agencies and noted that the new rule "will generally codify existing practices that similarly reflect the CPSS [Committee on Payment and Settlement Systems, now called the Committee on Payments and Market Infrastructure] – IOSCO Recommendations."[43]

The SEC has "fundamentally conformed the nonfinancial statement disclosure requirements for foreign private issuers to the nonfinancial statement disclosure requirements adopted by ... [IOSCO]."[44] It has also referred foreign investors considering investments in US stocks to IOSCO for information about the process[45] and has praised the organization for "moving regulators around the globe to work more closely together."[46]

Perhaps most tangibly, the SEC has adopted the International Disclosure Standards developed by IOSCO for nonfinancial statement information.[47] As one SEC official put it, the standards "represent an international consensus on the type of disclosure that should be provided when foreign issuers make a public offering of equity securities or list their equity securities on a foreign exchange."[48] IOSCO issued these standards in 1998; in 1999 the SEC promulgated changes to its Form 20-F, the "lynchpin of its foreign integrated disclosure system, to fully incorporate the Standards" filed by foreign issuers seeking to list on US exchanges.[49] Among other things, the standards and Form 20-F permit foreign firms to use International Financial Reporting Standards (IFRS), which were not created by IOSCO, but have increasingly been embraced by all of its members, except for the USA, as a uniform accounting measure. With Form 20-F, the SEC has permitted foreign listers to use IFRS, even though they are, in some ways, inconsistent with GAAP used in the USA.

The SEC also conducts self-assessments to monitor its compliance with IOSCO's concise and broadly defined Core Principles, as well as with specific initiatives such as the International Disclosure Standards.

The SEC's support of IOSCO has a lengthy pedigree. In 1988 the SEC issued a policy statement noting that "all securities regulators should work together diligently to create sound international regulatory frameworks that will enhance the vitality of capital markets."[50] To be sure, the agency does not change its own rules to reflect every particular IOSCO standard – the University of Pennsylvania's Beth Simmons has been skeptical of the closeness of the relationship between the international organization and the agency[51] – but it deems itself to be in compliance with the Core Principles and to have harmonized its international nonfinancial disclosure requirements with those of IOSCO.

The CFTC has also cited IOSCO as the authority and basis for agency action. The futures regulator, an associate member of IOSCO and, like the SEC, subject to APA review of its rulemakings, has also cited IOSCO pronouncements as the bases for its promulgations. The CFTC announced that it has "amended our nonfinancial statement disclosure requirements for offerings by foreign issuers to conform to the international disclosure standards adopted by IOSCO in 1998,"[52] and it has cited IOSCO guidelines as "appropriate" for automated clearing systems,[53] screen-based trading systems,[54] and electronic trading systems.[55] The CFTC has also submitted a proposed rule regarding compliance principles for derivatives clearing organizations that are consistent with the Principles for Market Infrastructures published by the Committee on Payments and Market Infrastructure and the IOSCO board.[56] Most recently, the CFTC has adjusted its rulemaking timeline for setting margin requirements for swap dealers on uncleared swaps in light of parallel Basel and IOSCO efforts on this practice.

The CFTC has also used IOSCO standards in specific rule applications, as well as in rulemaking. For example, in evaluating whether a Norwegian clearinghouse could operate on the International Maritime Exchange in Oslo, the agency "evaluated the oversight activities undertaken by [the clearinghouse's Norwegian regulator] in the context of the Principles and Objectives of Securities Regulation issued by [IOSCO]."[57] The CFTC accordingly did "not make any independent investigation or assessment of the Norwegian regulatory program," potentially important way that the network can serve as a market access and level playing field generating institution. If the CFTC deems compliance with the IOSCO standards as good enough to constitute compliance with American standards for listing, the network will occupy a useful niche when it comes to getting foreign firms involved in the American market.[58] IOSCO guidance publications have also been cited in the CFTC's interpretive guidance statements, which acknowledge the interaction between CFTC rules and IOSCO consultative documents.

The warmth of the relationship between the two US capital markets regulators and the global network should not be overstated. The SEC and CFTC have both approached IOSCO cautiously. In particular, accounting has proven to be an area where global regulatory efforts have been largely eschewed by American regulators. In the next section, we will explore in depth the example and the consequences of the attempt to push toward a uniform accounting system.

4.3 ACCOUNTING HARMONIZATION: PARTICIPATE IN GLOBAL GOVERNANCE OR PAY THE PRICE

IOSCO's failure to agree upon accounting standards, driven largely by the failure of the SEC to participate, illustrates the way that regulatory harmonization can take on a momentum that makes it difficult to remain isolated from the process. The accounting story is a cautionary tale for Americans because US regulators lost their ability to affect the effort by abandoning an already ongoing harmonization effort in the 1990s, and now have found that it has to begin the process of conforming to it.

International accounting standards – the idea that companies listed on stock exchanges from Stockholm to Shanghai might report their results in the same way – have always been an attractive regulatory goal. In the 1980s, capital market regulators agreed to endorse an effort by professional accounting organizations to try to attain global harmonization of accounting rules. But the effort proved controversial, as US regulators comfortable with the uniquely American approach to financial statements withdrew their support in the early 1990s.

That exit, however, did not stop the larger process of devising common accounting standards, which continued – outside the IOSCO. Instead, standardization efforts moved to Europe. The creation of international accounting standards after the SEC's rejection, has been managed by the International Accounting Standards Board, a public-private arrangement based in London and created in 2001. The IASB has devised a set of accounting standards, the International Financial Reporting Standards (IFRS), which has enjoyed quick adoption in European countries and elsewhere and was essentially created without US participation.

Perhaps unsurprisingly, IFRS differs from American accounting rules. It is a principles-, rather than rules-based accounting system, less technical than traditional US accounting, and relies more on the gestalt of a company's returns to assess its accuracy. The USA had – and, for the moment, still has – a challenging, rules-based set of accounting standards, GAAP, that differs from those of any other nation. GAAP, for example, only recognizes intangible assets at fair value. IFRS more flexibly measures such assets if they have an established track record and potentially offer a future economic benefit. IFRS in some cases permits write-downs to be reversed; GAAP never permits the reversal of a write-down.

Still, faced with a cascade of overseas adoptions of IFRS, GAAP principles have a tenuous future, despite the SEC's doubling down on their necessity in the 1990s. As foreign jurisdictions have gained more and more of the business of floating stocks and bonds and raising capital, US capital market regulators have given up hope that they might do so in ways consistent with the complex GAAP. As a result, as we have seen, the SEC has permitted foreign companies that list on US stock markets to use IFRS to file their US annual and quarterly reports. And the SEC will likely accede to IFRS eventually for all filers, should they wish to use it, making accounting a choose-your-own-system sort of enterprise.

Accounting is technical, and acronyms like GAAP and IFRS obscure almost as much as reveal what the distinction between rules-based and principles-based accounting really amounts to. But the import of the triumph of IFRS can be gleaned by abstracting away from it, and from the details of accounting. The commitment to an international effort in accounting has worked a sea change in the way companies report their results, which has come without much American involvement – even though it will, in the near future, affect US companies as much as others from foreign countries.

This story of accounting standards illustrates the dangers of not pursuing international efforts, both for the IOSCO and national regulators. The propensity towards momentum is not a universal law, to be sure, but regulators ignore cross-border efforts at their peril, because those efforts can set standards for even the most independent and recalcitrant jurisdictions, if circumstances are right.

4.4 BEYOND PEER REVIEW AND A PRAYER

IOSCO has not had the Basel Committee's regulatory impact, even though it is often compared to that organization (and, as members of the FSB, has been paired with it). Some members of the network have evinced frustration with the organization and its achievements. One IOSCO secretary-general has suggested that tools stronger than white papers might be necessary in the future for IOSCO to carry out its mission. That official, David Wright, a native of the UK, has called for a global international framework for financial regulation based on an international treaty, potentially with binding dispute-settlement and sanctioning powers. Wright has characterized the current model as "peer review and a prayer."[59]

Wright sees the WTO dispute-settlement process as a model for such a treaty. He has said that the current cooperation-based model is not sustainable because IOSCO's practice of peer-review, monitoring, and transparency will be too "soft" for the future global regulatory climate. He worries that while "ad-hoc firefighting and informal agreements" might be manageable now, with a few large players taking a large share of the world's capital markets, the system will grow increasingly unmanageable as emerging markets reduce the relative importance of big players. Wright sees a treaty as the best of three alternatives: the other two are "survival of the fittest," and the "loose-forms-of-cooperation, hope-for-the-best" model that currently exists.[60]

Such a proposal would, if taken up, represent a fundamental change in the way financial regulation has been pursued. Treaties and courts have long been avoided, sometimes for reasons of efficiency, and sometimes, to be sure, because it seemed unlikely that such institutions could be created in a world where multilateral treaties are difficult to conclude, and, in countries like the USA, ratified.

Some international lawyers have wondered whether the network form is a transitional one – a way of creating a framework of international cooperation that could be eventually institutionalized through a treaty. This is an origin story that some suggest shapes the emerging trade regime, where the not-clearly-legal GATT agreement was replaced by the WTO treaty, with its formalized dispute-settlement process. The adoption of formal procedures and increasingly discernable rules may be evidence not of the increasing elaboration of an alternative mechanism of international governance, as of the laying of foundations for a treaty that will serve as the capstone. In this telling, IOSCO would parallel the GATT in creating informal and increasingly institutionalized mechanisms of cooperation that would serve as the basis for a more formal settlement in the future.

Others believe that different institutional approaches may make sense for different regulatory regimes, and point to the strongly revealed preferences in finance for informal, networked regimes as evidence that the treaty process may not be a burden financial regulation must necessarily shoulder. In fact, there have been no efforts to create treaties, while the network form in capital markets has been with us for three decades without much evolution (in banking, it has existed for four decades without any effort to transform the regulatory network into a treaty). For what it is worth, in global securities regulation, the transitional era has been a long-lasting one.

Notes

1 *See* Paul Guy, *Regulatory Harmonization to Achieve Effective International Competition, in* REGULATING INTERNATIONAL FINANCIAL MARKETS: ISSUES AND POLICIES 291, 291 (Franklin R. Edwards & Hugh T. Patrick eds., 1992). The bylaws of IOSCO declare that "[a]t the time of the adoption of the Bylaws in 1996, all members of the Organization that were neither affiliate nor associate members became ordinary members of the Organization INT'L ORG. OF SECS. COMM'NS, BYLAWS pt. 2, para. 4 (2011) [hereinafter IOSCO BYLAWS]. The previous Bylaws provided that "[t]he securities commissions or similar agencies of the countries of the American Continent, as well as the Commission des valeurs mobilieres du Quebec and the Ontario Securities Commission, are charter members of the Organization." *See* INT'L ORG. OF SECS. COMM'NS, BYLAWS pt. 2, para. 2 (July 1995) (on file with the Texas International Law Journal). Originally, the members of the predecessor to IOSCO were a set of Western Hemisphere securities regulators. *See IOSCO Historical Background* www.iosco.org/about/index.cfm?section=background.

2 INT'L ORG. OF SEC. COMM'NS, 2002 ANNUAL REPORT 22 [hereinafter IOSCO, 2002 ANNUAL REPORT].

3 IOSCO BYLAWS, *supra* note 1, pt. 2, paras. 6–7.

4 *Getting Closer?*, ECONOMIST 82 (May 25, 1996); *Listing to Port*, FIN. TIMES 13 (May 28, 1998).

5 *See* An Act Respecting the International Organization of Securities Commissions, ch. 143, 1987 S.Q. 2437 (Can.) (incorporated under a private act as a nonprofit organization); Telephone Interview with Jean-Pierre Christel, Assistant Secretary General, IOSCO (January 10, 1996).

6 *See* Guy, *supra* note 1, at 291; INT'L ORG. OF SEC. COMM'NS, 2011 ANNUAL REPORT 51 [hereinafter IOSCO, 2011 ANNUAL REPORT], *available at* www.iosco.org/annual_reports/2011/.

7 By contrast, other international organizations have much more formal rules of order. The UN General Assembly, for example, has promulgated over 160 rules of procedure.

8 IOSCO 2002 ANNUAL REPORT, *supra* note 2, at 24.

9 *Id.*, pt. 5, para 40.1.

10 *Id.*, pt. 5, para 40.2.

11 IOSCO 2011 ANNUAL REPORT, *supra* note 6, at 10.

12 *See* Guy, *supra* note 1, at 292. IOSCO's bylaws require the Secretary General to, among other things, "keep[] the records of the Organization, ... assist[] the IOSCO Board and Committees of the Organization in their functions, ... [and to] represent[] the Organization in meetings with or presentations to other groups and bodies, subject to the review of the Chairman of the IOSCO Board ..."

IOSCO BYLAWS, *supra* note 1 pt. 7, para. 51. The Secretary General must also prepare an annual report for the organization. *See id.* pt. 7, para. 51.

13 IOSCO BYLAWS, *supra* note 1, at pt. 9 para. 67.

14 Gary N. Klieman, *Better Forum Needed to Negotiate Terms of Foreign Competition*, AM. BANKER, Jan. 4, 1996, at 5.

15 *See* Tony Porter, STATES, MARKETS, AND REGIMES IN GLOBAL FINANCE 122–23 (1993).

16 Even American regulators say that they benefit from the best practices style exploration of options that characterize some of the recommendations of the international organization. Interview with a Staff Attorney, CFTC (Jan. 23, 2004).

17 Indeed, IOSCO holds its meetings in secret. *See* A. A. Sommer, Jr., *IOSCO: Its Mission and Achievement*, 17 NW. J. INTL. L. & BUS. 15, 19 (1996) (observing that "all committee meetings of IOSCO are closed").

18 SECS. & EXCH. COMM'N, REPORT ON PROMOTING GLOBAL PREEMINENCE OF AMERICAN SECURITIES MARKETS PURSUANT TO SECTION 509(5) OF THE NATIONAL SECURITIES MARKETS IMPROVEMENT ACT OF 1996 § 5A (Oct. 1997) [hereinafter SEC, REPORT ON PROMOTING GLOBAL PREEMINENCE OF AMERICAN SECURITIES MARKETS], *available at* www.sec.gov/news/studies/acctgsp.htm.

19 *See "Convergence," More than Harmonization, Is Key Word in Cautious Working Group Sessions*, 2 INT'L SEC. REG. REP. (BNA) No. 20, at 8 (Sept. 27, 1989); *see also Go Slowly in Developing Common Rules, SEC Chairman Tells IOSCO Gathering*, 24 SEC. REG. & L. REP. (BNA) 1667 (Oct. 30, 1992) (discussing the need for securities regulators to take adequate time to produce good uniform rules or practices). IOSCO has gingerly pursued regulatory cooperation in the context of national differences since its inception. In 1988, it resolved that, "despite the national differences, which are narrowing, cooperation among the countries should be encouraged by IOSCO." *Regulators Agree to Move Cautiously on Enforcement, Information Exchanges*, 20 SEC. REG. & L. REP. (BNA) 1861 (Dec. 9, 1988).

20 Guy, *supra* note 1, at 297. Guillermo Harteneck, the president of Argentina's security commission, similarly told IOSCO that the implementation of harmonizing agreements "may change from country to country." *Harmonization Key for World Capital Markets, Officials at IOSCO Declare*, 63 BANKING REP. (BNA) No. 15, 609 (Oct. 20, 1994).

21 SEC, REPORT ON PROMOTING GLOBAL PREEMINENCE OF AMERICAN SECURITIES MARKETS, *supra* note 18.

22 INT'L ORG. OF SECS. COMM'NS, OBJECTIVES AND PRINCIPLES OF SECURITY REGULATION 3 (May 2003), *available at* www.cssf.cl/cssf/docs/ti-IOSCOPD154 .pdf.

23 *The Globalization of Securities Markets*, 86 AM. SOC'Y INT'L L. PROC. 349, 357 (1992) (remarks of Michael MacKenzie).

24 INT'L ORG. OF SECS. COMM'NS (IOSCO), 2005 ANNUAL REPORT 6 [hereinafter IOSCO, 2005 ANNUAL REPORT], *available at* www.iosco.org/annual_reports/annual_report_2005.

25 INT'L ORG. OF SECS. COMM'NS (IOSCO), 2006 ANNUAL REPORT 6, *available at* www.iosco.org/annual_reports/annual_report_2006/pdf/annual_report_2006.pdf.

26 *See generally* SEC Letter to IOSCO on Capital Adequacy, INT'L SEC. REG. REP., Nov. 3, 1992, at 11 [hereinafter SEC Letter]. The European regulators favored a "building block" approach which differentiates between general risk (such as changes in the market or economy) and specific risk (such as those presented by the specific security at issue). *See generally* HAL S. SCOTT & PHILIP A. WELLONS, INTERNATIONAL FINANCE: TRANSACTIONS, POLICY AND REGULATION 28–88 (1995). The SEC believed "that the building block approach will not yield sufficient levels of capital to protect markets in the face of major disruptions." SEC Letter, *supra*. The SEC itself imposed an alternative method of computing minimum capital for securities firms. *See id.* at 54–57.

27 *See* Securities Regulators Adopt Resolution to Reinforce International Cooperation, 26 Sec. Reg. & L. Rep. (BNA) 1431 (Oct. 28, 1994).

28 INT'L ORG. OF SECS. COMM'NS, RESOLUTION CONCERNING MUTUAL ASSISTANCE 1 para. a ("Rio Declaration") (1986), *available at* www.iosco.org/library/resolutions/pdf/IOSCORES1.pdf.

29 INT'L ORG. OF SEC. COMM'NS (IOSCO), 1989 ANNUAL REPORT 1. Tony Porter believes IOSCO's confidence is somewhat misplaced. In his view, the SEC not only persuaded the organization to adopt the Resolution on Reciprocal Assistance, but also has been the primary mover behind the increasing number of enforcement MOUs signed by securities regulators today. *See* TONY PORTER, STATES, MARKETS, AND REGIMES IN GLOBAL FINANCE 114–15 (1993).

30 Press Release, Secs. & Exch. Comm'n, SEC Announces IOSCO Unveiling of Multilateral Agreement on Enforcement Cooperation (Oct. 31, 2003), *available at* www.sec.gov/news/press/2003-145.htm.

31 INT'L ORG. OF SECS. COMM'NS, MULTILATERAL MEMORANDUM OF UNDERSTANDING CONCERNING CONSULTATION AND COOPERATION AND THE EXCHANGE OF INFORMATION 8 (May 2002, rev'd May 2012) [hereinafter IOSCO, MMOU], *available at* www.iosco.org/library/pubdocs/pdf/IOSCOPD386.pdf.

32 IOSCO, 2005 ANNUAL REPORT, *supra* note 24, at 2 (2005).

33 "The organisation considered recent developments among the membership in taking up the MOU including the progress being made as IOSCO seeks to meet the 2010 deadline by which members are required to become signatories." *Further progress with the IOSCO MOU*, 6 IOSCO UPDATE (Int'l Org. of Secs. Comm'ns, Madrid, Spain) May 2007, at 2, *available at* www.iosco.org/library/newsletters/pdf/IOSCO_Update_May_2007.pdf.

34 IOSCO, 2005 ANNUAL REPORT, *supra* note 24, at 2 (2005).

35 Press Release, Int'l Org. of Secs. Comm'ns, IOSCO Reinforces Standard on Cross-Border Cooperation (Sept. 18, 2013), *available at* www.iosco.org/news/pdf/IOSCONEWS299.pdf.

36 *See* Chris Brummer, *Stock Exchanges and the New Market for Securities Laws*, 75 U. CHI. L. REV. 1435 (2008).

37 IOSCO's Objectives and Principles are available at INT'L ORG. OF SECS. COMM'NS, OBJECTIVES AND PRINCIPLES OF SECURITY REGULATION (June 2010), www.iosco.org/library/pubdocs/pdf/IOSCOPD323.pdf.

38 Antonio Marcacci, *IOSCO: The World Standard Setter for Globalized Financial Markets*, 12 RICH. J. GLOBAL L. & BUS. 23 (2012).

39 TECHNICAL COMM. OF THE INT'L ORG. OF SECS. COMM'NS, COLLECTIVE INVESTMENT SCHEMES AS SHAREHOLDERS: RESPONSIBILITIES AND DISCLOSURE (2003), *available at* www.iosco.org/library/pubdocs/pdf/IOSCOPD158.pdf.

40 TECHNICAL COMM. OF THE INT'L ORG. OF SECS. COMM'NS, INVESTMENT MANAGEMENT RISK ASSESSMENT: MARKETING AND SELLING PRACTICES (2003), *available at* www.iosco.org/library/pubdocs/pdf/IOSCOPD156.pdf.

41 Roberta S. Karmel, *IOSCO's Response to the Financial Crisis*, 37 J. CORP. L. 849, 900 (2012).

42 SEC, Strengthening the Commission's Requirements Regarding Auditor Independence, 67 Fed. Reg. 76,780, 76,780 n.7 (proposed Dec. 13, 2002) (final rule codified at 17 C.F.R. pts. 210, 240, 249, and 274).

43 SEC Final Rule. 11/02/2012. www.federalregister.gov/articles/2012/11/02/2012-26407/clearing-agency-standards#h-37.

44 SEC, Disclosure in Management's Discussion and Analysis About the Application of Critical Accounting Policies, 67 Fed. Reg. 35,620, 35,637 (proposed May 20, 2002) (to be codified at 17 C.F.R. pts. 228, 229, and 249).

45 Press Release, Secs. & Exch. Comm'n, The Fleecing of Foreign Investors: Avoid Getting Burned by "Hot" U.S. Stocks (Mar. 2001), *available at* www.sec.gov/investor/pubs/fleecing.htm ("Are the Broker and the Firm Licensed? Contact your securities regulator to find out the International Organization of Securities Commissioners (IOSCO) provides contact information for most securities regulators on its website.").

46 Annette L. Nazareth, Dir., Div. of Mkt. Regulation, U.S. Secs. & Exch. Comm'n, Address at the Practicing Law Institute Conference on International Securities Markets (May 9, 2003), *available at* www.sec.gov/news/speech/spch050903aln.htm ("Our active participation in the work of IOSCO in the areas of credit rating agencies and analyst conflicts of interest is evidence of the fact that events here in the US have moved regulators around the globe to work more closely together.").

47 Recently, the SEC has admitted that its "decision to adopt the International Disclosure Standards was based on [a] conclusion that the standards were of high quality and that their adoption would provide information comparable to the

amount and quality of information that US investors receive today." SEC Concept Release: International Accounting Standards, Exchange Act Release Nos. 33-7801 & 34-4230, 65 Fed. Reg. 8896-02, 8897 (Feb. 23, 2000).

48 Felicia H. Kung, *The Rationalisation of Regulatory Internationalization*, 33 L. & POL'Y IN INTL. BUS. 443, 467 (2002). IOSCO's standards "cover the gamut of expected disclosure topics, including description of an issuer's business, operating and financial review and prospects, compensation paid to an issuer's directors and officers, and the identification of major shareholders and related party transactions." *Id.* I interviewed an SEC official, who characterized the standards as an important tangible change in the way the SEC conducts its regulatory business. Interview with a Staff Attorney, Secs. & Exch. Comm'n (Jan. 22, 2004).

49 Kung, *supra* note 48, at 468; INT'L ORG. OF SECS. COMM'NS, INTERNATIONAL DISCLOSURE STANDARDS FOR CROSS-BORDER OFFERINGS AND INITIAL LISTINGS BY FOREIGN ISSUERS (Sept. 1998), *available at* www.iosco.org/library/pubdocs/pdf/IOSCOPD81.pdf.

50 SEC Concept Release: International Accounting Standards SEC, 65 Fed. Reg. at 8897 (citing SEC, Regulation of International Securities Markets, Securities Act Release No 6807, 53 Fed. Reg. 469,63 (Nov. 14, 1988)).

51 *See* Beth A. Simmons, The International Politics of Harmonization: The Case of Capital Market Regulation, 55 INT'L ORG. 589, 595 (2001) ("The size of the internal US market gives US regulators an incentive to make unilateral regulatory decisions, even if foreign regulators do not follow suit.").

52 CFTC, A New Regulatory Framework for Clearing Organizations, 65 Fed. Reg. 76,008, 76,029 (2001), citing SEC, International Disclosure Standards, 64 Fed. Reg. 53,900 (1999).

53 CFTC, A New Regulatory Framework for Clearing Organizations, 66 Fed. Reg. 45,604, 45,613 (Aug. 29, 2001) ("The Commission believes that the guidelines issued by the IOSCO in 1990 and adopted by the Commission on November 21, 1990 (55 Fed. Reg. 48,670), as supplemented in October 2000, are appropriate guidelines for an automated clearing system to apply.").

54 CFTC, A New Regulatory Framework for Trading Facilities, Intermediaries and Clearing Organizations, 66 Fed. Reg. 42,256, 42,275 (Aug. 10, 2001) ("The Commission believes that the guidelines issued by the International Organization of Securities Commissions (IOSCO) in 1990 (which have been referred to as the 'Principles for Screen-Based Trading Systems'), and adopted by the Commission on November 21, 1990 (55 Fed. Reg. 48,670), as supplemented in October 2000, are appropriate guidelines for an electronic trading facility to apply to electronic trading systems.").

55 CFTC, Petition of the Chicago Board of Trade, the Chicago Mercantile Exchange, and the New York Mercantile Exchange for Exemption pursuant to Section 4(c) of the Commodity Exchange Act, 64 Fed. Reg. 46,356, 46358-59 (Aug. 25, 1999) ("The Commission notes that its review of newly created

electronic trading systems has been, and continues to be, based on principles developed by the international regulatory community – specifically the International Organization of Securities Commissions ('IOSCO'). Should the Commission's review of electronic trading systems be based on standards other than or different from those contained in the IOSCO principles?").

56 Interview with a Staff Attorney, Secs. & Exch. Comm'n (Jan. 22, 2004). However, cooperative enforcement work also involves the regulators who have signed on to the so-called "Boca Declaration," which was coordinated by the CFTC in 1997. *Id.*; *see also* Declaration on Cooperation and Supervision of International Futures Markets and Clearing Organizations, COMMODITIES FUTURES TRADING COMM'N (as amended Mar. 1998), *available at* www.cftc.gov/International/InternationalInitiatives/oia_bocadec0398.

57 CFTC, Recognition of Multilateral Clearing Organizations, 67 Fed. Reg. 2419, 2420 (Jan. 17, 2002).

58 *Id.*

59 David Wright, Sec'y Gen., Int'l Org. of Secs. Comm'ns, Remarks at the Atlantic Council, Washington, D.C. (Dec. 10, 2012), *available at* www.iosco.org/library/speeches/pdf/20121210-Wright-David.pdf.

60 *Id.*

5

Cooperation in Insurance: a Slow Start, but a Fast Present

The International Association of Insurance Supervisors (IAIS) represents the lowest level of elaboration achieved by a financial regulatory network to date, though it has recently made an effort to develop Basel Committee-style rules for capital requirements on internationally active insurers. There has been no iterated capital adequacy *a la* Basel, however. The IAIS also offers a paler replica of IOSCO's great achievement, the memorandum of enforcement cooperation. For much of its existence, IAIS has focused on best practices and rough principles of financial regulation, the standard foundation for the elaboration of network cooperation.

Why has regulatory coordination over insurance standards been so slow? The answers range from functional ones – the need in insurance might be less urgent – to quirks in the way American insurance regulation is structured, constraining its ability to act as a global leader, a role the Federal Reserve has assumed on the Basel Committee.

Until the European Union engaged in insurance supervision, there has been a lack of leadership in creating international standards. The United States has found it to be particularly difficult to pursue international standards given divisions over how best to handle insurance regulation domestically. Insurance regulation was left to the states by law until 2010, with the federal government playing almost no role. Coordinating the interests of state insurance regulators has made it difficult for the USA to speak with one voice in cross-border insurance regulation negotiations. The post-crisis creation of the Federal Insurance Office, which has been empowered to represent the USA in international negotiations, has begun to hasten regulatory harmonization.

Nonetheless, multinational collaboration on insurance standards has proceeded so slowly that the EU has pursued one of the traditional alternatives – the bilateral agreement – in the USA. The conclusion of a so-called covered agreement between the USA and EU in 2017, however, does not mean that the IAIS is irrelevant or that it has been sidelined; in fact, in the decade following the crisis, it has changed from an institution doing only the most basic sort of best-practices work into one pursuing the same sorts of accomplishments of securities and banking regulators.

Insurance companies were thought to be relatively safe financial intermediaries. There is less risk of cross-border contagion posed by insurance companies that fail, because runs on their financing are less likely – or, if one does fail, on its peers. Most of the largest insurance companies, with some exceptions, are less global than the largest banks or investment banks, with consumers more likely to prefer trusted and longstanding local brands. Insurers were regulated, especially in the USA, more to ensure that they did not deceive consumers, rather than for the risk that they might collapse and threaten the financial system. However, the financial crisis showed that as insurance companies have taken on more varied responsibilities, the largest of them can threaten the stability of the system. In particular, internationally active insurance groups were thought to pose a particular problem for insurance supervisors, who, like financial regulators, could only monitor parts of a firm, while its ability to make good on its insurance contracts depended on the solvency of the whole.

The problem famously occurred in the case of New York-based insurance giant American International Group, one of the largest companies in the USA. AIG collapsed in 2008. The firm provided all sorts of insurance to policyholders around the world. But its diverse array of products proved to be its undoing. (Its securities lending business, which AIG relied on to provide the kind of short-term financing that dried up during the crisis, also played a role.) A London subsidiary of AIG wrote insufficiently hedged credit default swaps, bolstered by the strong balance sheet of its parent. As the credit crisis deepened, AIG had to post more and more collateral to satisfy counterparties that it could make good on its long side of the swap agreements. Eventually, the collateral calls rendered the company insolvent, after which it received an enormous bailout from the American Treasury Department.

The AIG experience contributed to a decision on the part of global financial regulators to designate some insurance companies as systemically risky, much like some large banks. As of 2017, there were nine insurance conglomerates designated as systemically risky by the FSB. In the USA, the largest insurance companies were designated as systemically important financial institutions (SIFIs), that is, institutions whose failure could destabilize the US economy (a more recent deregulatory push in the USA has meant that these same insurers are being de-designated). While much of the work of traditional insurance regulation comes under the mantra of consumer protection rather than financial stability, IAIS has focused on the latter problem in keeping with the priorities of international financial regulation.

Over the years, the IAIS has expanded and drawn ever closer to the Basel Committee, which now houses its secretariat. It holds its annual meetings around the world, and like IOSCO, it charges high prices to those who would like to attend. In the wake of the financial crisis, it has received FSB membership, which attests to its centrality in the business of international financial regulation.

The IAIS has, especially in the wake of the financial crisis and its integration into the overarching financial-regulatory regime, become an organization of some consequence to insurance companies and their supervisors, despite its modestly effective history. It has engaged more deeply in international cooperation over regulation of financial institutions, as is the *raison d'etre* of the FSB and Basel Committee. Like Basel, the IAIS has started to pursue relevance through capital requirements for insurance firms, especially the largest ones. The story of the insurance network is one of modest accomplishment, but some promise – or threat – depending on your view of comprehensive global regulatory standards.

5.1 THE INSTITUTIONAL FORM OF THE INTERNATIONAL ASSOCIATION OF INSURANCE SUPERVISORS

As with Basel and IOSCO, the institutional details of the evolution of IAIS are a useful additional case study of how international financial regulatory harmonization works. IAIS has its idiosyncrasies, and its modest beginnings. Its subcommittees, principles, and white papers have been followed by recent efforts to act in a more comprehensive fashion. This section evaluates the form of its institutionalization, while the next sections, as with Basel and IOSCO, considers its achievements.

IAIS began as a nonprofit corporation incorporated in Illinois. It was founded in 1994, in part at the urging of the Basel Committee. Its first two general meetings were held in conjunction with the annual meeting of the US's National Association of Insurance Commissioners (NAIC). IAIS held its first annual meeting outside of the USA in 1996, in Paris. It began as a relatively nonexclusive organization; since then, it has grown. At first it represented insurance supervisory authorities in less than a hundred jurisdictions; by the middle of the 2010s, it had encompassed over 200 jurisdictions in some 140 countries, a base that represents 97 percent of global insurance premiums. Since its creation, IAIS has issued global principles of insurance regulation, conducted research on supervision problems, provided training and support on issues related to insurance supervision, and organized meetings for insurance supervisors, including an annual conference designed "[t]o further encourage multilateral discussions on topical issues for insurance supervisors and other insurance professionals."[1]

IAIS is composed of two membership classes: charter members and new members. Charter members, who consist of insurance regulators from sixty-seven countries and seventeen US states, joined the organization at the completion of its first annual meeting on June 16, 1994. Most of the original members send one delegation per country or state to the annual meeting; France and Germany each send two. New members form the second IAIS membership class. They continue to be admitted to the organization so long as they are an insurance industry supervisor or an umbrella group of supervisors.[2]

Today, members falling under the US umbrella hail from each of the fifty states, the US territories, and the District of Columbia; there are also separate representatives on behalf of the National Association of Insurance Commissioners, the US standard-setting body for the industry, and the FIO, which was created after the financial crisis.

The IAIS also accepts applications from observers, which can include government organizations with an interest in insurance supervision, "regardless of whether the organisation is directly responsible for insurance law or its administration," and "any other person, entity, or organisation, private or public, with an interest in the business or supervision of insurance . . ."[3] Observers are essentially a special category of membership for private-sector entities. They are individuals from industry and professional associations, insurance and reinsurance companies, consulting firms, and international financial institutions; as such, they (and those of their members who attend IAIS events open to them) are a source of dues. The first observers joined the IAIS in 2000.

Members may vote, generally on a one-member, one-vote basis, though occasionally, those votes are parceled out on a country, rather than a regulator basis. Observers may participate in IAIS functions, but may not vote or serve on the executive committee. Two-thirds of members at a general meeting must approve of proposed principles and standards for passage.

IAIS describes its mission as "promot[ing] effective and globally consistent regulation and supervision of the insurance industry in order to develop and maintain fair, safe, and stable insurance markets for the benefit and protection of policyholders and to contribute to global financial stability."[4] While the Basel Committee's goals include the establishment of uniform rules through the work of the organization, IAIS takes a broader view of its purpose, and emphasizes rulemaking less. The organization wishes to, among other things, "develop principles, standards, and guidance for the supervision of insurance markets . . . encourage broader contacts and co-operation amongst insurance supervisors . . . [and] engender awareness of common interests and concerns amongst insurance supervisors and identify potential risks that may affect insurance supervision."[5]

IAIS is composed of an association in general meeting to which all the members are invited, an executive committee that oversees the organization, and a modest general secretariat that consists of approximately thirty employees. When in general meeting, the association may seek a report on the work of the executive committee and elect members to it, change the bylaws, and approve the annual report and financial statement of the association.[6]

The executive committee, consisting of between nine and twenty-four members, is "limited to no more than one person per Member, and in principle per Jurisdiction . . . [and] shall be composed of an appropriate representation of the different geographic areas and different types of insurance markets, particularly in respect of the market sizes and development."[7] These members serve for two-year terms and are elected at the general meeting. The executive committee generally "takes all decisions necessary to achieve the objectives of the Association in accordance with the directions given by the General Meeting."[8] The general secretariat keeps records of the work of the IAIS, examines and makes recommendations on applications for membership, keeps the reports of the organization, and manages the resources (financial, material, and human capital) of the association in accordance with the organization's annual budget. IAIS first entered into a services contract with the NAIC to serve as the secretariat of the organization. At the beginning, the NAIC in turn delegated that responsibility to one of its employees, a recent law school graduate. In 1998, the organization moved to Basel; its now-larger secretariat is housed in the BIS.

IAIS's governing document is a set of bylaws thirteen pages long. Those bylaws "do not impose legal obligations on members or the countries which they represent"[9] and may be amended by a majority vote of the general meeting. Both IAIS and IOSCO have promulgated bylaws, but those laws are permissive and open-ended, rather than restrictive and definitive. IAIS's bylaws permit its executive committee to take "all decisions necessary to achieve the objectives of the organization,"[10] while its secretariat "carr[ies] out all other functions that are assigned" to it.[11]

IAIS's bylaws emphasize its role in "lias[ing] and cooperat[ing] with other international organizations," "facilitat[ing] . . . the exchange of supervisory information," "develop[ing] methodologies for the assessment of the observance of its principles and standards," as well as "represent[ing] a body of informed opinion within the field of insurance supervision."[12]

Membership dues finance the organization. The IAIS finished 2018 with $10.5 million in assets, having received $7.2 million in revenue over the course of the year. Of the revenue, approximately two-thirds was comprised of membership and observership fees.

The work of the IAIS is conducted through a committee system. The committees today address technical issues related to insurance supervision, implementation of IAIS principles, standards, and guidance, financial issues including the budget, audit and risk, and financial stability issues related to systemic risk. The organization conducts some of its affairs confidentially, though the annual meeting provides some open time to those who wish to pay a fee, and it has increasingly made its proposals available for notice and comment. Some of its committees meet in secret[13] or make presentations at general meeting sessions open only to organization members. The business meetings of the association have also been closed to nonmembers.[14]

As I have argued earlier in this book, the international financial regulatory organizations are characterized by their decentralized nature, and IAIS is no exception. Perhaps the best way to illustrate IAIS's decentralization is by identifying two ways that it is attempting to *centralize* its efforts. First, as mentioned above, the role of IAIS's secretariat was originally contracted to the NAIC, which in turn delegated that responsibility to a single employee who kept records of the organization and answered requests. Over time, however, the association reclaimed the secretariat role from the NAIC and by 2011 had "strengthen[ed] [its] staff resources" to twenty-nine full-time employees. Despite attempting to centralize its secretariat staff in one location, however, a number of secretariat employees are affiliated with, and operate from, institutions in other countries. Among those institutions represented by the secretariat staff are the Financial Supervisory Commission, Chinese Taipei; the Financial Services Agency, Japan; the Financial Supervisory Service, Republic of Korea; and the BIS.

Second, IAIS has tried to coordinate its priorities with those of other financial regulatory networks, as exemplified by its relatively new Macroprudential Policy and Surveillance Working Group, whose mission is to serve as "a macroprudential intelligence hub servicing IAIS Committees and supervisors in individual jurisdictions."[15] To that end, the group amorphously, but intelligibly enough, describes its duties as "liais[ing] with, and leverage[ing] on the work of, several other multilateral institutions engaged in the macroprudential analysis of the financial sector."[16]

5.2 THE SLOW-TO-START ACCOMPLISHMENTS OF THE IAIS

Before the financial crisis, the IAIS remained focused on the threshold work of international financial regulatory organizations; it tried to devise best practices for insurance regulators the world over to follow, but did little more than this. After the crisis, the organization began to transform itself into a body aspiring to the sorts of achievements that securities and banking regulators had already realized. It has pursued a comprehensive capital standard for very large insurance companies. It has played an increasingly important role in the FSB. And it has begun to move beyond general principles with its common framework for insurance group supervision, something much more rules-like and rule-based. These developments from IAIS are new, and they suggest that while insurance regulators have embraced international cooperation extremely cautiously, the hard-to-disentangle relationships between banks and insurance firms, especially outside of the USA, has meant that if anything insurance regulation is more ripe for a Basel-style revolution than capital-markets regulators.

The dynamics of IAIS's accomplishments are that their principles are agreed to by all, mostly. Their efforts to coordinate on enforcement the kind of thing US regulators prefer. But their emerging framework for regulation of internationally active firms may be following a European approach, with the threat of closure of European markets spurring on the development of international standards.

IAIS's contributions to the substance of insurance regulation take three forms: principles, standards, and guidance papers. Insurance Core Principles (ICPs) are values "that are fundamental to effective insurance supervision," and they pertain to areas such as insurer, intermediary, and consumer relations; capital adequacy and solvency; and reinsurance.[17] The ICPs are an accepted method used to evaluate insurance systems under the Financial Sector Assessment Program (FSAP), itself a joint effort of the World Bank and the IMF. Standards, on the other hand, define best practices with regard to specific matters within the insurance industry: for example, insurer licensing, onsite inspections, and controlling derivatives risks. Guidance papers, meanwhile, are intended to be complementary tools to principles and standards and are vaguely described by IAIS as "designed to assist supervisors and raise the effectiveness of supervision."[18]

IAIS's principles are arguably the most important vehicle by which it delivers regulatory guidance, and in keeping with principles often adopted by regulatory networks they lack specificity. The 2003 ICPs addressed, among other things: "The role and responsibilities of the boards of directors; the reliance on other supervisors for companies licensed in other jurisdictions; and the distinction between the standards to be met by companies incorporated in their jurisdiction, and branch operation of companies incorporated in other jurisdictions."[19] ICPs resemble other core principles. The FSB adopted them as part of its Compendium of Standards, which it describes as benchmarks for an effective system of financial regulation.

In 2005, IAIS published a paper on the organization of insurance supervision and identified two threshold requirements of an effective insurance supervisory system:

> (1) an environment that contains developed and efficient financial market[s] and an institutional and legal framework for financial services supervision; and (2) clearly defined principal, supervisory objectives, and . . . a supervisory authority . . . that[] has adequate powers.[20]

Specifically, this supervisor had to be able to impose "(1) financial requirements, (2) governance requirements, and (3) market conduct requirements" on insurers.

Before the crisis, the IAIS began two other initiatives aimed at developing a framework for an effective insurance supervisory system embodied in the IAIS Principles on Group-wide Supervision and a Group-wide Supervision Framework (GSF). These created a real tension with the USA, which supervises insurance companies on a state-by-state basis – that is, by subsidiary, rather than by considering subsidiaries parts of a whole. The Principles on Group-wide Supervision aimed to create an international framework that "contributes to ensuring appropriate streamlining, consistency, efficiency, and effectiveness of supervision on a group-wide basis."[21] The GSF, on the other hand, was a nebulous effort intended to gather all IAIS guidance materials on group-wide supervision – including Insurance Core Principle 23, the IAIS Principles on Group-wide Supervision of 2008, and the IAIS Framework for Insurance Supervision (core principles for insurance supervision, laid out in 2005) – under one umbrella.

In addition to this principles promulgation, IAIS has served as a forum for information exchange. Long ago, US insurance regulator David Walsh claimed that IAIS is "a very good vehicle for regulators to get to know one another and to develop the kind of relationship where you just pick up the phone and say, 'What's going on here?'"[22] IAIS's most significant effort along those lines in its first years of operation was its approval of the Recommendation Concerning Mutual Assistance, Cooperation, and Sharing of Information, established by its exchange of information subcommittee. In 1995, fifty-one members signed the document, which outlined cooperative efforts for information exchanges.[23] The Recommendation required signatories "to provide assistance on a reciprocal basis . . . for the prudential supervision of the insurance industry and obtaining information and documents related to market oversight or protection of each other's markets against fraudulent insurance transactions . . ."[24]

Twelve years later, in 2007, IAIS formally executed a document that updated its vision for information sharing among insurance regulators, by promulgating a new Multilateral Memorandum of Understanding (MMoU). The agreement resembles IOSCO's MOU in many ways. Described as a "global framework for cooperation and information exchange between insurance supervisors," the MMoU goes some way toward ensuring national treatment of insurance supervisors, both by dictating "minimum standards to which signatories must adhere," and by "subject[ing] [all applicants] to review and approval by an independent team of IAIS members."[25] MMoU signatories agree that "practical arrangements concerning cross-border cooperation and information exchange are essential not only in crisis situations, but also in insurance industry supervisors' day-to-day business, especially given their significant role in preserving financial stability."[26] With India's admission to the MMoU, the total number of signatories reached thirty-seven jurisdictions – a number that represents over 54 percent of insurance premium volume globally, the IAIS proudly reported. While the MMoU undoubtedly facilitates cross-border information sharing, participation in the exchange is completely voluntary: in fact, the agreement provides, like so many network commands, that "[t]he provisions of this MMoU are not intended to create any legally binding obligations or to modify or supersede any jurisdictional law. Nor does this MMoU create any directly or indirectly enforceable rights."[27]

Prior to reworking its proposal for information sharing, the IAIS revised its core principles in 2001. The ICPs were narrowed from twenty-eight to twenty-six core principles, though the amount of guidance provided, now spanning 400 pages, did not represent a thinning out of the supervisory framework.

Following the rollout of the new ICPs, IAIS began to increase the scope of its peer-review program, as networks have increasingly done since the FSB made peer review such an important component of its practice. For example, in the IAIS Self-Assessment and Peer Review on Insurance Core Principles 4, 5, 7, and 8, members were "strongly encouraged" to participate in the survey, which past members found "helpful to improve understanding and observance of the [Insurance Core

Principles]" and have used the information "to enhance their supervisory practices and legislative frameworks."[28]

After the crisis, things grew more complex. IAIS continued its efforts to establish an international framework for supervision, particularly for large, internationally active insurance firms. (The USA has a large number of small insurers that are influential with state insurance regulators and uninterested in the IAIS project.) The IAIS initiated a Common Framework for the Supervision of Internationally Active Insurance Groups ("ComFrame") in July 2010. ComFrame was developed with the expectation that it would "draw from and be built from" much of IAIS's earlier guidance on groupwide insurance supervision, including the ICPs and principles that had in 2008 been drawn under the umbrella of the GSF. The 2013 draft of ComFrame was subjected to comment until December 2013, after which it was field tested by volunteer internationally active firms for a period of years, followed by adoption at the end of the decade.

IAIS has described ComFrame as "an integrated, multilateral, and multidisciplinary framework for the groupwide supervision of internationally active insurance groups, or IAIGs."[29] The organization has stated that it intends ComFrame to complement its already existing Insurance Core Principles, standards, and guidance. While its ICPs are meant to provide guidance for the *intra*governmental regulation of insurance practices, ComFrame will provide structure for *inter*governmental interaction over IAIGs. The articulated objectives of ComFrame are focused on oversight of multinational insurers, and include efforts to, for example, "[e]stablish a comprehensive framework for supervisors to address group-wide activities and risks and also set grounds for better supervisory cooperation in order to allow for a more integrated and international approach."[30]

As is the case with most current network initiatives, ComFrame was opened for comment, and is being rolled out slowly, with plenty of attention to process. Insurance Europe, for example, expressed reservations about the project in its response letter to IAIS. The thiry-four-member insurance federation observed that the ComFrame draft failed to satisfactorily clarify "how ComFrame relates to local regulatory/legal requirements that meet the overall principles covered by ComFrame."[31] Similarly, three leading executives in the insurance industry were reported to have "sharply criticized" the project. Evan Greenberg, chairman, president, and CEO of Swiss-based global insurance provider Ace Ltd., observed that ComFrame has extended its reach beyond the initial goal of group-wide supervision and regulatory cooperation. "If [ComFrame is] ever implemented," Greenberg said, "it is likely to result in duplicative and, perhaps, burdensome requirements for insurers that will add excessive costs without clear benefit."[32]

Along the lines of ComFrame, IAIS developed a list, ultimately issued by the FSB, of "global systemically important insurers (G-SIIs)." To do so, the network looked to the size, complexity, and interconnectedness of insurance conglomerates, with the idea that sufficient scale on any such index would cause significant disruption to the global financial system and economic activity. In keeping with the focus of transnational insurance regulation on internationally active firms, the list of G-SIIs was focused on insurers doing business in multiple jurisdictions. Eventually, the FSB, with the assistance and input of the IAIS, settled on a short list of large insurance companies, reaching a high point of nine in 2016. The designated firms are subject to three broad regulatory requirements beyond those applicable to all insurers. Designated firms have higher loss absorbency requirements, requiring them to hold more capital; are subject to enhanced supervision by regulators; and had to participate in a process for planning for their orderly resolution, should the worst come to pass. The nine firms included three US companies, one Chinese, and five from Europe, meaning that the list covered some very large firms, but only a small proportion of the total global market for insurance services – the list was not designed to cover the waterfront. It nonetheless created an additional global regime for these firms that more local insurers did not need to consider.

The organization hopes through activities like ComFrame to prove its post-crisis relevance. The most important component of the ComFrame approach has been the effort to create a global insurance capital standard for internationally active insurance firms. The IAIS has made a recent push to develop and implement the standard, including, as per usual, rounds of comments and preliminary field testing, with an eye to implementing it by the end of the decade, a goal that's been pushed back as its development has led to some disagreement between regulators, particularly from Europe and the USA.

The delays should not obscure the potential of the achievement. The capital standard, at least as it has developed so far, looks much more like the Basel Committee's signature capital accord, instead of the sort of gauzy principles that mark the start of international financial regulatory cooperation. The capital standard is meant to apply on a groupwide basis to internationally active insurance firms, and constitutes a minimum standard for consolidated capital. The groupwide calculation means that domestic insurers cannot get away with a demonstration of the capital adequacy of a subsidiary within a regulator's jurisdiction; it makes insurance capital supervision necessarily international.

In particular, the capital standard creates multiple capital obligations for internationally active insurers. IAIS plans to impose a tier-1 capital requirement of provable resources designed to absorb losses on a going-concern basis, and a tier-2 requirement designed to absorb losses upon the failure and resolution of the firm. The capital standard includes plenty of technical details, from the accounting standards permitted to be used by firms when it comes to the assessment of capital to the kind of financial instruments that can be used to satisfy tier-1 and tier-2 requirements, to a number of other technical balance-sheet requirements.

As of this writing, the insurance capital standard is in *media res*, neither completed nor still on the drawing board. It is difficult to know exactly how it will be implemented, assuming that it is at all. The capital standard nonetheless illustrates a budding transformation in international insurance regulation. The details of the standard are, of course, something that makes it look like a capital-accord style rule, rather than the more flexible principles that IAIS spent most of its existence promulgating.

But the capital rule also reflects choices about how to evaluate the adequacy of firm capital in ways that not every regulator will find obviously palatable. US regulators, as we have seen, have resisted evaluating insurance companies on a consolidated, or groupwide basis, preferring to focus on each subsidiary. In its comment on the emerging ComFrame approach, the NAIC argued that "a single all-powerful group regulator is neither advantageous nor necessary. ComFrame must respect different jurisdictional approaches to group supervision and focus on a common outcome of providing group-wide information and perspective to all relevant supervisors."[33]

European regulators, on the other hand, have generally pushed for a capital standard, having achieved something like that through its efforts to unify European-wide insurance law under a single standard known as Solvency II. At least for now, European regulators have successfully been able to require that ICS use European accounting standards, with US standards available as an addition, for asset-valuation questions. They have pushed the network to develop post-crisis rules consistent with the European framework. And the existence of Solvency II as a requirement for insurance groups who hope to do business in Europe has meant that internationally active US firms have tried to comply with European rules already, while most domestically focused insurers continue to ignore them.

The decision to supervise firms on a groupwide basis shows how, if implemented, international financial regulation cannot only achieve specificity, but also make decisions in ways that privilege some participants in the process over others.

The ComFrame groupwide capital requirement, thereby parallels other major post-crisis initiative of the network, which is to identify systemically important companies, often in conjunction with banking and securities regulators that deal with insurers who have universal financial operations. As is common with SIFIs, insurance companies so designated would assume the burden of greater regulation, and additional capital requirements.

This process of subjecting the largest insurance firms to multinational standards has been driven by an interest in the so-called level playing field. As Thomas Sullivan, a senior advisor at the Fed for insurance regulation and a former state insurance commissioner has testified, "We believe in the utility of having the effect of global standards for regulation and supervision of internationally active financial firms. When implemented consistently, a class of global jurisdictions, such standards can help provide a level playing field for global financial institutions. Further, consistent global regulatory standards can help limit regulatory arbitrage and jurisdiction shopping and can promote financial stability."[34]

5.3 BILATERAL ALTERNATIVES TO NETWORKS: THE COVERED AGREEMENT

As we have seen in trade law, when multilateral efforts to expand the footprints of the global regime fail, those interested in furthering international cooperation often turn to bilateral or regional deals. Perhaps because the multilateral Doha trade round has failed to reach any conclusion, both the USA and Europe have increasingly pursued their interests through mooted trade deals with Canada (in the case of the European Union), a variety of non-China Pacific allies (in the case of the USA and the Trans-Pacific Partnership, though it recently pulled out of the deal), and one another.

The same dynamic applies to US and European insurance regulators, who have, perhaps because of the problems posed by coordinating their interests through the multilateral IAIS framework, pursued a bilateral agreement on some aspects of insurance supervision designed to reduce some regulatory barriers and provide market access to each other's large insurers. Critically, the US side of the bilateral negotiations was represented by the federal government's FIO, rather than by a committee of state regulators.

The result was a deal known as the US-EU Covered Agreement (or "covered agreement"), which was concluded in the final week of the administration of President Barack Obama in 2017. The covered agreement grew out of an effort in the wake of the financial crisis to make sure that globally active insurance companies were regulated as conglomerates, rather than as a series of operating subsidiaries, and that they faced a level playing field when it came to doing business at home or overseas. These goals were realized through a deal that reduced US capital-adequacy reinsurance regulations for European reinsurers, and dropped European requirements that US insurers maintain a "local presence" in various EU jurisdictions.

Dodd-Frank in general encouraged international regulatory cooperation; in addition to creating the FIO, it explicitly extended to it the power to work extraterritorially. Congress instructed it "to coordinate Federal efforts and develop Federal policy on prudential aspects of international insurance matters, including representing the United States, as appropriate, in the International Association of Insurance Supervisors;" to "consult with the States (including State insurance regulators) regarding insurance matters of national importance and prudential insurance matters of international importance;" and to "advise the [Treasury] Secretary on ... prudential international insurance policy issues."[35]

FIO was also given the power, in association with the United States Trade Representative, to conclude agreements on insurance regulation with foreign counterparties. These so-called covered agreements are defined in Dodd-Frank as

> [A] written bilateral or multilateral agreement regarding prudential measures with respect to the business of insurance or reinsurance that is

(A) entered into between the United States and one or more foreign governments, or regulatory entities; and

(B) relates to the recognition of prudential measures with respect to the business of insurance or reinsurance that achieves a level of protection for insurance or reinsurance commissioners that is substantially equivalent to the level of protection achieved under state insurance or reinsurance regulation.[36]

Covered agreements occupy a place in the middle of international efforts to solve problems posed by the modern insurance market. On one hand, trade negotiations are about reducing trade barriers and making it more feasible for insurers to access foreign markets; the efforts by the World Trade Organization to liberalize trade in services is the sort of arrangement that could most affect the ability of financial intermediaries to market their products overseas. Trade law relies upon its national treatment principle, which provides that WTO members "shall accord to the nationals of other Members treatment no less favourable than that it accords to its own nationals" for various products and services.[37] The goal is to remove discriminatory regulation of foreign imports as much as possible.

The IAIS efforts are also designed to level the playing field when it comes to the supervision of insurance companies. Here, the effort is not so much to remove regulations as to improve them. In this way, international financial regulation through a network like IAIS has a harmonizing purpose just as trade agreements do, though IAIS seeks to bring regulatory standards in member countries up to a more intensive standard, with national treatment serving as both a justification (we must measure up to other members of the network in our treatment of insurers) and a caution (we must treat our insurers the same way we treat foreign insurers).[38] IAIS, for example, has not yet had much luck creating capital standards for insurers, though it is moving quickly on a group capital standard. But it has worked on that issue, and has tried to persuade members to ensure that their regulatory powers meet a minimal standard, and that they are thinking about the solvency of their insurance firms in a similar way.

The covered agreement somewhat resembles a national-treatment effort in trade, contained within the more narrow confines of a limited agreement on international insurance regulation. In particular, there is currently a requirement that foreign reinsurance firms post 100 percent collateral to do business in certain US jurisdictions. Any reduction in the collateral requirements, which would open up the reinsurance market and introduce new competitors to the benefit of insurers and ultimately consumers, has been slow, necessitating a deal between the USA and the EU. The participation of the US Trade Representative (USTR) in the negotiations over the covered agreement underscores the relevance of the reinsurance arrangements for the more general reduction in trade barriers on both sides of the Atlantic.

But the USA also got something for its domestic reinsurers as well. The EU's local-presence requirement has been a burden on the ability of US reinsurers to access

Europe. The elimination of that burden will level the playing field for US and European reinsurers.

The agreement also contains provisions on group supervision, which is increasingly the mechanism used to supervise financial intermediaries, including banks and investment banks. The EU insists on group supervision as a condition for access to the European market, and by providing it, the USA has begun to regulate its globally active insurance companies much as it regulates its banks.

The covered agreement also provides for an information exchange that is likely to deepen contacts between regulators in the USA and EU and that is meant to add to the MMoU that already exists through IAIS's auspices. Over four decades of cooperation between central bankers and securities regulators has contributed to the capacity for a coordinated response, as we saw during the last financial crisis. In the midst of that crisis, the SEC coordinated a brief stock-shorting ban with its international counterparts at an IOSCO meeting, even though coordination was accomplished in the hallways rather than in the official session. By the same token, coordination of injections of capital through swap lines and other mechanisms by central bankers was facilitated by their already extant supervisory cooperation. In other words, cooperation on enforcement and understandings along those lines can create or deepen relationships that can facilitate international responses to crisis.[39]

The covered agreement was not created through the auspices of the insurance network, but by US regulators concerned about global harmonization of insurance standards; nonetheless, it seems to be cut from the same cloth. The covered agreement is an international alternative to network governance, but many think it will end up supporting the structure, even if IAIS was not behind its promulgation.

CONCLUSION

Cross-border insurance regulation cooperation is not a story of ever more elaborate coordination, like international banking regulation. Nonetheless, it has followed the network template in some cases. In another context, where the network template failed to make progress, important players in insurance regulation pursued a bilateral alternative that illustrates in another way the feasibility of financial regulation coordinated across borders.

Notes

1 *About the IAIS*, Int'l Ass'n of Ins. Supervisors, www.iaisweb.org/index.cfm?pageID=28.

2 International Association of Insurance Supervisors Bylaws 4 art. 6 (2013 ed.) [hereinafter IAIS Bylaws], *available at* www.iaisweb.org/Bylaws-45.

3 *Id.* at 5 art. 7. Currently, Insurance Europe (the European insurance and reinsurance federation) and the World Federation of Insurance Intermediaries participate in IAIS as observers. *See IAIS Observers*, INT'L ASS'N OF INS. SUPERVISORS, www.iaisweb.org/IAIS-observers–417.

4 INT'L ASS'N OF INS. SUPERVISORS, 2011–12 ANNUAL REPORT 2 (Oct. 25, 2012) [hereinafter IAIS 2011–12 ANNUAL REPORT], *available at* www.iaisweb.org/Annual-reports-44.

5 IAIS BYLAWS, *supra* note 2, at 2 art. 2.

6 *Id.* at pt. 7, para. 35.

7 *Id.* at 9 art. 14.

8 *Id.*at 9 art. 15.

9 *Id.* at pt. 1, para. 2.

10 IAIS BYLAWS, *supra* note 2, at 9 art. 15.

11 *Id.* at 12 art. 17.

12 *Id.* at. 2 art. 2.

13 Telephone Interview with Traci M Ribeiro, NAIC Policy Analyst/International (Jan. 19, 1996).

14 *See* NEWSL. OF THE INT'L ASS'N OF INS. SUPERVISORS, Mar. 1995, at 11.

15 IAIS 2011–12 ANNUAL REPORT, *supra* note 4, at 24.

16 *Id.*

17 *Principles*, INT'L ASS'N OF INS. SUPERVISORS, www.iaisweb.org/Principles-39.

18 *Guidance Papers*, INTERNATIONAL ASSOCIATION OF INSURANCE SUPERVISORS, www.iaisweb.org/Guidance-papers-41.

19 Wallace Wang, *Developing Reinsurance Markets in Emerging Economies: Regulatory Implications and Challenges*, 8 L. & BUS. REV. AM. 395, 421 (2002).

20 Elizabeth F. Brown, *The Development of International Norms for Insurance Regulation*, 34 BROOK. J. INT'L L. 953, 965 (2009) (quoting IAIS, A *New Framework for Insurance Supervision: Towards a Common Structure and Common Standards for the Assessment of Insurer Insolvency* 5-6 (Oct. 2005), *available at* www.iaisweb.org/view/element_href.cfm?src=1/87.pdf.

21 PRINCIPLES ON GROUP-WIDE SUPERVISION, INT'L ASS'N OF INS. SUPERVISORS 3 (Oct. 2008), *available at* www.iaisweb.org/view/element_href.cfm?src=1/5783.pdf.

22 Thomas Ressler, International Regulators to Hold First Meeting, Ins. Reg., Apr. 4, 1994, at 8, available in LEXIS, Market Library, Iacnws File.

23 NEWSL. OF THE INT'L ASS'N OF INS. SUPERVISORS, Summer 1995, at 1.

24 INT'L ASS'N OF INS. SUPERVISORS, RECOMMENDATION CONCERNING MUTUAL ASSISTANCE, COOPERATION, AND SHARING OF INFORMATION (1995), *reprinted in* NEWSL. OF THE INT'L ASS'N OF INS. SUPERVISORS, Summer 1995, at 5.

25 Press Release, IAIS, India Joins International Information Exchange Agreement (May 21, 2013), *available at* www.iaisweb.org/view/element_href.cfm?src=1/18526 .pdf.

26 INT'L ASS'N OF INS. SUPERVISORS, MULTILATERAL MEMORANDUM OF UNDERSTANDING ON COOPERATION AND INFORMATION EXCHANGE, 4 art. 1 (Feb. 2007) [hereinafter IAIS, 2007 MMoU], *available at* www.iaisweb.org/view/element_href.cfm?src=1/12350.pdf.

27 IAIS, 2007 MMoU.

28 Press Release, IAIS, Corporate and Risk Governance: The IAIS' Self-Assessment and Peer Review on ICPs 4, 5, 7 and 8 (Feb. 12, 2013), *available at* www.iaisweb.org/view/element_href.cfm?src=1/17501.pdf.

29 *Id.*

30 INT'L ASS'N OF INS. SUPERVISORS, COMFRAME CONCEPT PAPER 4 (July 1, 2011), *available at* www.iaisweb.org/view/element_href.cfm?src=1/12495.pdf.

31 *Insurance Europe Response to IAIS Consultation on ComFrame*, Aug. 31, 2012, at 5, *available at* www.insuranceeurope.eu/uploads/Modules/Publications/insurance_europe_response_to_iais_consultation_on_comframe.pdf.

32 Press Release, BestWire, Insurance Executives Blast ComFrame, IAIS During NAIC's International Insurance Forum (May 13, 2013), *available at* www.programbusiness.com/news/Insurance-Executives-Blast-ComFrame-IAIS-During-NAICs-International-Insurance-Forum.

33 www.naic.org/documents/committees_g_comframe_position_statements.pdf.

34 Thomas Sullivan, Testimony Before the Subcommittee on Housing and Insurance, US House of Rep., September 18, 2014.

35 31 U.S.C. § 313(c).

36 31 U.S.C. § 313(r)(2).

37 GATT Article III.

38 A further discussion of this point may be seen in David Zaring, *Finding Legal Principle in Global Financial Regulation*, 52 VA. J. INT'L L. 685, 707 (2012).

39 For more on this, see David Zaring, *International Institutional Performance in Crisis*, 10 CHI. J. INT'L L. 475, 485 (2010).

6

The Other Networks of Financial Regulation

In international financial regulation, some of the organizations that make policy have been more celebrated than others. Reams of scholarship have been produced about the Basel Committee, for example, and IOSCO has also enjoyed plenty of press. David Singer's book on the development of international financial regulation has focused on those two regulatory networks, along with the International Association of Insurance Supervisors, the IAIS.[1] Abraham Newman and Elliot Posner also highlighted the three networks, although it identified others as well.[2] Ethan Kapstein also focused on the Basel Committee in his own book-length work[3] as did Tony Porter in his.[4] Tim Buthe and Walter Mattli have written about the IAIS, the International Organization for Standardization and the International Electrotechnical Commission.[5] Of course, these examples constitute a limited sample; they are books written by international relations scholars. The law reviews feature a similar focus on network scholarship.[6]

While largely warranted, this attention could obscure other important contributions to the networked form of financial regulation. This chapter reviews the accomplishments of the networks that form the periphery, rather than the core, of financial regulation, and places them into the larger context of international financial regulation. It is organized around their roles in the signature post-crisis regulatory institution: the Financial Stability Board's "Compendium of Standards," which looks to core principles from networks beyond the Basel Commission, IOSCO, and IAIS that it views as fundamental for a well-working system of financial oversight.[7] The Financial Stability Board has offered membership to other networks.[8] These networks have played important roles in regulating money laundering, deposit insurance, and other subjects. In light of the incorporation of these institutions into the architecture of financial administration, it is worth focusing on what they do and how they do it.

The existence of so many financial regulatory institutions, even if some are quite small and amount to little more than task forces within the ambit of the Basel Committee, suggests that financial regulation still remains a task-specific, disaggregated enterprise. Consider, for example, deposit insurance. It is conceivable that the

Basel Committee or IAIS could develop principles for effective deposit insurance on their own; deposit insurance contributes to financial stability, which is the *raison d'etre* of the Basel Committee, and is an insurance product that insurance supervisors, in theory, understand (perhaps only in theory – deposit insurance is more commonly thought of as a tool for bank regulators). The fact that Basel and the IAIS haven't done so is a testament to the regulatory fragmentation of financial oversight.

We also see evidence that financial regulatory networks remain lean, with tiny budgets and little capacity to add new functions to their extant roles.[9] Instead, new networks are spun off from old ones, beginning perhaps as task forces, then developing into distinctive low-key cross-border enterprises.

The networks themselves form more ground-level supervision and are consistent with the view of the financial regulatory space developing into something that looks like a transnational disaggregated agency. They fill in gaps of the new regulatory regime, offering briefer, issue-specific sets of principles and opportunities for meetings meant to foster the exchange of ideas, and the transnational development of regulatory expertise. They also underscore the increasing elaboration of the transnational financial regulatory regime.

The rest of this chapter considers six networks, all of which play a role in the FSB's new standard-setting enterprise, three of which are members of the FSB itself. The goal is to provide a factual basis for the claim that financial regulatory networks often appear almost identical. They are leanly staffed, rely on their members for personnel, have small budgets, and serve as conduits for the exchange of information and often as an initial matter the development of core principles. Identifying these common developments in the organization and accomplishments of each network runs the risk of repetition. Nonetheless, little attention is being paid to the networks discussed here as part of the architecture of financial regulation, even though they have been charged with important roles in the supervision of financial institutions, and they underscore an abiding affection for the network form.

Above all, these networks contribute to an emerging architecture. The old efforts to deal with cross-border externalities of finance, which were limited in their ambition and breadth, have been reformed in the wake of the financial crisis. Instead, a new order that is hierarchical, procedurally regular, and politically supervised has emerged. This new order pervades the Basel Committee, IOSCO, and IAIS in particular, but also very much applies to more interstitial outfits that have received less attention in the scholarly literature.

Those values, of course, are the values of the administrative state. Political supervision, increasingly regularized output, and bureaucratic order make international financial regulation look increasingly like an administrative agency stretched across a global multilateral context.[10]

6.1 THE OVERLOOKED NETWORKS

There are two important ways that overlooked regulatory networks have been integrated into the new order of international financial regulation. First, some of them have been integrated through membership in the FSB.[11] Good examples are the Committee on the Global Financial System (CGFS) and the less esoteric, more practical Committee on Payments and Market Infrastructure. Also part of the FSB is the International Accounting Standards Board (IASB), an important network that includes private participants as well as public overseers, and which is attempting to devise a global set of standards for accounting. These lesser-known networks are joined by the Basel Committee, IOSCO, and IAIS on the FSB, along with various G20 member agencies, and the European Commission, the IMF, the Organisation for Economic Co-operation and Development (OECD), and the World Bank.[12]

The second way networks play a role in the new financial architecture is by providing a set of standards endorsed by the FSB and the G20 as appropriate minimum metrics of effective financial supervision. The Compendium of Standards also includes submissions by multinational organizations such as the IMF, the World Bank, and the OECD.[13]

By being taken up by the FSB, these overlooked networks have demonstrated their attractiveness to regulators concerned with systemic stability of the financial system. It is accordingly useful to spend some time discerning how these networks do their job.

6.2 THE QUIET STANDARD SETTERS

Many overlooked networks that now participate in the project of international financial regulation draw their strength from two kinds of endorsements by the FSB. Some provide standards that have been approved by the board, while others have been invited to join it.

Often regarded as offshoots of the Basel Committee, three such networks exemplify both rulemaking in the post-crisis era, and the role of interstitial organizations in filling gaps in cross-border financial regulation. The FSB's Compendium of Standards characterizes their work, as well as the work of nine other financial regulatory networks, as "internationally accepted as important for sound, stable, and well-functioning financial systems."[14] The standards endorsed by the FSB are meant to "strengthen domestic financial systems by encouraging sound regulation" and improve "international financial stability by facilitating better-informed lending and investment decisions, improving market integrity, and reducing the risks of financial distress and contagion."[15] The board identified twelve policy areas that it views as "key for sound financial systems and deserving of priority implementation."[16] Some of these principles are provided by networks that do little else – for instance, the International Auditing and Assurance Standards Board and

International Association of Deposit Insurers. The Financial Action Task Force provides similar principles to fighting money laundering and terrorism finance.

We see in these institutions the telltale models of network organization, devised for the purpose of coordinating regulatory approaches and developing best practices for more obscure parts of the financial regulatory system.

6.3 INTERNATIONAL ASSOCIATION OF DEPOSIT INSURERS

The International Association of Deposit Insurers (IADI) has become the principle forum for deposit insurers across the globe.[17] Like most networks, it facilitates the gathering of knowledge and the sharing of expertise. In its case, this expertise involves deposit insurance, a component of financial stability that for many years was by no means widespread, and even today, is much less central to many countries than it is to the USA. The IADI is not a large network; it features agencies from only those countries that offer deposit insurance to their citizens, or those that are considering doing so.[18]

The number of jurisdictions considering deposit insurance has increased in the wake of the financial crisis. One of the principal functions of deposit insurance is to prevent customer runs or panics that destabilize the financial system. Deposit insurance provides depositors comfort that their funds are not at risk, even if the economy is insalubrious or there are concerns over the viability of a particular bank. By IADI calculations, over a hundred countries have some form of deposit insurance, a number dramatically larger than the fewer than a dozen in 1974 (and a claim that appears to come perilously close to overstatement).[19] Europe, through the EU, adopted deposit insurance requirements meant to apply to all member countries in a 1994 directive by the European Parliament and the council.[20] Nonetheless, during the financial crisis, the quality and extent of deposit insurance was thought to be one of the regrettable features of the financial systems in many jurisdictions.

Deposit insurance usually works through dues paid by insured financial institutions to a government-run deposit insurer.[21] The insurer, in turn, tries to make sure that financial institutions are operated relatively safely and soundly to preserve its resources. In the USA, the Federal Deposit Insurance Corporation (FDIC) plays this role – scrutinizing the stability of banks that it insures. But it also plays the role of a balance sheet-obsessed corporation, in that it collects dues, marshals a fund, and pays money out in the case of insolvencies.[22] The FDIC, unlike some other deposit insurers, also plays a key role in taking insolvent financial institutions through bankruptcy. The fund guarantees consumer deposits, and, in the event of a pending insolvency or collapse, sells the assets of the bank or winds up operations as quickly as possible.

IADI was founded on May 6, 2002,[23] and is based, like the Basel Committee, IAIS, the Committee on Payment Systems, and others, at the Bank for International Settlements in Basel.[24] With the assistance of the Basel Committee, IADI has developed joint core principles for effective deposit insurance systems – principles to which all seventy-one of its member organizations[25] are supposed to commit. Those principles were promulgated on June 18, 2009.[26]

The IADI, like many networks, is governed by an executive council.[27] It has a tiny secretariat and does much of its work, like other networks, through standing committees. While only deposit insurance organizations can become IADI members, the association also invites other organizations in countries that are considering developing deposit insurance systems to participate as associates[28]; the goal is to proselytize as well as exchange information. The IADI also allows other not-for-profit entities that have a direct interest in the effectiveness of deposit insurance to be involved as observers[29]; this may be a function of stakeholder participation and fundraising. The IADI, like other low-key networks, has little access to funding; membership and registration fees to the annual meeting are part of its fundraising effort.[30] Other organizations that have cooperative arrangements with IADI are considered partners that work with it to further the association's objectives.[31]

Unlike other regulatory networks, the IADI does not maintain a monopoly on issuing guiding principles. It has endorsed guidance developed by IADI members and third parties such as the Asia Pacific Economic Cooperation and the Financial Stability Forum, making clear that at least part of what it does is to serve as an information clearinghouse.[32]

Although IADI is not a member of the FSB, its published principles and guidance papers have been designated by the FSB as standards that help to stabilize national and international financial systems. In fact, the Core Principles for Effective Deposit Insurance Systems is listed by the FSB as part of its Compendium of Standards.[33]

Deposit insurance core principles were developed with the assistance of the Basel committee and reflect a commitment to a series of preconditions and some principles for the use of deposit insurance. As the IADI has said, "[a] deposit insurance system will be most effective if a number of external elements or preconditions are in place."[34] These preconditions are aspirational, and include incontestable values like macroeconomic stability, strong prudential regulation, and sound governmental agencies. No one is against those sorts of policies, and so it is difficult to know how constraining they are meant to be. Once in place, however, the network has developed some principles meant to be assessed by outsiders, and understandable in jurisdictions hoping to implement deposit insurance. These principles are broad in their own right, but include requirements and checklists that do in fact constrain agencies. For example, in its Enhanced Guidance papers, the network outlines specific procedures that deposit insurers must take in setting coverage levels and primary methods for reducing moral hazards in deposit insurance.[35] The principles begin as broad proclamations of deposit insurance objectives like "the stability of the financial system and [the protection of] depositors" as well as the importance of "appropriate design features and ... other elements of the financial safety net" designed to mitigate moral hazards.[36] The deposit insurer is required to "be operationally independent, transparent, accountable, and insulated from undue political and industry influence."[37] The principles also address more specific procedures like mandatory membership for "all financial institutions accepting deposits from those deemed most in need of protection (e.g. retail and small-business depositors) to avoid adverse selection" and a primary role of banks in paying for deposit insurance "since they and their clients directly benefit from having an effective deposit insurance system."[38]

In addition, the principles also speak in more specific terms of characteristics of an effective deposit insurance system. For one thing, they discuss the drawbacks of a "blanket guarantee" of deposits and the desirability of a quick transition within countries from blanket guarantee to limit guarantee systems.[39] They also advise regulators to ensure that the necessary funding is in place to support a deposit insurance system, and counsel that "[p]rimary responsibility for funding the deposit insurance system [should be] borne by member banks and [ideally] is enforceable by the deposit insurer."[40] Finally, the principles recommend that legal protection against lawsuits should be afforded to "[t]he deposit insurer and individuals working for the deposit insurer . . . for their decisions and actions taken in 'good faith' while discharging their mandates," but that those individuals should also be required to adhere to applicable conflict-of-interest rules and codes of conduct.[41]

IADI looks like a lot of other networks, albeit with a relatively narrow issue area. It shows the prevalence of the network form in financial regulatory space, and the consistency that characterizes the evolution of that form.

6.4 INTERNATIONAL AUDITING AND ASSURANCE STANDARDS BOARD

If IADI represents a relatively small network of financial insurers with quasi-governmental roles, the IAASB is an ethics regulator: the IAASB validates the professional status of the accounting industry. Ethics regulators of professions define and police malpractice, the sine qua non of professional status – MBA programs and consultancies often regret the lack of a malpractice sanction. They worry that it is a sign that business management and consultancy is not truly a profession.

The predecessor to the IAASB, the International Auditing Practices Committee (IAPC), was founded in March 1978.[42] It published the International Standards on Auditing (ISAs) in 1991.[43] Today, the IAASB attempts to set "high quality" international standards for auditing and quality control and that auditing practices (rather than accounting standards, which are the province of the very important IASB discussed *infra*), are followed in a similar manner.[44] To facilitate this process, the IAASB began what it calls the Clarity Project in 2004 with the goal of updating and clarifying the ISAs – integrating new drafting conventions, eliminating ambiguities, and "improving the overall readability and understandability of the ISAs."[45]

The IAASB reports to a group of auditing practice supervisors, who themselves are players in a network known as the Public Interest Oversight Board (PIOB).[46] The

PIOB is meant to ensure that the IAASB follows some degree of due process and acts in ways consistent with the public interest.[47] And so standards of conduct for accountants are the product of the IAASB (and, for that matter, the PIOB, which is more explicitly comprised of government accounting supervisors). The IAASB publishes an annual handbook that summarizes new standards and pronouncements pertaining to international audits and quality control.[48] Additionally, the organization also develops specialized standards for specific auditor functions. The IAASB has developed, for example, the ISAE 3000 assurance standards to provide for how an engagement of assurance may be carried out[49] and ISAE 3420 that prescribes how to report on the compilation of pro forma financials included in a prospectus.[50] The IAASB in this sense is a global professional organization for accountants. Its principal achievement has been defining the objectives and scope of the audit of financial statements, an ongoing process with multiple rounds of comments and drafts.[51] Again, all countries interested in passing IMF Financial Sector Assessment Program (FSA) scrutiny must adopt these principles.

In developing and adopting new standards, the IAASB follows a traditional notice and comment process.[52] It tends to begin with a consultation process involving stakeholders. Then the draft of a pronouncement is posted on the organization's website and comments are invited.[53] Eventually, final pronouncements are published, along with a summary of comments received.[54] In addition to this "rigorous due process," the IAASB aspires towards transparency.[55] All meetings are open to the public and all relevant papers, along with audio recordings of those meetings, are published on its website.

These standards are meant to be professional standards that would apply to auditors. The aspiration is for "high-quality international standards for auditing, quality control, review, other assurance, and related services."[56] For example, on audit documentation, the ISA requires auditors to perform very specific recordkeeping and verification measures.[57] "The auditor shall document discussions of significant matters with management" and "[i]f the auditor identified information that is inconsistent with the auditor's final conclusion regarding a significant matter, the auditor shall document how [he] addressed the inconsistency."[58] Substantial leeway is given to individual auditors who are free to "design and perform tests of controls to obtain sufficient appropriate audit evidence."[59]

As is often the case with auditing requirements, there are many standards, encompassing guidance documents, principles, and white papers. As part of the Clarity Project, the IAASB board staff has supplemented the clarified standards with questions and answers publications as well as non-authoritative videos and slideshows to flesh out details. Every year, the IAASB also publishes a handbook summarizing all amendments and pronouncements as well as an annual report that covers newly issued standards and reports on the status of ongoing projects.[60] The board also publishes implementation guides meant to aid practitioners in understanding and applying the international standards in their work.[61]

This IAASB resembles other networks, but its success (along with the IASB) suggests that financial regulators view the accounting profession as a critical gatekeeper. The IAASB is subject to oversight by two regulatory networks – networks composed of privately employed accountants in addition to government officials – and provides an example of a network expanding from standard-setting for regulators to standard-setting for private watchdogs who assist regulators, an expansion in the reach of the form, if a modest one.

6.5 FINANCIAL ACTION TASK FORCE ON MONEY LAUNDERING

Established in 1989 by the G-7 Summit, the Financial Action Task Force (FATF) is an intergovernmental body that sets standards and promotes "measures for combating money laundering, terrorist financing, and other related threats to the integrity of the international financial system."[62] Unlike other regulatory networks, FATF operates under "a fixed life-span," meaning that the task force will dissolve at the set end date without a decision to continue by its ministers.[63] Under the most recent mandate, approved in April of 2012, the FATF is scheduled to operate until 2020.[64] The task force currently has a membership of thirty-four countries and two regional organizations – the European Commission and the Gulf Co-Operation Council.[65] The FATF relies heavily on its eight associates, "a global network of FATF-Style Regional Bodies," to promote compliance and adoption of FATF recommendations within their regions.[66] The FATF also includes a number of observer organizations interested in anti-money-laundering measures, like the African Development Bank and Interpol.[67]

The FATF's mission is to develop a set of standards to fight against money laundering and terrorist financing. The 40+9 Recommendations were completed in October 2004 – the original forty recommendations, issued in 1990, were structured as an action plan to combat money laundering and the nine special recommendations were developed later after combatting terrorist financing was added to FATF's mission in 2001. The recommendations were thoroughly reviewed and updated in 2012 to reflect new threats and technologies. For example, one recommendation "requires that the laws and regulations that govern nonprofit organizations be reviewed so that these organizations cannot be abused for the financing of terrorism."[68] In keeping with the times, the FATF also recently issued guidance regarding the role of "prepaid cards, mobile payments, and Internet-based payment services" in terrorist financing.[69] Though the technology discussed may be relatively novel, the recommendations are hardly groundbreaking – the report calls for "effective recordkeeping," "customer due diligence," conventional licensing arrangements, and basic international cooperation.[70] In addition to frequent meetings, the FATF has also brought together experts to evaluate existing recommendations and identify areas for improvement.

In addition to developing standards, the FATF also functions like a third-party inspector of its members' money laundering and terrorist financing countermeasures and their progress in adopting FATF recommendations. The task force also monitors non-member jurisdictions through its International Co-operation Review Group to identify countries where measures to counter money laundering and terrorism financing are lacking or insufficient. It has a shaming mechanism similar to one implemented by IOSCO; FATF publicly identifies "high-risk and non-cooperative" jurisdictions and "call[s] upon its members and urge[s] all jurisdictions to strengthen preventive measures and apply effective countermeasures against" those problematic jurisdictions.[71]

Perhaps the most important way that FATF enforces its standards is by keeping a black list and a grey list. The black list consists of countries that are not meeting the standards of the network in combatting money laundering and terrorist financing; it includes Iran and North Korea. The grey list includes countries that have committed to an action plan to remedy their deficiencies – Pakistan, Sri Lanka, Syria, and Yemen are among the fewer than ten jurisdictions on this list. Once listed, FATF can call on its member countries to apply enhanced due diligence or countermeasures to firms doing business in those countries, potentially inhibiting investment in them.

The organization has thus had a real effect on countries – reducing investment, isolating pariahs, and so on. It also reports to the G20 and publicizes its efforts. It has become an important tool in the war on terror.

6.6 STANDARD SETTERS AND THE FSB

Three other networks play more elaborate roles in international financial regulatory architecture. One of these networks is quite important in its own right, while two others resemble networks that are not members of the FSB but have been asked to provide it with standards.

The International Accounting Standards Board (IASB) has enjoyed a relatively high profile, even if it has not often been in the center of the financial regulation revolution. In a short time, it has transformed the practice of accounting and been the central, if not the sole, driver of regulatory change. The IASB has overseen the transformation of accounting standards in all countries, with one major exception: the US Signatory nations have agreed with IASB's landmark product, the International Financial Reporting Standards (IFRS).

The two other networks that have joined the FSB have a much lower profile. The Committee on Payments and Market Infrastructure plays an interstitial role in reforming settlement processing. It promulgates principles meant to govern how payments processes work. The Committee on the Global Financial System has done little more than promulgate a particularly gauzy set of principles; it seems like an offshoot of the Basel Committee and is meant to monitor macroprudential safety and stability.

These networks, like others, offer core principles that are standard fare for such institutions. They also seek to build capacity on behalf of member agencies or chartered accountants across the world. But with regard to financial stability, the two prominent networks, the FATF and IASB, fit into financial regulations only orthogonally. Anti-money laundering is not a threat to the stability of the financial system, though it can weaken and destabilize, like termites in a house. With the exception of the Bank for Credit and Commerce International, which engaged in massive money laundering and was shuttered in 1991, a large, interconnected bank is unlikely to find itself insolvent because of exposure to criminality and tax fraud. And while US and European banking regulators have often imposed safety and soundness sanctions on firms that fail to prevent money laundering through their offices, the theory behind sanctions is that the failure to detect that activity suggests a lack of adequate internal controls, and, concomitantly, increased operational risk.

By the same token, accounting standards are critically important for publicly traded companies, particularly for publicly listed banks. But they are not designed in and of themselves to ensure financial system stability. Rather, they serve as a mechanism that can suggest whether a bank, for instance, is in fact stable, with reference to its profit-and-loss statement.

These more obscure members of the FSB have important roles to play in systemic stability. Payment systems are often ignored by financial regulators, but have often proved to be critical vectors in the spread of financial panic and contagion. Herstatt Risk is a form of payment systems risk. And, of course, a committee concerned with macroeconomic stability is almost by definition engaged in a project that has also animated Basel, IOSCO, and IAIS.

Nonetheless, these smaller networks have different missions. Their ambits are technical, and though their jurisdictions can be risky, they operate more in the shadows than some other more prominent groups of financial regulators.

6.7 THE INTERNATIONAL ACCOUNTING STANDARDS BOARD

The IASB is a network that has done for accounting what IOSCO has not been willing to do in securities regulation: develop international financial reporting standards, global rules for bookkeeping that apply regardless of the market or entity.

The attractiveness of common accounting standards is straightforward in a global context. Common standards allow investors to evaluate the returns of publicly traded companies around the world.[72] In fact, common standards would allow those companies to prepare a single set of returns that would satisfy regulators in any market in which their stock is listed, and "[g]iven the increasingly global nature of investment and finance . . . such a language [as embodied in common standards] would help communications between investors and issuers in capital markets, improving transparency and understanding of the financial position and performance of the issuers."[73]

Despite these incentives, the SEC essentially opted out of the informal effort to create common standards that would work for any company and any exchange.[74] The US securities regulator presumably assumed that it had no need for foreign standards. It announced "concerns with respect to the IASB governance structure," among other things.[75] This kind of reaction capsized IOSCO's 1980s efforts to develop a standard; the SEC has also failed to seriously participate in the informal network that succeeded IOSCO – the IASB – though it did participate in the arm's-length IOSCO committee that monitored IASB's progress.[76] But while US regulators could insist on unique American standards during the twentieth century, its preeminence has grown more tenuous in the twenty-first century because of the global acceptance of a principles-based system rooted in European practice.[77]

Like IOSCO, IASB began as an informally constituted committee. It was formed in 1973 by the (primarily private) standard-setters of Australia, Canada, France, Germany, Ireland, Japan, Mexico, the Netherlands, the UK, and, indeed, the USA.[78] Like IOSCO, IASB looks like a network – it is informal, only partially public, and not subject to the requirements and limitations of international law. These are differences the SEC has noted: "IOSCO is a committee of securities regulatory agencies, [while] the IASC is an independent, private-sector organization,"[79] which has moved increasingly to publicize its deliberations in an effort, some commentators believe, to win acceptance for IFRS by the USA.[80]

The organization tried to develop the sort of accounting standards that could replace diverse standards being used around the world. It did so one painful standard at a time, with regular meetings all over the world, and the ready cycling in of representatives from various jurisdictions in the standard development process.[81] Neither the SEC nor American accountants played a particularly important role in this process.

During the late 1980s, the USA abandoned accounting standardization, and killed IOSCO's initial efforts along these lines. The result resulted in the move of IOSCO headquarters from North America to Europe and recentered the global accounting effort around IASB's efforts. As former SEC Commissioner Roberta Karmel has said:

> [A]t this time, the SEC also determined not to adopt a process-oriented approach to IASB standards ... Rather, it intended to assess each IASB standard after its completion, and then recognize acceptable standards ... [It only] decided instead to consider all IASB standards after the IASB completed its core standards work program.[82]

None of this stopped the IFRS, however. The adoption of the standard throughout the EU in 2005, and decisions by Australia, Hong Kong, and South Africa that followed, proved to be a tipping point, with over a hundred countries now requiring or permitting IFRS.[83] As John White, once the director of the SEC's corporate finance division, has noted, the European accounting system the IASB adopted seems to have caught on better with world markets than the arguably more rigorous US GAAP.[84]

A part of the IFRS Foundation, the IASB is an independent standards-setting body responsible for the development of new accounting standards. The board currently has sixteen members – all accounting and auditing professionals – and all meetings are open to the public and available via webcast. Some meetings, or particular sessions of meetings, are held jointly with the US Financial Accounting Standards Board (FASB). After every monthly meeting, tentative decisions reached by the IASB are published in a monthly IASB update. Public engagement and stakeholder involvement play prominent roles in IASB standard setting, with all IASB rules published for public comment.[85] As part of the development of IFRS, the board publishes all proposed rules and amendments as well as provides guidance on rules in specific areas. The IFRS Interpretations Committee assists in the standardization process. The committee consists of fourteen members with a variety of professional backgrounds and reviews current issues in the accounting profession and provides guidance on their resolution. Committee meetings are also available to the public and broadcast on the website.

In order to guarantee the organization's independence, the foundation is funded by a number of national economies. The support they provide varies with the country's gross domestic product. The idea is to ensure the independence of the board; for this reason, the IASB recently rejected the EU's attempt at imposing funding conditions.[86]

Though independent, the IASB is held accountable through its unique governance structure and transparent procedures. The organization operates under a constitution and is overseen by a monitoring board. The trustees are primarily responsible for appointing members to and establishing operating procedures and due process for the IASB, the interpretations committee, and the advisory council. The work of the trustees is overseen by the trustees' due process oversight committee; the trustees are accountable to the monitoring board.

Accordingly, even without the support of the USA, international convergence on accounting standards took place anyway. A December 2002 survey of fifty-nine countries' accounting standard-setters revealed that 90 percent of the standard-setters intend to converge to IFRS.[87] "Most countries are moving towards IFRS," one observer has said. These countries have generally found the standards to be congenial and reputable.[88]

In the end, the SEC was left with little choice on accounting standards – it decided it had to defer to the successful global network, though it has been slow to embrace it. In 2006, it established a "database on application of IFRS," where "[IOSCO] members can exchange information about problems and non-compliance with [the standard]."[89] IOSCO "assesses the data[,] and where it reveals varying interpretations, refers the[m] to the [IASB]," the organization responsible for developing IFRS standards.[90] IOSCO has a longstanding relationship with the

IASB, and it claims that it continues to "contribut[e] actively to the work of the IASB, through participation in various expert committees and responses to consultation,"[91] and "continue[s] to monitor the work of the IASB."[92] Still, the SEC has been unwilling to sign up for multinational accounting standards (at least until recently) and is only now making its presence felt after the standards were developed, and after the SEC has declared its intention to adopt them.[93]

In the end, the SEC bowed to the power of this network. It allowed foreign firms listed in the USA to file returns using IFRS. As former SEC Chair Christopher Cox admitted in 2006, "Our recent decision to accept IFRS financial statements in SEC filings was crafted in such a way as to support the efforts of the IASB, and many other nations, to establish IFRS as a single, global set of standards, and not so many national flavors."[94]

The story of this network is thus a story of a move from enforcement cooperation, which permits countries to opt in and opt out as they wish, and to retain their regulatory standards, to something in which the costs of exit – or, in the SEC case, nonparticipation – are too high to bear, because the advantages of standardization, a major advantage of network effects, have been realized by IASB, as they haven't been by IOSCO. That's because the IASB created a standard that "tipped" in a network sense, making it all-but impossible to resist. As a result, the IASB is a network that moved from offering club goods to, perhaps, one where the obvious benefits of its standard, IFRS, makes it impossible to exit.

6.8 THE COMMITTEE ON PAYMENTS AND MARKET INFRASTRUCTURE

The CPMI is a network organized to assist the Basel Committee on a critical issue: systemic stability. Intriguingly, the network exists independently of the committee, marking a preference among financial regulators for a degree of fragmentation and specialization in their efforts. In other respects, however, it resembles other networks that concern themselves with banking.

The CPMI was founded in 1990 as a continuation of the G10's Group of Experts on Payments Systems and the ad hoc Committee on Interbank Netting Schemes. The CPMI (the Committee on Payment and Settlement Systems was renamed in 2014) is one of the permanent committees of the BIS that, until 2009, reported to the G10 governors. Since then, the CPMI has expanded to include twenty-five central banks and, as such, the committee now reports to the governors of the BIS' bimonthly Global Economy Meeting. The committee "addresses general concerns regarding the efficiency and stability of payment, clearing, settlement and related arrangements" as well as "issues related to these systems or arrangements" and their impact on major financial markets and monetary policy.[95] The CPMI periodically publishes reviews of payment and settlement systems in selected countries – generally called Red Books. The most recent edition of the Red Book was published in 2003, though its statistics are updated annually and published separately.

In order to pursue its work, the committee cooperates with other international organizations – including IOSCO, the Basel Committee, and the FSB – and with other global payment system institutions to address common concerns. For example, the CPMI and IOSCO have been working together to monitor implementation of the Principles for Financial Market Infrastructures (PFMIs), which the two organizations issued jointly in 2012.[96] In late 2013, CPMI and IOSCO released the PFMIs for public comment, noting that they were developed with the fundamental notion that "financial market infrastructures (FMIs) should provide relevant information to participants, relevant authorities, and the broader public."[97] In conjunction with publication of the PFMIs, the CPMI has also developed guidance for disaster preparedness plans in the face of financial threats,[98] the concern being that the absence of such "comprehensive and effective recovery plans [could cause] the disorderly failure of such FMIs [and] could lead to severe systemic disruptions."[99] Due to the international nature of its work, the CPMI also maintains relationships with non-CPMI central banks and publishes reviews of payment-system developments in those countries.

The CPMI, because it is staffed by the payments experts of central bankers, may buy those bankers another vote on the Financial Stability Board; it may also be a gesture taking the technical world of payment systems seriously in reforming global finance. But its independence is intriguing. For example, while the CPMI does accept requests to complete specific studies from the governors of the Global Economy Meeting, it also undertakes investigations at its own discretion, setting up working groups as it deems necessary.[100]

6.9 COMMITTEE ON THE GLOBAL FINANCIAL SYSTEM

The very existence of the Committee on the Global Financial System (CGFS) as the deep-thinking network in the financial regulatory arsenal suggests a taste for task-specificity among financial regulators. The CGFS, which was founded in 1999, focuses on helping its members recognize, analyze, and respond to threats that imperil the stability of the financial markets and the global financial system.[101] The CGFS monitors financial stability and, as the Basel Committee puts it, "supports central banks in their pursuit of monetary and financial stability."[102] The committee has thirty-one member institutions, and is currently overseen by William C. Dudley, until recently president and chief executive officer of the Federal Reserve Bank of New York.[103] Interestingly, Dudley previously led the CPMI from 2009 through 2012.[104]

Unlike the CPMI, the CGFS covers a broad policy area. As the name implies, the committee is conceived as a "forum for the monitoring and examination of broad issues relating to financial markets and systems."[105] The committee focuses on monetary and financial stability and works to increase transparency of the financial markets. As part of its activities analyzing the stability of the global financial system, the CGFS has published numerous reports and papers, two of which have been included by the FSB in its Compendium of Standards.[106] The CGFS's 2013 publication on asset encumbrance, financial reform, and the demand for collateral assets notes a global increase in requiring collateral in financial transactions in the wake of the financial crisis.[107] In keeping with the CGFS focus on transparency, the report urges that banks be required "to provide regular, standardised public disclosures on asset encumbrance" and "should be asked to perform regular stress tests that evaluate encumbrance levels under adverse market conditions."[108]

6.10 CONCLUSION: A TASTE FOR THE NETWORK FORM

The story that emerges from this overview of regulatory networks is one of rational organizations – albeit, rational organizations that evolve along path-dependent lines. The network form is not clearly institutionally superior to all other kinds of cross-border organization, impressive although its accomplishments in financial regulation have often been. Some networks, like the one focused on payment systems, represent organizational distinctions that simply do not exist among domestic regulators, none of whom have payment-system agencies.

But the underlying story here is of a taste for the network form, and a willingness to endure disparate networks connected through the centralized mechanism of the FSB. Although all networks are different in their remit, they are organized in pretty much the same way, and take on similar kinds of tasks, particularly as they begin their work. To be sure, the Basel Committee and the IASB have organized their fields in ways that other networks have not. But over the development of the six networks considered here – each of which has made contributions to financial stability that have not always been recognized – clear patterns emerge.

These patterns are consistent with the view that the network form is preferred in international financial regulation; that rulemaking is the ordinary output of these networks, each of which promulgated principles to start; that the process of peer review is meant to organize and regulate the networks; and that there may be some agreements among basic principles that each of these networks developed – a taste for consensus, for example, and a general belief in national treatment.

Of course, there may be other reasons for the precise architecture of the networks that we see. The FATF would surely not be so prominent were it not for the war on terror. The payment systems network may be a gesture, rather than a commitment. And the accounting network's integration into the whole may be a sign of the political importance of the accounting profession, along with the industries that depend on it. By the same token, the number of banking related networks may simply be a reflection of turf expansion by banking regulators.

None of this means that the network form is ordained by reason, and forged in inevitability. But it does mean that bureaucratic organization is increasingly shaping the disaggregated international financial regulatory space.

Notes

1 DAVID ANDREW SINGER, REGULATING CAPITAL: SETTING STANDARDS FOR THE INTERNATIONAL FINANCIAL SYSTEM (Cornell Studies in Money Ser., 2010).
2 ABRAHAM L. NEWMAN & ELLIOT POSNER, VOLUNTARY DISRUPTIONS: INTERNATIONAL SOFT LAW, FINANCE, AND POWER 31–62 (2018).
3 ETHAN B. KAPSTEIN, SUPERVISING INTERNATIONAL BANKS: ORIGINS AND IMPLICATIONS OF THE BASLE ACCORD (Essays in Int'l Fin. Ser., 1991).
4 TONY PORTER, STATES, MARKETS & REGIMES IN GLOBAL FINANCE (1993).
5 TIM BÜTHE & WALTER MATTLI, THE NEW GLOBAL RULERS: THE PRIVATIZATION OF REGULATION IN THE WORLD ECONOMY (2011).
6 *See* Douglas W. Arner & Michael Taylor, *The Global Financial Crisis and the Financial Stability Board: Hardening the Soft Law of International Financial Regulations*, 32 U. NEW S. WALES 488 (2009) (focusing on the role and effectiveness of the FSB), Emiliio Avgouleas, *Rationales and Designs to Implement an Institutional Big Bang in the Governance of Global Finance*, 36 SEATTLE U. L. REV. 321 (2013) (discussing Basel, IOSCO, and the IMF with reference to the financial crisis), Chris Brummer, *How International Financial Law Works (And How it Doesn't)*, 99 GEO. L.J. 257 (2011), Ross Buckley, *Reforming the International Monetary Fund*, 3 GLOBAL POLICY 102 (2012), Eric J. Pan, *Challenge of International Cooperation and Institutional Design in Financial Supervision: Beyond Transgovernmental Networks*, 11 CHI. J. INT'L L. 243 (2010), Pierre-Hugues Verdier, *The Political Economy of International Financial Regulation*, 88 IND. L. J. 1405 (2013), David Zaring, *Best Practices*, 81 N.Y. U. L. REV. 294 (2006); Maximillian L. Feldman, Note, *The Domestic Implementation of International Regulations*, 88 N.Y.U. L. REV. 401 (2013).
7 *See About the Compendium of Standards*, FIN. STABILITY BD., www.financialstabilityboard.org/cos/index.htm (describing the Compendium of Standards as a "list[of] the various economic and financial standards – by both subject area and issuing body – that are internationally accepted as important for sound, stable and well functioning financial systems"); *Compendium of Standards – Issuing Body – Last 5 Years*, FIN. STABILITY BD., www.financialstabilityboard.org/list/fsb_cos_issuing_body/index.htm (listing the various standards that comprise the Compendium of Standards by issuing body).
8 *See, e.g., Links to FSB Members*, FIN. STABILITY BD., www.financialstabilityboard.org/members/links.htm (listing as members of the FSB "[i]nternational standard-setting bodies" including the Committee on the Global Financial System (CGFS), the Committee on Payment and Settlement Systems (CPSS), and the International Accounting Standards Board (IASB), among others).
9 The International Association of Deposit Insurers, for example, had a total operating revenue of less than $1.3 million USD for the fiscal year ended March 31, 2012 – one-third of which constituted a contribution from BIS. IADI,

2011/2012 ANNUAL REPORT 32, *available at* www.iadi.org/annual_reports/IADI_AnnualReport_2011-low.pdf (reported in Swiss Francs; converted using December 3, 2013 Bloomberg conversion ratio of 1.1057). BIS, on the other hand, had about $1.35 billion in operating income for the same time period. BANK FOR INT'L SETTLEMENTS, 83RD ANNUAL REPORT 2012/2013 127 (June 23, 2013), *available at* www.bis.org/publ/arpdf/ar2013e.pdf (reported in Special Drawing Rights currency; converted using December 3, 2013 International Monetary Fund conversion ratio of 1.53439).

10 *See, e.g.*, David Zaring, *Finding Legal Principle in Global Financial Regulation*, 52 VA. J. INT'L L. 685 (2012) (arguing that, international regulatory cooperation in the financial industry is developing along parallel lines to domestic agencies and that this development can be described in terms of six fundamental legal principles).

11 *See Links to FSB Members*, FIN. STABILITY BD., www.financialstabilityboard.org/members/links.htm.

12 *Id.*

13 *Compendium of Standards Issuing Body by Category*, FIN. STABILITY BD., www.financialstabilityboard.org/list/fsb_cos_issuing_body/index.htm.

14 *About the Compendium of Standards*, FIN. STABILITY BOARD, www.financialstabilityboard.org/cos/.

15 *Why Are Standards Important?*, FIN. STABILITY BOARD, www.financialstabilityboard.org/cos/wasi.htm.

16 *Key Standards for Sound Financial Systems*, FIN. STABILITY BOARD, www.financialstabilityboard.org/cos/key_standards.htm.

17 Wally Suphap, *Toward Effective Risk-Adjusted Bank Deposit Insurance: A Transnational Strategy*, 42 COLUM. J. TRANSNAT'L L. 829, 855 (2004) (noting that, while there is not global deposit insurance oversight organization, the IADI is the largest, and seemingly most active, of its type).

18 *See How to Join IADI*, INT'L ASS'N OF DEPOSIT INSURERS, www.iadi.org/aboutIADI.aspx?id=49.

19 *Deposit Insurance Systems Worldwide*, INT'L ASS'N OF DEPOSIT INSURERS, www.iadi.org/iadi_members.html.

20 Council Directive 94/19/EC 1994 O.J. (L 135) 5–14 (EC).

21 Edward J. Kane & Asli Demirguc-Kunt, *Deposit Insurance Around the Globe: Where Does It Work?* 7 (Nat'l Bureau of Econ. Research, Working Paper No. 8493, 2001), *available at* www.nber.org/papers/w8493.

22 *Deposit Insurance Summary*, FED. DEPOSIT INS. CORP., www.fdic.gov/deposit/deposits/dis/.

23 *History*, INT'L ASS'N OF DEPOSIT INSURERS, www.iadi.org/aboutIADI.aspx?id=45.

24 INT'L ASS'N OF DEPOSIT INSURERS, www.iadi.org/.

25 *Overview of the Association*, INT'L ASS'N OF DEPOSIT INSURERS, www.iadi.org/aboutIADI.aspx?id=48.

26 Press Release, Bank for Int'l Settlements, Core Principles for Effective Deposit Insurance Systems: Paper Issued by Basel Committee and IADI (June 18, 2009), *available at* www.bis.org/press/p090618.htm.

27 Statutes of the International Association of Deposit Insurers 7 (Revised Oct. 25, 2012) [hereinafter IADI Statutes], *available at* www.iadi.org/aboutiadi.aspx?id=71; *see also* Int'l Ass'n of Deposit Insurers, 2011–2012 Annual Report 18, *available at* www.iadi.org/annual_reports/IADI_AnnualReport_2011-low.pdf.

28 *How to Join IADI*, *supra* note 18.

29 *Id.*

30 Article 5 of the IAID Statutes lists among as its "financial resources" the initial fund contribution by its members, the annual fee collected from participants; and donations, grants or other sources of revenue. IADI Statutes, *supra* note 27, at 5. Beginning in the 2009–2010 fiscal year, dues were payable in Swiss Frances (CHF). *How to Join the IADI*, *supra* note 18. Members pay an initial fund contribution of CHF 11,390 (approximately $12,732 USD as of December 2013) and an annual fee of the same amount; Associates and Observers pay an initial fund contribution of CHF 5,695 (approximately $6,366 USD) and an annual fee of CHF 8,542.50 (approximately $9,549 USD) and Partners pay no fees. *Id.* The 2011–2012 IADI annual report indicated that the organization had collected CHF 784,487 ($876,914 USD) as of fiscal year end March 31, 2012. Int'l Ass'n of Deposit Insurers, 2011–2012 Annual Report, *supra* note 27, at 28. The annual fee for the 2013 IADI annual conference, held in November 2013 in Buenos Aires, Argentina, was $850 USD per delegate. Letter from Int'l Ass'n of Deposit Insurers to IAIDI Members, Support Staff, and Colleagues, *available at* www.iadi.org/docs/Dear%20IADI%20Members%20and%20Support%20staff_AGM%20Notice.pdf.

31 *Overview of the Association*, Int'l Ass'n of Deposit Insurers, www.iadi.org/aboutIADI.aspx?id=48.

32 *IADI Research and Guidance Papers*, Int'l Ass'n of Deposit Insurers, www.iadi.org/Research.aspx?id=55.

33 *Key Standards for Sound Financial Systems*, *supra* note 16.

34 Basel Comm. on Banking Supervision & Int'l Ass'n of Deposit Insurers, Core Principles for Effective Deposit Insurance Systems: A Methodology for Compliance Assessment 5 (Dec. 2010) [hereinafter Basel & IADI, Core Principles], *available at* www.bis.org/publ/bcbs192.pdf.

35 *See, e.g.*, Int'l Ass'n of Deposit Insurers, Enhanced Guidance for Effective Deposit Insurance Systems: Mitigating Moral Hazard (May 2013), *available at* www.iadi.org/docs/IADI_Mitigating_Moral_Hazard_Enhanced_Guidance_2013-05.pdf. For more enhanced guidance papers providing guidance on a variety of areas relating to developing sound deposit insurance systems, see *IADI Research and Guidance Papers*, www.iadi.org/Research.aspx?id=55.

36 Basel & IADI, Core Principles, *supra* note 34, at 10.

37 *Id.* at 12.
38 Basel & IADI, CORE PRINCIPLES, *supra* note 34, at 15, 18.
39 *Id.* at 17.
40 *Id.* at 18.
41 *Id.* at 20.
42 *About IAASB*, INT'L FED'N OF ACCOUNTANTS, www.ifac.org/auditing-assurance/about-iaasb.
43 *Id.*
44 *Id.*
45 *Clarity Center*, INT'L FED'N OF ACCOUNTANTS, www.ifac.org/auditing-assurance/clarity-center.
46 INT'L AUDITING & ASSURANCE STANDARDS BD., 2012 ANNUAL REPORT 3 [hereinafter IAASB, 2012 REPORT], *available at* www.ifac.org/sites/default/files/publications/files/IAASB%20ANNUAL-2012-V10-SPREADS.pdf.
47 *Id.*
48 *See, e.g.*, INT'L AUDITING & ASSURANCE STANDARDS BD., 2013 HANDBOOK OF INTERNATIONAL QUALITY CONTROL, AUDITING, REVIEW, OTHER ASSURANCE, AND RELATED SERVICES PRONOUNCEMENTS (Sept. 19, 2013) [hereinafter IAASB, 2013 HANDBOOK], *available at* www.ifac.org/publications-resources/2013-handbook-international-quality-control-auditing-review-other-assurance-a.
49 INT'L AUDITING & ASSURANCE STANDARDS BD., INTERNATIONAL STANDARD ON ASSURANCE ENGAGEMENTS 3000, *available at* www.ifac.org/publications-resources/2013-handbook-international-quality-control-auditing-review-other-assurance-a.
50 INT'L AUDITING & ASSURANCE STANDARDS BD., INTERNATIONAL STANDARD ON ASSURANCE ENGAGEMENTS 3420, *available at* http://www.ifac.org/publications-resources/2012-handbook-international-quality-control-auditing-review-other-assurance-a.
51 *Audit Quality*, INT'L FED'N OF ACCTS., www.ifac.org/auditing-assurance/projects/audit-quality.
52 *About IASB*, INT'L FED'N OF ACCTS., www.ifac.org/auditing-assurance/about-iaasb.
53 *See, e.g.*, *IAASB Consults on Five-Year Strategic Objectives and Work Priorities*, INT'L AUDITING & ASSURANCE STANDARDS BD., www.ifac.org/news-events/2013-12/iaasb-consults-five-year-strategic-objectives-and-work-priorities.
54 *See, e.g.*, *IAASB Reports on Findings from Post-Implementation Review of the Clarified ISAs*, INT'L AUDITING & ASSURANCE STANDARDS BD., www.ifac.org/news-events/2013-07/iaasb-reports-findings-post-implementation-review-clarified-isas.
55 INTERNATIONAL AUDITING AND ASSURANCE STANDARDS BOARD FACT SHEET 1 (Dec. 2013), *available at* www.ifac.org/sites/default/files/uploads/IAASB/IAASB%20FactSheet.pdf.
56 *Id.*

57 INT'L FED'N OF ACCTS., INTERNATIONAL STANDARD ON AUDITING 230: Audit Documentation 145-46 (Dec. 15, 2009), *available at* www.ifac.org/sites/default/files/publications/files/A012%202012%20IAASB%20Handbook%20ISA%20230.pdf.

58 *Id.* at 146.

59 INT'L FED'N OF ACCTS., INTERNATIONAL STANDARD ON AUDITING 330: THE AUDITOR'S RESPONSES TO ASSESSED RISKS 326 (Dec. 15, 2009), www.ifac.org/sites/default/files/publications/files/A020%202012%20IAASB%20Handbook%20ISA%20330.pdf.

60 *See* IAASB, 2013 HANDBOOK, *supra* note 48; IAASB, 2012 REPORT, *supra* note 46.

61 *See, e.g., Guidance & Support Tools*, INT'L AUDITING & ASSURANCE STANDARDS BD., www.ifac.org/publications-resources/clarified-international-standards-auditing-clarity-resources-brochure.

62 *Who We Are*, FATF, www.fatf-gafi.org/pages/aboutus/.

63 *What We Do*, FATF, www.fatf-gafi.org/pages/aboutus/whatwedo/.

64 FINANCIAL ACTION TASK FORCE MANDATE 2012–2020, 8 (Apr. 20, 2012), *available at* www.fatf-gafi.org/media/fatf/documents/FINAL%20FATF%20MANDATE%202012-2020.pdf.

65 *Id.* at 9.

66 Press Release, FATF, FATF Steps Up the Fight Against Money Laundering and Terrorist Financing (Feb. 16, 2012), *available at* www.fatf-gafi.org/topics/fatfrecommendations/documents/fatfstepsupthefightagainstmoneylaunderingandterroristfinancing.html.

67 *FATF Members and Observers*, FATF, www.fatf-gafi.org/pages/aboutus/membersandobservers/.

68 *Best Practices: Combating the Abuse of Non-Profit Organizations (Recommendation 8)*, FATF, www.fatf-gafi.org/documents/guidance/bpp-npo-2013.html.

69 FATF, GUIDANCE FOR A RISK-BASED APPROACH: PREPAID CARDS, MOBILE PAYMENTS AND INTERNET-BASED PAYMENT SERVICES 3 (June 2013), *available at* www.fatf-gafi.org/media/fatf/documents/recommendations/Guidance-RBA-NPPS.pdf.

70 *Id.* at 12.

71 *High-Risk and Non-Cooperative Jurisdictions* FATF, www.fatf-gafi.org/topics/high-riskandnon-cooperativejurisdictions/.

72 Sir David Tweedie, Chairman & Thomas R. Seidenstein, *Setting a Global Standard: The Case for Accounting Convergence*, 25 NW. J. INT'L L. & BUS. 589, 591 (2005) ("[A] common financial language, applied consistently, will enable investors to compare the financial results of companies operating in different jurisdictions more easily."); *see also International Financial Reporting Standards Questions and Answers*, AICPA IFRS RESOURCES, www.ifrs.com/updates/aicpa/ifrs_faq.html#q5.

73 Comments on Concept Release on Allowing U.S. Issuers to Prepare Financial Statements in Accordance with International Financial Reporting Standards, Exchange Act Release No. 33-831, 2007 WL 4985355, at *1 (Nov. 12, 2007) (comments of Richard Martin, Head of Financial Reporting, Association of Chartered Certified Accountants).

74 *See* Harold S. Bloomenthal & Samuel Wolff, 3F FEDERAL SECURITIES & CORPORATE LAW § 27:82.52 (2d ed. 2013) (describing the SEC's evaluation of the viability of adopting IFRSs and explaining that the last formal efforts came on July 13, 2012 with the publication of a Final Staff Report on a Work Plan for incorporating IFRS, a document that left the question of whether and how adoption might take place unanswered).

75 John W. White, Director, Div. of Corp. Fin. U.S. Sec. & Exch. Comm'n, 35th Annual Securities Regulation Institute, San Diego, California (Jan. 23, 2008), *available at* www.sec.gov/news/speech/2008/spch012308jww.htm.

76 James D. Cox, *Regulatory Duopoly in U.S. Securities Markets*, 99 COLUM. L. REV. 1200, 1208 (1999) (describing this event in some detail, and noting that the stature of IASC during the mid-1990s presented the SEC with a difficult decision concerning whether to recognize its accounting standards for SEC filings and how the SEC therefore engaged with IASC, directly and through the International Organization of Securities Commissions (IOSCO), laying out basic criteria it would have to meet and providing a "stream of comment letters" on IASC proposals).

77 Roberta S. Karmel, *The EU Challenge to the SEC*, 31 FORDHAM INT'L L.J. 1692 (2008) (discussing the mutual recognition principle in financial regulation, its origins in the European Union (EU) and the pressure by the EU and various other players on the U.S. to engage in mutual recognition efforts).

78 George Mundstock, *The Trouble with FASB* 28 N.C. J. INT'L L. & COM. REG. 813, 842 (2005) (noting that the forerunner to the IASB, the IASC, was created in 1973).

79 *Pursuant to Section 509(5) of the National Securities Markets Improvement Act of 1996: Report on Promoting Global Preeminence of American Securities Markets*, U.S. Sec. & Exch. Comm'n (Oct. 1997), www.sec.gov/news/studies/acctgsp.htm.

80 The restructuring "include[s] changes in the IASC's objectives and strategy, due process, standards implementation and enforcement, and funding mechanisms." Maureen Peyton King, Note, *The SEC's (Changing?) Stance on IAS*, 27 BROOK. J. INT'L L. 315, 332 (2001).

81 In this it benefited from the support of the International Federation of Accountants (IFAC), another network, though one entirely private, and not one with its own designs on accounting standardization – it was happy to delegate that process to IASB.

82 Karmel, *supra* note 77, 1701.

83 Christopher Cox, Chairman, U.S. Sec. & Exch. Comm'n, "International Business – An SEC Perspective" Address to the American Institute of Certified Public Accountants' International Issues Conference, Washington, D.C. (Jan. 10, 2008), *available at* www.sec.gov/news/speech/2008/spch011008cc.htm.
84 White, *supra* note 75 ("[T]he rest of the world is already heading in this direction and their endpoint is IFRS – not US GAAP.").
85 *About the IFRS Foundation and the IASB*, IFRS, www.ifrs.org/The-organisation/Pages/IFRS-Foundation-and-the-IASB.aspx.
86 The European Parliament wanted to condition funding upon the serious consideration of prudence-based accounting by the IASB. Huw Jones, *IASB Accounting Body Rejects EU Parliament's Funding Conditions*, Reuters (Oct. 14, 2013, 3:01 PM), www.reuters.com/article/2013/10/14/us-accounting-iasb-idUSBRE99D0KU20131014.
87 Donna L. Street, *GAAP Convergence 2002: A Survey of National Efforts to Promote and Achieve Convergence with International Financial Reporting Standards* 2, available at www.ifad.net/content/ie/ie_f_gaap_frameset.htm
88 Stuart H. Deming, *International Accounting Standards*, 40 INT'L LAW. 363, 366 (2006).
89 *Review of Financial Reporting by Issuers – Cycle* 5, FIN. MKTS. AUTH. N.Z., http://seccom2.test.netco.co.nz/publications/documents/cycle-5/11.shtml?print=true.
90 *Id.*
91 IOSCO, 2005 ANNUAL REPORT 6, *available at* www.iosco.org/annual_reports/annual_report_2005/.
92 IOSCO, 2006 ANNUAL REPORT 6, *available at* www.iosco.org/annual_reports/annual_report_2006/annual_report_2006.html.
93 72 Fed. Reg. 37962-01, 2007 WL 1985828.
94 Bradley Cox, Chairman, U.S. Sec. & Exch. Comm'n, Address to the American Institute of Certified Public Accountants' International Issues Conference (Jan. 10, 2008), *available at* www.sec.gov/news/speech/2008/spch011008cc.htm.
95 *CPSS: History, Organisation, Cooperation*, BANK FOR INT'L SETTLEMENTS, www.bis.org/cpss/cpssinfo01.htm.
96 Press Release, Bank for International Settlements, Implementation of PFMIs Monitored by CPSS and IOSCO (Apr. 17, 2013), *available at* www.bis.org/press/p130417.htm.
97 *Cover Note, Publication of a Consultative Document on Public Quantitative Disclosure Standards for Central Counterparties*, Bank for Int'l Settlements (October 15, 2013), www.bis.org/publ/cpss114covernote.pdf.
98 *Recovery of Financial Market Infrastructures – Consultative Report*, BANK FOR INT'L SETTLEMENTS (Oct. 2013), www.bis.org/publ/cpss109.htm.
99 COMMITTEE ON PAYMENT AND SETTLEMENT SYS. BOARD OF THE INT'L ORGANIZATION OF SEC. COMMISSIONS, CONSULTATIVE REPORT – RECOVERY OF

FINANCIAL MARKET INFRASTRUCTURES 1 (Aug. 2013), *available at* www.bis.org/publ/cpss109.pdf.

100 *CPSS: History, Organisation, Cooperation*, BANK FOR INT'L SETTLEMENTS, www.bis.org/cpss/cpssinfo01.htm.

101 For background on the Committee for Payment & Settlement Systems, see Bank for Int'l Settlements, www.bis.org/cpss/index.htm. For a scholarly discussion, see Carl Felsenfeld & Genci Bilai, *The Role of the Bank for International Settlements in Shaping the World Financial System*, 25 U. PA. J. INT'L ECON. L. 945, 989–90 (2004).

102 Bank for Int'l Settlements, 81st Annual Report 2010/11 101 (June 26, 2011), *available at* www.bis.org/publ/arpdf/ar2011e.htm.

103 *Committee on the Global Financial System*, BANK FOR INT'L SETTLEMENTS, www.bis.org/cgfs/.

104 *William C. Dudley*, FED. RESERVE BANK OF N.Y., www.newyorkfed.org/aboutthefed/orgchart/dudley.html.

105 *Fact sheet: Committee on the Global Financial System*, BANK FOR INT'L SETTLEMENTS, www.bis.org/about/factcgfs.htm.

106 *Compendium of Standards – Issuing Body – Committee on the Global Financial System (CGFS)*, FIN. STABILITY BOARD, www.financialstabilityboard.org/list/fsb_cos_issuing_body/tid_85/index.htm.

107 *Asset Encumbrance, Financial Reform and the Demand for Collateral Assets* (Committee on the Global Fin. Sys., CGFS Papers No. 49, May 2013), *available at* www.bis.org/publ/cgfs49.pdf.

108 *Id.* at 2–3.

7

International Financial Regulation and International Law

International financial regulation is a complex, evolving phenomenon, and one that, as we have seen, has changed significantly since the financial crisis. Nonetheless, it can usefully be compared with public international law as it is traditionally understood. This chapter evaluates the differences – and surprising similarities – between financial regulation, which does not count as "hard" law, and international law, which does count as hard law. As it turns out, both depend on domestic institutions to enforce their rules, both institutions are negotiated and iterative, rather than fixed and stable, and both are best at facilitating mutually beneficial cooperation, rather than resolving zero sum disputes.

Understanding how international financial regulation achieves its legitimacy through a series of domestic processes, rather than an international one gleaned from state practice and treaty commitments, provides a different perspective on public international law, which draws attention towards the way states actually feel and respond to real obligations and international commitments. The defining "lawness" of international law is supposed to come about through its recognition as such by states. The magical nature of this elevation to legal obligation has often mystified observers, and made communicants of old-time international law religion believers in a kind of legal transubstantiation: the interpretation of discretionary acts as evidence of legal obligation, and therefore of the existence of law itself.[1]

Particularly in the case of custom, where states comply with their legal obligations not because of some explicit treaty or contractual commitment but rather because of a more diffuse sense that through their actions they recognize the commitment to be legally binding – the moment at which inclination turns into legal obligation is very difficult to discern.

Consider the United States Supreme Court's view in *The Paquete Habana*,[2] in which the Court reversed a government policy of capturing enemy fishing vessels at war prizes. As the court famously observed: "Like all of the laws of nations, it rests upon the common consent of civilized communities ... it is recognition of the historical fact that by common consent of mankind these rules have been acquiesced in as of general obligation."[3] The language is famous but difficult to pin down. The search is for state-level "common consent," although it is not always easy to know how that consent, evidenced by the conduct of the amalgam of actors known as the state, would be expressed. Understanding that consent exists because of a sense – again, by the state itself – of "general obligation" is just as tricky to pin down.

As a result, it is not surprising that the evidence resorted to in *The Paquette Habana* to discern *opinio juris* – the belief that an action was taken because of legal obligation – by the United States appears quite selective. To discern evidence of custom, the Supreme Court examined, among other things, orders issued by English King Henry IV in the early fifteenth century during a war with France, a treaty made between the Holy Roman Empire and France in the sixteenth century, treaties between the USA and Prussia and Mexico, a British case concerning a Dutch fishing vessels, and Japanese state practice in relation to Chinese vessels.[4] All this is quite interpretive and, as with any kind of precedent-selection rubric, suspicions of selection bias and aggressive interpretation rear their heads.

For these reasons, customary international law, with its uncomfortably pliable methods of discerning state practice, has become the sort of international law most likely to be assaulted by critics of the enterprise.[5] Few international lawyers doubt that nations rely on custom in some cases. If the USA was unable to rely on customary international law as a mechanism to provide an approach to treaty interpretation consistent with the Vienna Convention on the Law of Treaties, then it would have had a difficult time concluding any treaties. Still, custom is international law at its most mysterious.

Even treaties, though more straightforward to limn, turn on difficult contract-like questions as to whether there has been a meeting of the minds between states – as if states had minds.[6] It is just as difficult to attribute a purpose to a state, though treaties are regularly interpreted to give effect to those purposes.[7] Indeed, Article 31 of the Vienna Convention of the Law of Treaties, the canonical statement of how international lawyers are supposed to approach the task of treaty interpretation, provides that "[a] treaty shall be interpreted in good faith in accordance with the ordinary meaning to be given to the terms of the treaty in their context and in the light of its object and purpose."[8]

And the less said about another important source of international law – *jus cogens*, or peremptory norm – the better.[9] These peremptory norms are essentially supercharged customary norms from which derogation is not permitted; they are also principles of international law accepted by the international community, and as such subject to all of the interpretive difficulties of custom, albeit with even fiercer debates as to which norms, precisely, have arisen to the exalted status of peremptory. The Restatement (Third) of Foreign Relations Law mentions prohibitions on genocide, slavery, and torture, but hardheaded lawyers might wonder how often at least two of those norms are honored in the breach.[10] The International Law

Committee admitted in 1963 "there is not as yet any generally accepted criterion by which to identify a general rule of international law as having the character of *jus cogens*."[11]

In each of these cases, much of the interpretive difficulty involves trying to think about what a state is thinking. States do not think; the people serving them think, negotiate treaties, take actions that they believe to be legally required, and so on. As Peter Malanczuk observed in his international law treatise, "[t]here is clearly something artificial about trying to analyze the psychology of collective entities such as states."[12] International law doctrine is based on recognition of the modern sovereign state as the only subject of international law. That system has, of course, changed with the advent of human rights and investor protections of individual claims, which make substate actors worthy of the attention of public international law. But still the state remains central in international legal efforts.[13]

Observers of international financial regulation do not spend their time wondering what France "believes" or what the United States "wants" from a capital adequacy arrangement. In international financial regulation, legitimation does not happen mysteriously on the international level, where the difference between what is legal and what is not is often discerned by descending into the subconscious of a state and the reasons for its compliance with or disregard of a particular principle of international relations. International financial regulation is never legal once agreed to in Basel, or by a resolution of the International Organization of Securities Commissioners. As Daniel Lefort, the general counsel of the Bank for International Settlements has observed, the international part of the regulatory process formulates broad supervisory standards and guidelines and recommends statements of best practices in the expectation that individual authorities will take steps to implement them through detailed arrangements – statutory or otherwise – which are best suited to their own national systems.[14] In other words, it obtains its legitimation through domestic institutions, through agencies that agree on an international standard and then go home and implement it.

If anything, international financial regulation has taken the domestic legalization component of what it does to an extreme. While international financial policymakers tend to deny that they make law, the domestic component applies the law vigorously. Regulatory networks rely upon peer review to ensure compliance with their mandates, which relies on domestic regulators surveilling one another.[15]

In this way, international financial regulation exemplifies a truly dualist international legal system. The dualism/monism distinction is one of the traditional battlegrounds of international law; the question is whether an international law is the governing domestic law of a country that has signed on to it, or whether international law only binds domestic actors like courts when duly enacted through domestic legislation or some other domestically cognizable legal act.[16] A dualist view "assumes that international law and municipal law are two separate legal systems, which exist independently of each other."[17] Monists understand international law and domestic law as components of a single legal institution, with international law occupying a position of supremacy over the local variant.[18] But in international financial regulation, thinking of the international component as supreme misses the point, even when international agreements provide the contents of domestic regulation. The international arena is where policy is formulated. But it is the domestic arena where it is implemented and made into binding legal instruments.

This process is anything but monist. Rather, the international and the local perform different functions in international financial regulation, and it is the local where legal obligations are maintained. The radically dualist nature of international financial regulation calls into question some of the monists' beliefs that international law supposedly trumps domestic law.

In the *Free Zones* case, thought to be a stalwart of the monist vision, the Permanent Court of International Justice held that "it is certain that France cannot rely on her own legislation to limit the scope of her international obligations."[19] International financial regulation works the opposite way. France depends on her own legislation to give any force whatsoever to the scope of her international financial regulatory obligations. Similarly the rule found in Article 27 of the Vienna Convention of the Law of Treaties providing that "a party may not invoke the provisions of its internal law as justifications for its failure to perform a treaty" is subject to a similar revision when the question is one of financial regulation.[20]

The dualist nature of international financial regulation is not American per se, but consistent with the American approach to international law. US courts have held that American treaty commitments are not actionable before the judiciary unless there has been a clear statement suggesting that the treaty is "self-executing."[21] In recent years, the Senate has frequently stipulated that the president could not consider a treaty ratified until Congress has passed implementing legislation.[22] America's branches of government, in other words, tend to treat all international agreements, and not just agreements among regulators, as something that only becomes effective when implemented at home via an authoritative domestic lawmaker.

But if international financial regulation is dualist and regulatory, it is not unique. Many regimes depend upon information exchange and bureaucratic reporting. The pattern applies even to matters of international law that some would argue have risen to the level of *jus cogens*,[23] or something quite close to it.

Consider human rights. The parties to the International Covenant on Economic, Social, and Cultural Rights (ICESCR), which includes rights to self-determination, to be treated "without discrimination of any kind as to race, colour, sex, language, religion, political or other opinion, national or social origin, property, birth or other status," and to a panoply of other social rights, has been signed and ratified by the vast majority of countries around the world.[24] The states that have ratified the ICESCR Convention, however, have committed only to monitoring through a body known as a committee on economic and cultural social rights established by a so-called

Economic and Social Council.[25] The monitoring mechanism does not provide for state-against-state, or individual-against-state complaints, and the council does not offer dispute-resolution services. Instead, the council provides opportunities for states to show they have taken steps domestically to implement commitments they have undertaken as part of the convention.[26]

Similarly, a state that ratifies the International Covenant on Civil and Political Rights, which includes rights against discrimination, freedom from torture and slavery, and the liberty and security of the person, is monitored by the United Nation's Human Rights Committee. As the committee has stated, "When there are inconsistencies between domestic law and the Covenant, Article 2 requires that the domestic law practiced be changed to meet the standards imposed by the covenant substantive guarantees."[27] But the committee is comprised of nothing more than "independent experts," and their chief task is dialogue.[28] The committee monitors implementation by receiving reports and, in light of the reports and the research of its members, measures the steps the states have taken to implement the terms of the treaty.[29] The committee then sends written comments to each state regarding their implementation of the ICCPR.

Many mechanisms for the protection of fundamental human rights value domestic implementation, and make it the process to do the actual work of realizing international commitments – a process students of international financial regulation will find familiar – while leaving international oversight to a flexible peer review and monitoring regime. This is not to suggest that international law in its classical variant is the same as international financial regulation, but rather that in both domestic institutions make international commitments real inside each country.

The reliance on domestic institutions reflects the relatively disaggregated way that the state is understood in all kinds of international law, be it soft, hard, or precatory. Rather than one billiard ball of state-level interests, states contain multitudes, and looking inside is what international law scholars interested in international financial regulation do. They are not the first to do so. The American diplomat and international jurist Phillip Jessup defined "transnational law" in 1956 as "all law which regulates actions or events that transcend national frontiers," including "[b]oth public and private international law ... [plus] other rules which do not wholly fit into such standard categories."[30]

Applying the legal process approaches developed in domestic law in the 1950s produced articles and casebooks to international law that went beyond the state, inquiring into the interests within each state best served by international legal obligations. By the 1970s, the role of multinational corporations in the international system animated much legal scholarship. Henry Steiner and Detlev Vagts' *Transnational Legal Problems* groundbreaking international business transactions casebook also looked within the state to efforts by investors and firms to do business across borders.[31] Scholarship like Slaughter's on transnational networks has increased the attention by scholars to look within the state.

These scholars have disaggregated the state in an effort to better understand how the legal system worked. To understand America's approach to international governance, a consideration of what was going on within the country's borders, rather than assuming a monolithic and consistent sense of interests, was more revealing. One of the things it showed is that these interests sometimes use the legal system to facilitate agreement, rather than to resolve disputes. International law sometimes enabled coordination, as well as contests.

In fact, one of the points of any legal system is to permit parties to coordinate their interests – contracts, for example, are premised on such a confluence of interest – but it is often viewed derisively by some international law critics.[32] Why call it law if the parties to the project would have done it anyway? The experience of international financial regulation reminds us of the way that coordination games create winners and losers, just like tort cases and mergers and acquisitions. In this sense, it is just as interesting as the kind of law that proscribes conduct such as fraud, monopolization, or the unwarranted use of force, even if there are some who criticize both regulation and international law for being principally concerned with obligations that increase the size of pies, rather than merely dividing them.

International law often comes in for a great deal of criticism based on its coordinative role. Eric Posner and Jack Goldsmith particularly have raised some questions about its customary variant.[33] They argue that "international law does not pull states toward compliance contrary to their interests. International law emerges from states pursuing their interests to achieve mutually beneficial outcomes, and it is sustained [only] to the degree to which it continues to serve those interests."[34] Posner and Vermeule have also questioned its importance when international problems grow very severe, as they do in times of war or crisis.[35]

In this view, international law is really not much of anything; it merely celebrates the sort of mutually beneficial cooperation that rational actors would embrace regardless of its legality, and, presumably, if there was no such thing as international law.

The Goldsmith and Posner view builds on a rich tradition of skepticism in political science about international law. A primary school in international relations, the rational choice realists, have always suspected that international law is little more than a meaningless exercise in labeling by hopeful academics and other hangers-on, a position articulated by Hans Morganthau in the post-World War II period,[36] and many others since.[37] Realism, along with its legal sympathizers, treats states as self-interested unitary actors of varying strengths locked in an anarchic struggle to survive, and unconstrained by legal principle when it conflicts with self-interest.[38]

But from the perspective of international financial regulation, the anarchic struggle is not so obvious – not after four decades of effort to create international institutions capable of regulating world finance. In light of this experience, students of international finance find the act of branding coordination enterprises as somehow unrelated to the project of international law – or international relations – bizarre.[39] International financial regulation, after all, is regulation, interpreted by lawyers, and devised by bureaucrats, in an increasingly legalized process. It looks a lot like law.

At the same time, it emphasizes coordination. The rules must be agreed upon, rather than imposed. International financial regulation operates through consensus, and its coercion mechanisms are modest and horizontal.

But coordination has long made for law that anyone would recognize as "real." And coordination has to occur at *some* equilibrium, which may favor one interested party over others. The process of international financial regulation is replete with winners and losers, and with compliance as well. It would be donning blinders to observe the world if you ignored all cases where legal or regulatory instruments were deployed in the service of coordination and cooperation.

Regardless of legal implications, looking at international law through a regulatory lens prompts the observer to consider just how much international law, often thought of as a mechanism for states to contract with one another, is comprised of coordination.

International law has been quite a successful mechanism for resolving some cross-border externalities created by globalization, with its problems of environmental degradation, economic contamination, and trade and investment frictions and inequalities. Here international law, and indeed often international soft law, which takes on many international legal characteristics, coordinates outcomes among states that simply must be resolved through a variety of institutional arrangements. In environmental law and international trade, this has often involved treaties. Meanwhile international financial regulation has taken recourse in building networks and soft legal institutions.

While very few of these regimes have the power to impose losses on participants, coordination does create losers and winners, as international financial regulation exemplifies.

Can a legal system claim to be a system if its rules cannot be reduced to writing? International lawyers have traditionally worried that the answer is no. The search for rules reducible to writing is a feature of classic international legal scholarship.[40] Particularly puissant scholars have been garlanded with appointment to the International Law Commission, and charged with writing international law, at least in draft form, for states to consider adopting.[41]

The traditional vision of the role of the scholar posits that international law is reducible to rules. If one thinks it through carefully enough, this vision may stem from the work of the natural law aficionados that founded the discipline. In the seventeenth century, Hugo Grotius argued that the fundamental tenets of international law could be derived from principles of justice that had a validity transcending time and context and were discoverable through reason.[42] Grotius argued that natural law, and the international law that depended upon it, "would have a degree of validity even if we should concede that which cannot be conceded without the utmost wickedness, that there is no God, or that the affairs of men are of no concern to Him."[43]

The search for the rules of international law has accordingly been an abiding passion for legal theorists. But it also threatens to set overly precise standards for a discipline that, on account of its horizontal structure, is likely to arrive at those sorts of standards very slowly, and only after much disagreement, tentative agreement, and revisitation of the issue. As Peter Malanczuk has observed: "The horizontal system of [international] law operates in a different manner from a centralized one and is based on principles of reciprocity and consensus rather than on command, obedience, and enforcement."[44]

This is not a surprise to observers of international financial regulation. The horizontal nature of international financial regulation means that it resembles an argument more than it does a list of rules, and reflection on the way it works suggests that the desire to fix international law principles on ratified paper should be tempered. After all, neither international financial regulation nor public international law offers a monopoly on violence (which makes them different from a conventionally Weberian definition of a legal system).[45] And like international financial regulation, international law features ambitious claims about what the law requires, and plenty of pushback against those ambitious claims by skeptics of legal evolution.

International financial regulators frequently appear to agree on very little. They meet and argue about rules that they would like to impose across the world's financial markets. The debates can be heated. When there is resolution on issues – when, say, a capital adequacy rule meets with consensus by the world's banking regulators – the issue must be revisited when the facts require, as they often do. For example, the capital adequacy accord promulgated by the Basel Committee, the signature achievement of international financial regulation, has gone through three complete revampings, and intermediate clarifications and reconceptualizations almost too numerous to mention have been made. Students of international financial regulation do not think that the accord is unimportant, even though it is constantly revisited. Indeed, international financial regulation is structured to make that sort of revisitation constant.

In international financial supervision, we have seen at the beginning limited work – efforts by regulators to stay in touch with one another, and to divide responsibilities over multijurisdictional financial enterprises. That was then paired with efforts to cooperate across borders, but only to assist financial regulators in carrying out their domestic responsibilities.[46] Later yet came deeper and more far-reaching efforts to do things in the same way and with the same approach. The evolving cooperation was first accomplished through developing core principles of financial institutional supervision. (These "Principles" are quite short, broadly defined guidelines that all regulators are meant to apply to their own organizations, and to regulated industries within their purview; they come in numbers of twenty-one, twenty-eight, or occasionally as many as forty; and they are one of the first acts of every new financial regulatory network.) In some cases, supervision has become even more elaborately cooperative, and has resulted in the creation of complex rule systems that leave little room for domestic discretion.

Of course, progress in international financial regulation, like its domestic counterpart and like many other international problems, is periodic and sporadic, if unprompted by crisis. Throughout this period, finance has constantly innovated, creating brand new markets – derivatives trading only became a big business in the last twenty years – and getting, if anything, ever-more global.[47] Regulators have struggled to keep pace, which has required them to constantly move targets and goalposts of their missions.

Other international lawyers might benefit from thinking about their own bailiwicks through a paradigm of revisitation, rather than one that looks for a treatise-like fixity of rules. International law fosters a debate about bedrock commitments more often than it might appear. It is useful to think of public international law, like international financial regulation, as one that resolves questions over obligation through contestation rather than through mandate. Doing so insulates public international law from a persistent criticism that it is often breached, without consequence to the breacher. This critique is surely true, even if states observe most of their treaty obligations most of the time.[48] In any particular time and, indeed, in particularly important times, powerful states may break their legal obligations in the interests of national security or other national interests. Well-known US examples of this phenomenon include airstrikes in Libya in 2011, one pursuant to an aggressive interpretation of a UN Security Council resolution seeking an immediate ceasefire in an ongoing Civil War, and the response to the International Court of Justice's decision in the *Nicaragua Harbors* case.[49]

While some argue that occasional noncompliance by the powerful means that international law is not relevant to interactions of states, others recognize that all those lawyers deployed and all that time spent on legal instruments must amount to something. Thinking of international law in this way – as a way of debating value without expecting uniform compliance with these values – explains some of the potential of international law a bit more persuasively, and illuminates some of the tensions behind something that occasionally looks like a pitfall of international legal scholarship, where thoughtful academics are announcing the discovery of new favored rights, for example, rights to be free of war,[50] to be free of want,[51] or to access to healthcare.[52] Better to think of this work as an effort to start a debate, rather than to derive a proof.

The point is not meant to be overly constructivist. Constructivists argue that legal meaning is created through communities of like-minded thought, rather than from any logical necessity; it is a sociological, arguably a "soft" form of obligation that turns more on thought processes than on external requirements. But this study is not a constructivist enterprise; it recognizes that legal obligation is not always relative, and not always supported by anything more than a bit of we-feeling among elites when it crosses borders. But recognizing the negotiated nature of a governance regime is not meant to deny that there is legal obligation present in the international system.

One useful way of looking at what various parts of international law are supposed to do is to think about the fundamental question those components are meant to answer. For international financial regulation, the institution builders and rule makers are asking, "what does a safe and sound global financial system require?" Answering that question has been a negotiated process. It is not one that reaches a terminal result but one that evolves over time, which is why the international financial system is replete with the re-evaluation of standards.

The Financial Stability Board, for example, uses peer review to check on the commitment of its members and counterparties to the coordinated outcomes meant to be created through financial regulatory cooperation.[53] Peer review exemplifies the negotiated nature of international financial regulation because, like all other sorts of peer review, it inquires into, rather than demands allegiance to, the values of the system.[54] In this way, there has never been a time when the question, "what does a safe and sound global financial system require?", has been clearly and unanimously answered. And of course, throughout all of these evolutions in style and degree of international governance, regulators have pursued their own interests and the interests of the industries they oversee. Indeed, many political scientists, such as David Singer and Abraham Newman, have identified this sort of state influence as being a critical component that explains the content of the rules of international financial regulation.[55]

In sum, instead of permanent rules representing ideals of sound international governance, financial regulation is a messy debate. In fact, it is really not very different than other kinds of more formal international laws.

One could look at international criminal law, perhaps the most active area of public international law over the last twenty years, and analyze it quite similarly. It too, has an animating question: What activities by states and individuals should be regarded as international crimes? The answer is a subject of debate, even after the Rome Statute criminalized terms like "atrocities," and "aggression," and attempted to define them.[56] But even after that treaty's conclusion, there has been a great deal of negotiation about what should be beyond the pale and what should be regretfully tolerated, as allowable state and leader conduct.

Consider the crime of aggression. First mentioned in the London Charter governing the Nuremburg trials, aggression was included on a laundry list of "crimes against peace," and ever since it has been difficult to discern where the outer bounds of such a crime lie.[57] The UN General Assembly adopted a resolution in 1974 that included both a general definition of aggression and a list of examples.[58] The general definition provided that: "Aggression is the use of armed force by a State against the sovereignty, territorial integrity, or political independence of another State, or in any other manner inconsistent with the Charter of the United Nations."[59] The specifics include blockades, airstrikes, and more capacious and arguable provisions such as "allowing territory ... to be used by [another] State for perpetrating an act of aggression against a third," or "substantial involvement" in the "sending" of "armed bands."[60] The resolution has unsurprisingly been criticized ever since as "both too narrow and too broad."[61]

International criminal lawyers hoped that the definition of international crime would be settled by an international process and that a tribunal would then be created to interpret and enforce it. But, while the Rome Statute listed the crime of aggression as a cause of action over which the ICC would have jurisdiction, it was not until 2010 that the meaning of the term "aggression" was finally defined.[62] Then, at a Rome Statute review conference held in Uganda, the parties to the statute settled, after a fashion, on a definition after years of debate and negotiation.[63] Article 8 defines the crime of aggression as, among other things, "the planning, preparation, and initiation or execution, by a person in a position effectively to exercise control over or to direct a political or military activity of a state, of an act of aggression which, by its character, gravity, and scale, constitutes a manifest violation of the charter of the United Nations."[64] The article also includes activities that qualify, ranging from invasion to infiltration.

International criminal law is both at the heart and at the cutting edge of public international law. Still, the parallels between its form of governance and that of international financial regulation are striking even as the provenance of their legality differentiates them. Aggression remains one of the least defined and most debated aspects of international criminal law, and while this chapter is not the place to sort out what, precisely, aggression is or should be, its indeterminateness is one of its features, and is one of the reasons why the development of international criminal law provokes support (because of the belief that it can evolve), and opposition (for the same reason). And if that is the case, it underscores parallels between the negotiated and debated nature of informal international regulation like international financial regulation and the much more formal public international law represented by the Rome Statute and its court.

Just as with financial regulation, state interests go into this process of negotiation, and despite the creation of dispute-resolution processes and tribunals, much of international criminal law turns on its own stylized process of peer review, whereby multiple states act in judgment of the delicts committed by peer states in the dock. The similarities go on from there. Just as international financial regulation is developed through financial crises, the mechanisms of criminal law have been prompted by atrocities. For instance, the International Criminal Tribunal for the former Yugoslavia (ICTY) handled a different set of war crimes cases than did the

International Criminal Tribunal for Rwanda (ICTR), with the ICTY focusing more on leaders, and the ICTR on mid-level participants in the hostilities.[65]

Nor need the nature of the debates in international financial regulation or in international criminal law resemble unrealistically pious searches for truth. Again, in both cases, state interests play important roles in determining content and participation. The USA has stayed out of the ICC because it worries about consequences for its soldiers posted abroad.[66] American regulators along with their British counterparts first pursued a capital-adequacy agreement in international financial regulation because the US and UK banking industries were worried that they would be unable to compete with large Japanese banks. No one is suggesting that simply because international financial regulation and international law work through contestation and disagreement, that self-interest is abandoned. Indeed, self-interest explains why the dialogue is constant and the disagreements often sharp.

Moreover, the contestation is underscored by the consensus orientation of both international financial regulation and international law. The constant undercurrent of debate and revisitation is encouraged by the need to convince everyone, and is a feature of both international financial regulation and international law. For international financial regulation, there is a need to motivate domestic agencies to seek harmonization. International law's preference for consensus is presumably rooted in its (not always explicable) commitment to the idea of sovereign equality of nations, the belief that Vanuatu and China are functionally similar in the eyes of the law. In both cases, consensus is driven by the horizontal nature of global governance.

Rather than being set in stone, international financial regulation involves a debate about values and interests in the service of discovering an answer to a question about safe and sound finance. But an argument over the answer is not so different from the way more formal variants of international law often work. The insight is not meant to be a fundamental rethinking of what international law is all about. Instead, it aims merely to remind scholars that despite the predilection for doctrinal analysis, and particularly the doctrinal analysis of insecure international lawyers, precision and reduction to writing have often been favored. But in reality international governance happens through imprecision and a constant revisiting of the writing. International lawyers would do well to remember this and international financial regulation has taken it to an art form.

Because of the importance of coordination, contestation, and domestic institutions, international law looks very much like international financial regulation. The comparison underscores the horizontal nature of international legal obligation, and emphasizes the way that soft law, in the international system, has more similarities to hard law than one might expect, given that the concepts were initially conceived as opposites.[67] These insights are the kind still ignored by leading textbooks of international law. But they have not always been. The New Haven School argued that international law was more than doctrine, and could be better understood as a process of authoritative decision-making. Myres McDougal and Harold

Lasswell, the founders of the school, wrote that "our chief interest is in the legal process, by which we mean the making of authoritative and controlling decisions."[68] Their disciples agreed. "[I]nternational law is most realistically observed, not as a mere rigid set of rules but as the whole process of authoritative decisions in which patterns of authority and patterns of control are appropriately conjoined," argued Eisuke Suzuki.[69] No less an authority than World Court judge Rosalyn Higgins agreed that "international law is a process, a system of authoritative decision-making . . . a process for resolving problems."[70]

It is an attractive approach to international law. Rather than seeking doctrine where doctrine is necessarily contested (and always has been when it comes to international law), the New Haven school sensibly inquired as to what would act as the legally required, decision-making organs. Paying attention to the process of how policy preferences are transformed into legal obligations makes it clearer the surprising similarities between international financial regulation and international law. By the same token, the process of transforming international policy to domestic regulation illustrates the critical role substate actors play in making international law, in either its hard or soft variants. The process of coordination around a mutually beneficial standard also represents a turn to process rather than to content. The continual debate and revision of principles, too, is a function of process, rather than to any particular piece of substantive regulation.

The New Haven School has largely been forgotten because of its inability to pick from far too many methods of investigating the international system. Its explicitly utopian streak also did it little good. But process need not be interrogated with a value system favoring world peace at its forefront. It must not be forgotten that in international law, legal procedures are fuzzy, varied, and often quite ad hoc. But similarities in process animate each of the three lessons international financial regulation offers for the kind of public international law considered in this chapter. Those similarities are real, enlightening, and, far too often, ignored. It is time to consider them anew, and, at the same time, to engage in new research efforts into the new international legal process, both hard and soft.

Notes

1 *Cf.* Thomas M. Franck, *Legitimacy in the International System*, 82 AM. J. INT'L L. 705, 740 (1988) ("The excommunicate priest who elevates the host before the altar in a fraudulent Eucharist is left holding only bread and wine because his invalid orders cannot effect the miracle of transubstantiation.").

2 175 U.S. 677 (1900).

3 *Id.* at 711.

4 *Id.*

5 *See* Jack L. Goldsmith & Eric A. Posner, *Further Thoughts on Customary International Law*, 23 MICH. J. INT'L L. 191, 200 (2001); Jack L. Goldsmith & Eric A. Posner, *Understanding the Resemblance Between Modern and Traditional Customary International Law*, 40 VA. J. INT'L L. 639 (2000); Jack L. Goldsmith & Eric A. Posner, *A Theory of Customary International Law*, 66 U. CHI. L. REV. 1113 (1999).

6 *See* Curtis J. Mahoney, *Treaties as Contracts: Textualism, Contract Theory, and the Interpretation of Treaties*, 116 YALE L.J. 824, 857 (2007).

7 For a critique of the effort to try to discern the object and purpose of the treaty by looking to state practice, see George Letsas, *Strasbourg's Interpretive Ethic: Lessons for the International Lawyer*, 21 EUR. J. INT'L L. 509, 512 (2010).

8 Vienna Convention on the Law of Treaties art. 31–1, May 23, 1969 1155 U.N.T.S. 331 (entered into force Jan. 27, 1980).

9 Jus cogens is the Latin term for non-derogable principles of international law.

10 *See* RESTATEMENT (THIRD) OF FOREIGN RELATIONS LAW § 702, cmt n.

11 Second Report on the Law of Treaties, [1963] 2 Y.B. Int'l L. Comm'n 16, U.N. Doc. A/CN.4/107. For a discussion, and an effort to move towards more specificity in jus cogens, see Evan J. Criddle & Evan Fox-Decent, *A Fiduciary Theory of Jus Cogens*, 34 YALE J. INT'L L. 331, 337 (2009).

12 PETER MALANCZUK, AKEHURST'S MODERN INTRODUCTION TO INTERNATIONAL LAW 44 (7th ed. 1997).

13 *Id.*

14 *See* Lefort, *supra* note 14, at ¶ 172.

15 For a discussion of peer review, see J.B. Ruhl & James Salzman, *In Defense of Regulatory Peer Review*, 84 WASH. U. L. REV. 1, 18 n.82.

16 *See* Louis Henkin, *The Constitution and United States Sovereignty: A Century of Chinese Exclusion and Its Progeny*, 100 HARV. L. REV. 853, 864–66 (1987); Harold Hongju Koh, *Transnational Public Law Litigation*, 100 YALE L.J. 2347 (1991); J. G. Starke, *Monism and Dualism in the Theory of International Law*, 17 BRIT. Y. B. INT'L L. 66 (1936).

17 MALANCZUK, *supra* note 12, 63.

18 For a discussion of dualists and monists, see Melissa A. Waters, *Creeping Monism: The Judicial Trend Toward Interpretive Incorporation of Human Rights Treaties*, 107 COLUM. L. REV. 628, 631 (2007).

19 Free zones of Upper Savoy and District of Gex (Fr. V. Switz.), 1932 P.C.I.J. (Series A/B) No. 46, at 167 (June 7).

20 Vienna Convention on the Law of Treaties art. 27, Jan. 27, 1980, 1155 U.N.T.S. 331. Per discussion, see MALANCZUK *supra* note 12, at 64.

21 *See* Medellin v. Texas, 552 U.S. 491, 491 (2008).

22 VALERIE EPPS & LORIE GRAHAM, EXAMPLES AND EXPLANATIONS: INTERNATIONAL LAW § 11.2.4 (2011), at § 3.13.1.

23 Vienna Convention on the Law of Treaties, May 23, 1969, U.N.Doc. A/CONF.39/27, *reprinted in* 8 I.L.M. 698–99 (1969) (art. 53 defines "peremptory norm of general international law (jus cogens)" as "a norm accepted and recognized by the international community of States as a whole as a norm from which no derogation is permitted and which can be modified only by a subsequent norm of general international law having the same character"); *see also* Nadine Strossen, *Recent U.S. and International Judicial Protection of Individual Rights: A Comparative Legal Process Analysis and Proposed Synthesis*, 41 HASTINGS L.J. 805, 822 (1990) ("there is much scholarly support for the view that most international human rights norms constitute at least binding rules of customary law if not, indeed, noderogable rules or jus cogens."). Though beyond that, it is hard to know what, exactly, just cogens include. As Jules Lobel observed, "[s]ome dispute exists over what norms are fundamental. The International Law Commission, in adopting the notion of jus cogens in the Vienna Convention on the Law of Treaties, did not elaborate on its content, in part because even the drafting commission could not agree on what norms constituted jus cogens." Jules Lobel, *The Limits of Constitutional Power: Conflicts Between Foreign Policy and International Law*, 71 VA. L. REV. 1071, 1148 (1985).

24 International Covenant on Economic, Social, and Cultural Rights art. 2, G.A. Res. 2200A, U.N. Doc. A/RES/2200A (Dec. 16, 1966). The United States has only signed, but not yet ratified, the convention.

25 Shortcomings of the council and challenges to its effectiveness have been apparent since its creation. For a general discussion of the obstacles confronted by the council, see Phillip Alston, *Out of the Abyss: The Challenges Confronting the New U.N. Committee on Economic, Social and Cultural Rights*, 9 HUM. RTS. Q. 332 (1987). As Barbara Stark has observed, "[a]s part of ICESCR compliance, ratifying nations prepare self-monitoring reports that document their efforts, successes, and failures to 'progressively achieve' the goals set out in ICESCR. These 'country reports' are reviewed by the Committee on Economic, Social and Cultural Rights (the 'Committee')." Barbara Stark, *Economic Rights in the United States and International Human Rights Law: Toward an "Entirely New Strategy,"* 44 HASTINGS L.J. 79, 89 (1992).

26 For a description of the council's current enforcement mechanism and suggestions for improvement, see Audrey R. Chapman, A *"Violations Approach" for Monitoring the International Covenant on Economic, Social and Cultural Rights*, 18 HUM. RTS. Q. 23 (1996); Michael J. Dennis & David P. Stewart, *Justiciability of Economic, Social, and Cultural Rights: Should There Be an International Complaints Mechanism to Adjudicate the Rights to Food, Water, Housing, and Health?*, 98 AM. J. INT'L L. 462 (2004).

27 Human Rights Committee, General Comment No. 31, ¶13, U.N. Doc., CCPR/C/21/Rev. 1/Add 13 (May 26, 2004).

28 The membership of the committee is listed on the committee's website. *Human Rights Committee – Membership*, Office of the U.N. High Comm'r for Human Rights, www.ohchr.org/EN/HRBodies/CCPR/Pages/Membership.aspx. Its current American member, for example, is an international law professor at Harvard Law School. *See* Gerald L. Neuman (United States of America), Office of the U.N. High Comm'r for Human Rights, www2.ohchr.org/english/bodies/hrc/membersCVs/neuman.htm (presenting the credentials of Professor Neuman).

29 As the HRC puts it on its website, "All States parties are obliged to submit regular reports to the Committee on how the rights are being implemented. States must report initially one year after acceding to the Covenant and then whenever the Committee requests (usually every four years). The Committee examines each report and addresses its concerns and recommendations to the State party in the form of 'concluding observations'." *UN Human Rights Committee, Monitoring Civil and Political Rights*, Office of the U.N. High Comm'r for Human Rights, www2.ohchr.org/english/bodies/hrc/.

30 Philip C. Jessup, Transnational Law 2 (1956).

31 Henry J. Steiner & Detlev Vagts, Transnational Legal Problems (2nd ed. 1976).

32 *See* Andrew T. Guzman, *The Design of International Agreements*, 16 Eur. J. Int'l L. 579, 585 (2005)).

33 Goldsmith & Posner, *A Theory of Customary International Law, supra* note 5.

34 Jack Goldsmith & Eric A. Posner, *The New International Law Scholarship*, 34 Ga. J. Int'l & Comp. L. 463, 467 (2006). This view about international law come from a social scientific view of state interest focused on the rational actor. As Goldsmith and Posner have argued, "international law emerges from and is sustained by nations acting rationally to maximize their interests (i.e., their preferences over international relations outcomes), given their perception of the interests of other states, and the distribution of state power." Rather than hewing to international legal obligations because they are law, "self-interest and the logic of the strategic situation do a much better job of explaining the behaviors associated with international law." Jack L. Goldsmith & Eric A. Posner, *International Agreements: A Rational Choice Approach*, 44 Va. J. Int'l L. 113, 134 (2003).

35 Eric A. Posner & Adrian Vermeule, the Executive Unbound: after the Madisonian Republic (2011).

36 *See, e.g.*, Hans J. Morganthau, Politics Among Nations: The Struggle for Power and Peace 3–15 (1960). Morgenthau's work built on earlier skepticism by E. H. Carr. Edward Hallett Carr, The 20-Year Crisis, 1919 through 1939: An Introduction To the Study of International Relations (1940).

37 *See* Kenneth N. Waltz, Theory of International Politics 88 (1979) (stating that "[i]nternational systems are decentralized and anarchic"); *see also* Adamson Hoebel, The Law of Primitive Man (1967).

38 Many realists argue that international institutions have no effect on the important aspects of international life – namely, the competition between states. *See* John J. Mearsheimer, The *False Promise of International Institutions*, 19 INT'L SECURITY 5, 7 (1994); John J. Mearsheimer, *A Realist Reply*, 20 INT'L SECURITY, 75, 82 (1995).

39 And not just from an international financial regulatory perspective, it is perhaps worth noting. *See* Robert B. Ahdieh, *Foreign Affairs, International Law, and the New Federalism: Lessons from Coordination*, 73 MO. L. REV. 1185, 1204 (2008); Mariano-Florentino Cuellar, *Reflections on Sovereignty and Collective Security*, 40 STAN. J. INT'L L. 211, 242 (2004); Andrew T. Guzman, A *Compliance-Based Theory of International Law*, 90 CAL. L. REV. 1823, 1857 (2002).

40 *See* Jill McC. Watson, *Briefer Notice*, 95 AM. J. INT'L L. 747 (2001) (reviewing ARTHUR WATTS, THE INTERNATIONAL LAW COMMISSION: 1949–1998 (1999); George K. Walker, *Sources of International Law and the Restatement (Third), Foreign Relations Law of the United States*, 37 NAVAL L. REV. 1, 3 (1988).

41 Michael Owen, *The ILC Articles on State Responsibility: The Paradoxical Relationship Between Form and Authority*, 96 AM. J. INT'L L. 857, 859 (2002).

42 HUGO GROTIUS, DE JURE BELLI AC PACIS LIBRI TRES: PROLEGOMENA, in 2 THE CLASSICS OF INTERNATIONAL LAW ¶11 (Francis W. Kelsey trans., James Brown Scott ed., 1925). For a discussion, see William P. George, *Grotius, Theology, and International Law: Overcoming Textbook Bias*, 14 J.L. & RELIGION 605, 606–07 (2000).

43 GROTIUS, *supra* note 42, at ¶11.

44 MALANCZUK, *supra* note 12.

45 The concept comes from Max Weber, under which the government "upholds the claim to the monopoly of the legitimate use of physical force in the enforcement of its order." 1 MAX WEBER, ECONOMY AND SOCIETY 54 (Guenther Roth & Claus Wittich eds., 1978) (1956). For a discussion, see Benedict Sheehy & Jackson N. Maogoto, *The Private Military Company-Unraveling the Theoretical, Legal & Regulatory Mosaic*, 15 ILSA J. INT'L & COMP. L. 147, 164 (2008) ("It is the State's monopoly of violence that underpins the international legal system and justifies the emphasis on State sovereignty").

46 An example would be IOSCO's Multilateral Memorandum of Understanding. IOSCO discussed in Chapter 4. INT'L ORG. OF SECS. COMM'NS, MULTILATERAL MEMORANDUM OF UNDERSTANDING CONCERNING CONSULTATION AND COOPERATION AND THE EXCHANGE OF INFORMATION 8 (May 2002, rev'd May 2012) [hereinafter IOSCO, MMOU], *available at* www.iosco.org/library/pubdocs/pdf/IOSCOPD386.pdf.

47 As former CFTC chair Brooksley Born observed, "[d]uring the past decade, the world derivatives markets have grown exponentially in size and importance." Brooksley Born, *International Regulatory Responses to Derivatives Crises: The Role of the U.S. Commodity Futures Trading Commission*, 21 NW. J. INT'L L. & BUS. 607, 608 (2001).

48 As Louis Henkin has memorably observed, "[m]ost nations observe most international law most of the time." LOUIS HENKIN, HOW NATIONS BEHAVE 47 (2nd ed. 1979).

49 *See* Katrina J. Church, *The Briar Patch of Reality: A Legal Analysis of the Mining of Nicaragua's Harbors*, 18 N.Y.U. J. INT'L L. & POL. 169 (1985–1986)).

50 *See, e.g.*, David A. Soley, *Hunt v. Galtieri: A Hypothetical Scenario for Holding International Aggressors Civilly Liable in American Courts*, 33 EMORY L.J. 211, 224 (1984).

51 *See* Aravind R. Ganesh, *The Right to Food and Buyer Power*, 11 GERMAN L.J. 1190 (2010).

52 *See* Puneet K. Sandhu, *A Legal Right to Health Care: What Can the United States Learn from Foreign Models of Health Rights Jurisprudence?*, 95 CAL. L. REV. 1151, 1159 (2007).

53 The Board is, in conjunction with the IMF, dedicating a substantial portion of its resources to "peer review," designed to see that its member countries are making progress towards implementing the programs it has pursued internationally. These peer reviews feature self-reporting by the regulators to other members of the FSB, and are paired with, and modeled off of, the IMF's own Financial Sector Assessment Program. Jeffery Atik, *Basel II: A Post-Crisis Post-Mortem*, 19 TRANSNAT'L L. & CONTEMP. PROBS. 731, 758 (2011)(describing the IMF program). The IMF describes the purpose of the program as "a comprehensive and in-depth analysis of a country's financial sector … [i]n jurisdictions with financial sectors deemed by the Fund to be systemically important, financial stability assessments … and are supposed to take place every five years." *Supporting Documents Country FSAPs*, INT'L MONETARY FUND (Nov. 14, 2013), www.imf.org/external/NP/fsap/fsap.aspx.

54 For a discussion of peer review, see J. B. Ruhl & James Salzman, *In Defense of Regulatory Peer Review*, 38 ENVTL. L. REP. NEWS & ANALYSIS 10,553, 10,554 (2008). For criticism of the peer review process, at least as applied to the world of international trade law, see J. H. JACKSON ET AL., LEGAL PROBLEMS OF INTERNATIONAL ECONOMIC RELATIONS (3d ed. 2009).

55 *See* DAVID ANDREW SINGER, REGULATING CAPITAL: SETTING STANDARDS FOR THE INTERNATIONAL FINANCIAL SYSTEM (2007); David Bach & Abraham Newman, *Transgovernmental Cooperation and Domestic Policy Convergence: Power, Information, and the Global Quest Against Insider Trading* 36 (Am. Political Sci. Ass'n Annual Mtg., 2009) *available at* http://ssrn.com/abstract=1450395.

56 For one account of the effort to define the term "atrocity," see William A. Schabas, *Retroactive Application of the Genocide Convention*, 4 U. ST. THOMAS J.L. & PUB. POL'Y 36, 41 (2010).

57 Charter of the International Military Tribunal – Annex to the Agreement for the Prosecution and Punishment of the Major War Criminals of the European Axis ("London Agreement"), art. 6(a), Aug. 8, 1945, *available at* www.unhcr.org/ref

world/docid/3ae6b39614.html. The charter governing the Tokyo trials of Japanese leaders contained a very similar laundry list.

58 G.A. Res. 3314 (XXIX), U.N. GAOR, 29th Sess., Supp. No. 19, U.N. Doc. A/Res/3314 (XXIX) (Dec. 14, 1974).

59 *Id.* art. 1.

60 *Id.* art. 3.

61 Epps & Graham, *supra* note 22, § 11.2.4 (2011).

62 David Scheffer, *Atrocity Crimes Framing the Responsibility to Protect*, 40 Case W. Res. J. Int'l L. 111, 113 (2008).

63 For a discussion, see Claus Kress, *The Kampala Compromise on the Crime of Aggression*, 8 J. Int'l Crim. Just. 1179, 1183 (2010).

64 Int'l Criminal Court, Assembly of States Parties, Resumed Seventh Session Feb. 9–13, 2009, Annex I, Report of the Special Working Group on the Crime of Aggression, at 11, art. 8 *bis*, ¶ 1, ICC-ASP/7/SWGCA/2 (Feb. 20, 2009).

65 Morten Bergsmo, Catherine Cissé, & Christopher Staker, *The Prosecutors of the International Tribunals: The Cases of the Nuremberg and Tokyo Tribunals, the ICTY and ICTR, and the ICC Compared*, *in* The Prosecutor of a Permanent International Criminal Court 121 (1999).

66 Or so, at least, has been the conclusion of Congress, which passed the Servicemember's Protection Act for this reason. *See* Lilian V. Faulhaber, *American Servicemembers' Protection Act of 2002*, 40 Harv. J. on Legis. 537 (2003).

67 For other works, along this line, see Gidon Gottlieb, *The Nature of International Law: Toward a Second Concept of Law*, in 4 The Future of the International Legal Order 331 (Cyril E. Black & Richard A. Falk eds., 1972); Oliver J. Lissitzyn, The International Court of Justice 5–6 (1951); *cf.* Lea Brilmayer, *International Law in American Courts: A Modest Proposal*, 100 Yale L.J. 2277, 2280 (1991) ("the distinction between horizontal and vertical interpretations of international law is already implicit in the case law. In this sense, the horizontal/vertical distinction is old wine in new bottles."); Steven R. Ratner, *Corporations and Human Rights: A Theory of Legal Responsibility*, 111 Yale L.J. 443, 545 (2001) (noting that "in most areas of the law, states have obligations without either the possibility or probability that they might be called before an international court").

68 Myres McDougal et al., Studies in World Public Order (1987); Myres S. McDougal & W. Michael Reisman, International Law in Policy-Oriented Perspective, in The Structure and Process of International Law: Essays in Legal Philosophy, Doctrine and Theory 103 (Robert Macdonald ed., 1983); G. L. Dorsey, *The McDougal Laswell Proposal to Build a World Public Order*, 82 Am. J. Int'l L. 41 (1998); Myres S. McDougal, *International Law, Power and Policy: A Contemporary Conception*, 82 Recueil des Cours 137, 157 (1953); *see also*

David Kennedy, *My Talk at the ASIL: What Is New Thinking in International Law?*, 94 AM. SOC'Y OF INT'L L. 104 (2000).

69 Eisuke Suzuki, *The New Haven School of International Law: An Invitation to a Policy-Oriented Jurisprudence*, 1 YALE J. WORLD PUB. ORD. 1, 30 (1974); *see also* John Norton Moore, *Prolegomenon to the Jurisprudence of Myres McDougal and Harold Lasswell*, 54 VA. L. REV. 662, 667 (1968) ("[T]he most useful conception of law is a broad one encompassing the entire process by which judges, legislators, litigants and many others pursue particular values through the whole panoply of authoritative community decision-making.").

70 ROSALYN HIGGINS, PROBLEMS AND PROCESS 267 (1994); see *also* Harold Hongju Koh, *Is There a "New" New Haven School of International Law?*, 32 YALE J. INT'L L. 559, 573 (2007) (The New Haven school does not describe the world's different community decision processes through a dichotomy of national and international law, in terms of the relative supremacy of one system of rules or other interrelations of rules. Instead, it describes them in terms of the interpenetration of multiple processes of authoritative decision of varying territorial compass.).

8

International Financial Regulation and China

One way to put the sorts of theoretical claims in this book to the test is to run the rule over them with a case study or two. Our story has mostly been concerned with the governance offered by the United States and European Union, who have dominated the financial regulatory networks, when it comes to staffing, debate, and outputs. International financial governance is a thing that has been worked out by the agencies in the world's financial capitals, working in increasingly systemic concert. But what about the rest of the world?

One question posed by the international regime of financial regulation is how newcomers will respond to it. China, with its one-party government, cultural uniqueness, and relatively recent embrace of financial capitalism presents a distinctive test of the willingness of the developing world to buy into a system of globalized governance that has largely been devised by others. But if this lack of a seat at the table when the fundamental terms of financial regulation were formulated suggests that there may be reasons why China – and the rest of the developing world – would want to stay out of the regime, there are, as we will see, incentives encouraging them to join it.

Thus far, China has not complained about its lack of power over the international regulatory process that it has joined. It has embraced both G20 membership and financial regulatory cooperation, and joined the relevant networks, adding successful bids to host annual meetings. In 2006, the International Association of Insurance Supervisors met in Beijing and in 2012 the International Organization of Securities Commissions did as well. In 2014, China hosted the Basel Committee's international conference in Tianjin, where the committee signed off on one of its signature post-crisis regulatory initiatives, the net stable funding ratio. In 2016, China entertained members of the G20 at a summit in Hangzhou.

China's active participation has not come without a rumbling of discontent, or a sense that financial regulatory principles to which the United States, Japan, and the European Union have already agreed were either illegitimate, or inappropriately applied to China's young, fast-growing, and somewhat chaotic financial sector.

Nonetheless, it is hardly alone in being presented as a growing and powerful economy with rules that it must adopt, but did not help to formulate. Brazil, Russia, and India are all similarly situated with regard to financial regulatory networks. By considering why China might embrace the rules, and why it might resist them, one can get a sense of the dynamics for the developing world of acceptance of the financial regulatory settlement.

There is no doubt that countries like China have a limited voice in the institutions that make up international financial regulation; China is only one vote among twenty at the G20, and its peers tend to have smaller voices in fora where voting is allocated by economic size, such as the Financial Stability Board. China did not get a chance to participate in the formulation of the Basel I and II capital adequacy standards. It has never been a leading member of IOSCO or IAIS, and did not play an important role in devising international accounting standards, or the common approach to antiterrorism finance, despite its willingness to host the conventions of the organizations that did develop these standards. Its regulators have never occupied leadership positions in any of the financial regulatory networks.

Nor has it been a particularly active participant in critical debates. The policymaking struggles for each of the networks have tended to be characterized as differences between the USA, the United Kingdom, and the rest of Europe, along with, occasionally, Japan. Basel's capital adequacy rules, for example, have always been supported by US and British regulators, who have persuaded the rest of the world to go along, including sometimes-recalcitrant continental supervisors. To the extent that insurance regulation has begun to achieve substantive regulatory ends, much of the credit belongs to a push by the EU to come up with insurance solvency rules and capital standards for all insurance companies that seek to do business within its jurisdiction. American insurance supervisors have somewhat unwillingly gone along with this process, concluding a covered agreement with the EU designed to ensure market access for big, internationally active, US insurers, and adopting a form of the EU's solvency guidelines for insurers in the IAIS capital standard, while generally protesting all-too-rapid recent developments in supervision.

China has never been a central part of these big policymaking disputes, though it claims it has been "fully engaged" in international financial regulatory reform since the financial crisis.[1]

The developing world could accordingly reject the regulatory system this book has essayed by arguing that it never got a chance to write the rules. But discarding a settled agreement about how to approach a growing and very multinational industry poses its own problems. China has an enormous financial sector, with a fast growing and very competitive insurance industry, four enormous state-run banks, a terrifyingly large shadow banking sector, and as of 2018, the world's most valuable fintech startup. These institutions need to be regulated, and it is not obvious that China should reinvent the wheel. Moreover, as we will see, China has real financial stability problems in each of its financial sectors; its capital markets are rife with fraud; its insurance sector is growing too quickly and relies on dodgy financial products; its banks are far too big to fail; while its shadow banking sector does much of the work of corporate finance, and yet is relatively unregulated.

A review of how these sectors work shows that they are perilous, but in the relatively simple and straightforward ways that financial institutions in fast-developing economies tend to be. The banks do not depend on derivatives or trading operations; the shadow banking sector has followed a relatively straightforward credit intermediation function by taking money from investors and loaning it out to businesses, at interest; and the insurance industry, if a bit aggressively creative in product development, is not seeking to reinvent the business. Following the rules of international financial regulation is accordingly not such a hard lift for these institutions.

After a brief overview of the financial situation in which China finds itself, we will explore some of the reasons why the country, and by extension other developing nations, might sign on to the financial regulatory regime. The attractions of adoption are not negligible. The halo of membership has encouraged developing world regulators to adopt what have been presented to them as cutting-edge best practices, with all the potential attraction for foreign investment that membership in such a high-standards club can provide. Governments like China often see no need to reinvent the wheel when it comes to coming up with a plan for financial sector supervision; borrowing the law from an already sophisticated jurisdiction is a classic way that legal regimes spread; comparativists call these laws "transplants." Occasionally, developing world regulators happily announce that they will adopt standards they have little interest in actually enforcing. Lastly, the World Bank and International Monetary Fund have applied pressure to embrace the core principles of financial regulators during negotiations to join the World Trade Organization, and during financial sector reviews.

China supervises its banks through the China Bank Regulatory Commission (CBRC) and the Bank of China, its insurance firms via the China Insurance Regulatory Commission (CIRC), and its securities markets by the China Securities Regulatory Commission (CSRC). China has chosen to develop its young system along the lines of that of the USA, by regulating through sector-based commissions known in China as *Yihang Sanhui* (one bank, three commissions), which reflects the government's policy of handling financial firms through "separate operation, separate regulation."[2] But this state of affairs is apparently in flux. China has begun a process of consolidation by announcing a plan to merge its banking and insurance regulators.

The Chinese financial sector itself is fraught with promise and peril. China's big four state-owned commercial banks – the Agricultural Bank of China, the Bank of China, the Construction Bank of China, and the Industrial and Commercial Bank of China – are all enormous, and all appear on the Basel Committee's list of globally systemically important banks. They are very close (to say the least) to meeting the undesirable standard of being too big to fail – that is, so big that they would have to be bailed out by the government in tough times, rather than be allowed to go out of business. Moreover, they are all quite young; each bank was either founded or reformed in the late 1970s or early 1980s.

The history of China's banking sector has given Chinese economic policymakers pause. Once the big four Chinese banks were formed, some of their branches were used by local officials to pursue uneconomic projects, which meant that a high proportion of the loans issued by these banks were nonperforming or underperforming. Moreover, they made a lot of loans. In 2003, on average, the banking system showed an overall equity to asset ratio of just 3.25%.[3] The Asian financial crisis of the 1990s, although it did not consume the Chinese economy, also worried Chinese officials over the risks of failing to modernize the financial sector. The government accordingly revised its banking laws in the mid-1990s. It continued to try to develop its capacity partly to gain admission to the WTO, which implemented a transitional review mechanism for China that specifically considered, among other things, the quality of supervision of the country's banking system. To meet its WTO mandated goals, China implemented the second Basel Capital Accord quickly, although its capacity to really make the capital rules work remained in doubt before the financial crisis (some concluded that Basel II remained only partly implemented in China, and, for that matter, India).

Perhaps for this reason, China in the judgment of its peers has welcomed some degree of regulatory reform, and implemented the Basel III rules. The committee's 2013 review of China's implementation of Basel III found that Chinese regulators were "substantially compliant" with Basel; for its part, the CBRC claimed that "China has a strong commitment to global regulatory reform and standards for the purpose of building a sound and resilient financial system."[4] Indeed, the regulator claimed that its capital rules exceeded Basel's minimum requirements, suggesting it had no objection to Basel's approach. In February 2015, it finally implemented a deposit insurance regulation, bringing the jurisdiction in line with those of others that already had deposit insurance, including the USA and its Federal Deposit Insurance Corp. It has not joined the International Association of Deposit Insurers, however. And China has resisted foreign efforts to encourage it to broadly open up its banking system. Instead of limited market access, it continues to exercise a large governmental role over its largest banks.

The problem for China is that its shadow banking sector has become enormous, and a critical source of financing for the country's small- and medium-sized enterprises. As Duke Law School's Stephen Schwarcz has observed, shadow banking can increase risk, particularly where limited liability gives investors "strong incentives to take risks that might generate outsized personal profits, even if that greatly increases systemic risk."[5]

China's shadow banking system includes an array of financial enterprises ranging from the formal to the less so. Ant Financial exemplifies both the promise of the

Chinese financial system, and the way that shadow banking can pose questions that regulators find difficult to answer. Ant quickly became an enormous financial firm largely by processing payments for Alibaba, the giant Chinese online retailer. It also used the data it had obtained on Alibaba's customers – their product interests, payment records, social networks, and so on – to offer them almost all of the financial services that the internet can make possible.[6] Ant originates loans, manages money, and owns a money-market fund with assets that amounted to $228 billion in 2017.[7] It also offers consumer loans to millions of users on Alibaba's e-commerce platforms; it does not yet take deposits, but could if the Chinese central bank grows comfortable with electronic compliance know-your-customer requirements. Moreover, Chinese regulators have already given the firm an online banking license.[8] It is, as the Wall Street Journal has put it, "the world's biggest unicorn," with an equity value of $150 billion as of 2018. Given that size, Ant would qualify as "systemically important," that is, potentially too big to fail, if it were located in the USA.[9] But Ant's extremely fast growth means that it has been difficult for any regulator to know what to make of it. Chinese regulators assumed that it had bank-like characteristics in giving it a fintech license. But it does not yet take deposits, the activity most central to banks.

The shadow-banking sector is not just about fintech. It includes trust guarantee companies, brokerages, informal lenders, and other cooperative arrangements. It has grown rapidly, and is substantially less regulated than Chinese banks, and yet is thought to be playing a crucial credit intermediation role, one that the banks will not play for a large proportion of Chinese private enterprise. Because the shadow banking system – the largest proportion of which in China are trust products – is the most likely source of financing for less creditworthy borrowers, the concern is akin to the mania for junk bonds in other jurisdictions. The coupons are large, but investors may not understand that the high interest comes with high risk, often in the form of high leverage. That is, the shadow-banking sector is making loans to companies already deeply in debt, with no assurance that they will be able to make all of their interest payments. That means, in turn, that they have to borrow at high interest rates, meaning that trust products can promise high returns – but no guarantees of payment. Globally, shadow banking is something that regulatory networks have discussed, but not a subject on which there has been much consensus about what to do. The FSB has looked at shadow banking, but largely in the context of shadow banking that occurs in developed economies, including consideration of the risks of money-market funds, securitizations, and the like, none of which are particularly central to Chinese shadow banking. Even there, the FSB has moved cautiously, with interest mostly in gathering data rather than imposing global standards. China cannot really look abroad for guidance about how to tame its runaway trust companies, though it has told its banks to stop recommending the products to clients.

If banking has toggled between a large regulated sector and a growing unregulated sector, insurance is currently a combination of a regulated industry that is nonetheless expanding quickly. It is a very competitive sector of the financial economy, led by some very large companies in terms of market capitalization, such as China Life, HNA, and Ping An, and a large number of smaller, relatively new firms. These insurance companies have invested the resources entrusted to them aggressively, both inside and outside of China, creating questions about asset quality, which, in turn, have raised questions about their solvency, especially in the case of an economic downturn.

Chinese insurers also offer customers a variety of controversial products along with standard ones, raising the possibility that the insurance sector may be "runnable," that is, susceptible to a panic if a prominent insurer fails to make good on a popular, but poorly understood, and relatively new product. Insurers, for example, offer customers variable annuities and are deeply interested in branding their products (and dealing with their customers) via "fintech." The CIRC has tried to address the solvency of the system by implementing a China Risk Oriented Solvency System (C-ROSS), which is meant to comport with IAIS's ComFrame approach and be acceptable to European regulators applying their Solvency II regime to Chinese firms. C-ROSS has led Chinese insurers to add capital to their balance sheets, in some cases dramatically – reports of $3.15 billion of capital added by fourteen insurers have been mooted. Nonetheless, Chinese insurance regulators have, when visiting their counterparts abroad, tried to slow the march towards an insurance firm capital standard applied on a groupwide basis. They have attempted instead to find common cause with US supervisors, who have also never been interested in groupwide supervision, dealing instead with large insurers on a state-by-state basis, and so have, at least in this case, entered one of the financial regulatory policy debates on the side of slightly less global uniformity.

China's securities markets are, if anything, just as controversial an area of financial supervision. The markets have grown dramatically in size and value, many members of the emerging Chinese middle class speculate in them, and day-to-day conduct of those markets is often controversial, featuring irregular trading halts in stocks both when they decline and when they soar, sometimes for lengthy periods. China's securities markets have grown over the course of two decades to be among the largest in the world, with large and active exchanges in both the Shanghai and Shenzhen exchanges. The country has tens of millions of investors, and ranked first or second in initial public offerings between 2007 and 2012. Interestingly, this vast size and scale has been managed despite the fact that Chinese securities laws offer little protection for investors. Many firms have been marked by fraud, and some lower-quality ones have taken their offerings to Hong Kong or Singapore to access capital markets without going through the burdens, such as they are, of Chinese securities market registration.

The result has been wild and woolly. Chinese shares lost half their value between 2001 and 2005, followed by another 20% decline at the beginning of the 2010s. The gains have also been dramatic – meaning that China's stock market, despite being quite young, is now the world's second largest, in terms of market capitalization. Chinese issuers are being added to global emerging market funds, the Chinese IPO market is as active as any other (at least if judged by the number of IPOs), and the bond market has quietly grown into the world's third largest.

All of this has presented challenges for China's securities regulator. The World Bank and IMF's 2017 review of China's adoption of IOSCO's Objectives and Principles of Securities Regulation found that the Chinese regulatory approach approximately complied with the principles. However, the review identified a number of problems. Perhaps most importantly, the CISC was said to be both under-resourced and under-equipped, with insufficiently threatening sanctions. The World Bank and IMF recommended budget and staffing increases, and legal reforms that would give regulators new tools to punish firms for securities misstatements. It also warned of a fragmented system of supervision, especially since Chinese financial firms often blurred the lines between debt, equity, and insurance. It identified derivatives and wealth-management products as two areas where regulatory lines of responsibility were unclear.

Chinese banks have asset-quality problems, given all those nonperforming loans, but they are largely funded through depositors, and the revised capital rules are relatively depositor friendly. Moreover, some of the more technical Basel rules, such as stable funding requirements and short-term funding matches, did not really apply to relatively uncomplicated Chinese banks. Nor were Chinese banks dependent upon their derivatives businesses. In this sense, China was happy to adopt a set of capital rules that, while not entirely easy to implement, did not portend wholesale changes in the industry. The global regulatory regime thus presents some strange dynamics for Chinese banks and regulators going forward. It seems likely that Chinese lenders will be internationally active, and so therefore they should be covered by international settlement represented by Basel. However, its system is very different than that which exists in the USA or the UK. Chinese policymakers often push their banks to lend, as they did during the global financial crisis and as they have repeatedly done when pursuing development projects at home. We can imagine that Chinese lending overseas will often be designed to support foreign policy objectives and that banks, rather than solely existing for the benefit of their shareholders, will be tools of Chinese foreign policy. It will be interesting to see how this different agenda gets incorporated into Basel, or whether, as banks grow into the mechanisms of international oversight and interaction, they begin to approach issues more along Western lines.

As for securities markets, the country's basic compliance with IOSCO's core principles, along with the limited deeper efforts on harmonization that securities regulators have been able to undertake, means that China may find membership in the securities organization to be consistent with its approach to doing business thus far. In insurance, China is likely to find international capital standards difficult to comply with. As we have seen, however, it does have an ally in slowing the rush to international harmonization in the USA.

China has taken up international financial regulatory standards by the letter of the law, with some questioning whether they have also been embraced in spirit. To many countries, including China, the adoption of off-the-shelf international state-of-the-art standards is a way to market still-developing economies to foreign investors. Like many developing countries, China has welcomed seats at the table of international policymaking. It would have been hard to exclude the country from G20 membership in any case after the financial crisis, but it is clear that China, along with the other new members, has relished their access to leading organizations of international financial regulation. China isn't alone in moving quickly to host meetings and conferences of the financial regulatory networks. The new invitees into the post-crisis financial-reform process have generally quickly adopted Basel standards. And they have similarly embraced the requirements of other networks. These markers all suggest to outsiders that there is a commitment to the rule of law, or law-like institutions in these frontier markets. The halo of membership pulls these countries to adopt international financial regulatory standards.

But there is also a push (although China is less affected by this) for some countries. For many developing countries, the requirement that core principles must be adopted in exchange for World Bank or IMF assistance helps spread networks' financial regulatory rules. The conditionality of financial sector congruence with the basic requirements of the regulatory networks has undoubtedly led to the widespread sign-on by quite undeveloped economies to sometimes-complex requirements of sophisticated regulators who populate the financial networks' technical committees. Moreover, these jurisdictions, including China, probably see acceptance of the letter of the core principles as being relatively costless. Enforcing all those requirements of independence, process, and market surveillance is not an easy thing. But claiming that regulatory independence, fair process and enforcement, and a desire to oversee credit risk at home is simple enough, and plausibly consistent with the interests of all regulators.

For those who worry about the possibility that the spread of financial regulations devised in the West amounts to neocolonialism, it is worth considering what the realistic alternatives would be. China, with its rich and unique domestic history of bureaucratic experience, has never been shy about borrowing basic principles of regulatory organization from Central Europe and the Communist world. Especially as capital has proven to be quite global, it is difficult to imagine that many jurisdictions would be able to develop truly unique ways of attracting investments that would not match conventional methods investors have grown accustomed to. Comparativists often assess the quality and comprehensiveness of the transplantation of rules from one jurisdiction to another. But surely one of the real drivers behind the transplantation thesis – the theory that law spreads when law importers wholesale adopt the rules of legal exporters – is the fact that there may not be many options when it comes to the most basic principles of financial institution supervision. In this sense, transplantation may be inevitable as developing countries recognize just how elaborate their financial systems are becoming. China will, as we have seen, always do some things in its own way. But, in other ways, it is probably grateful to have a consensus set of off-the-shelf basics for managing its financial markets.

Notes

1 China Banking Regulatory Commission, *China's Basel III Graded "Compliant,"* www.cbrc.gov.cn/EngdocView.do?docID=187603855FBA4860BE9DB191EA44B433.

2 Robin Huang, *Institutional Structure of Financial Regulation in China: Lessons from the Global Financial Crisis*, 10 J. Corp. L. Stud. 219 (2010), https://ssrn.com/abstract=1512105.

3 Violaine Cousin, *Basel I, II, III – We Want It All At Once*, All China Rev., May 1, 2014, www.allchinareview.com/basel-i-ii-iii-we-want-it-all-at-once/.

4 Basel Committee on Banking Supervision, *Regulatory Consistency Assessment Programme (RCAP) Assessment of Basel III regulations – China*, Sep. 2013 www.bis.org/bcbs/implementation/l2_cn.pdf at 5.

5 Steven Schwarcz, *Shadow Banking and Regulation in China and Other Developing Countries*, 31 Boston University Review of Banking and Financial Law 619 (2012).

6 *Ant Financial's $100 Billion Valuation Would Put It in the Same League as the World's Biggest Banks*, Quartz, Feb. 10, 2018, https://qz.com/1204717/chinas-ant-financial-plans-to-raise-5-billion-reportedly-at-a-valuation-of-100-billion. ("Investors think prospects for next-generation companies like Ant Financial are comparable to top-tier institutions like Goldman Sachs, which had a $94 billion market cap at the time of writing.").

7 Shuli Ren. *Ant's Quiet Kingpin in the Storm*, Bloomberg, Dec. 26, 2017, www.bloomberg.com/gadfly/articles/2017-12-27/lucy-peng-must-bend-with-the-wind-to-get-ant-financial-its-break.

8 *Id.*

9 Julie Steinberg, "Jack Ma's Ant Financial to Raise $9 Billion, Become World's Biggest Unicorn," The Wall Street Journal, Apr. 10, 2018, www.wsj.com/articles/jack-mas-ant-financial-to-raise-9-billion-become-worlds-biggest-unicorn-1523353351. Also see Shuli Ren, "An Ant Financial IPO? Not So Fast," Bloomberg, Feb. 2, 2018, www.bloomberg.com/gadfly/articles/2018-02-02/an-ant-financial-ipo-got-you-excited-not-so-fast.

9

The Next Financial Crisis

Forecasting how the emerging regime of global financial regulation will respond to the next financial crisis offers a sense of its limits, and underscores the way that law-like constraints mesh with the need for administrative discretion. Traditionally, crisis response is the sort of government work that is most amenable to discretion, and therefore least amenable to management through a set of pre-existing, agreed upon rules and principles. Because crises are difficult to predict, flexibility may be necessary to effectively respond. The values of effective crisis response – promptness, overwhelming force, perhaps a degree of surprise – are not amenable to ordinary values of bureaucratic order.

This, however, does not mean that crisis response is a law-free zone. There are few crises that have not been dealt with by a response inflected by the legal and process constraints of ordinary administration, even if the requirements of crisis interdiction have forced regulators more concerned with effectiveness than with process to act with flexibility and – at times – the circumnavigation of standards that would constrain them in ordinary situations.

The internationalization of financial regulation means that legal constraints will be unique. As we have seen, the legal portions of any response will be domestic, rather than international, and regulation, as opposed to treaties or even statutes, will form much of the underpinnings of the international response. The international response will be organized by coordination rather than the kind of domestic regulation designed to minimize shocks to the financial system. How that coordination unfolds creates the procedural and institutional vehicles of crisis response. And precedents created by the response to the last crisis, such as central banks lending to one another, will make the response to the next crisis more predictable.

None of this suggests that when the next crisis arrives law and tradition will supplant politics and discretion. In past crisis response, as opposed to preparation for a crisis, international law and domestic administrative law have shown their limitations; the difficulties of both when it comes to so-called cross-border resolution authority – the power to quickly fail and recapitalize major, interconnected financial institutions – has been particularly obvious.

That does not mean that crisis response is orthogonal to the project of international financial regulation. Financial crises are the greatest test of financial regulators, who spend most of their time trying to avoid them, in part because responding to a crisis is so challenging. Understanding and assessing how this unique creature of international governance will respond to catastrophe helps us to take its measure.

If we know anything about global financial crises, it is that they are ubiquitous. Since the end of the Cold War, financial crises with cross-border implications have erupted in Mexico, East Asia, the United States, and Europe. And, of course, banks have collapsed in other countries as well, many with knock-on effects ranging from the spectacularly corrupt BCCI, which operated in seventy-eight countries at the time of its 1992 collapse, to 2014's Banco Espirito Santo, a nominally eurozone bank, headquartered in Portugal, brought low by the credit practices of its Angolan unit. Nor is it only the financial system that can become unstable. The power dynamics of the world are shifting, as China, a country with a relatively young but already enormous domestic financial industry emerges and joins various multinational frameworks.

For policymakers, then, the approach to the next financial crisis will be an exercise in damage minimization rather than in absolute prevention. The damage minimization will be institutionalized in two ways. First, the cross-border crisis response – the actions governments take once it becomes apparent that the global economy is reeling – will be focused on relationships built by the regularized interaction of heads of state, central bankers, and finance ministers through the G20. As I have argued elsewhere, the G20 has provided the political oversight over the emerging system of financial regulation, and so the immediate response to the next crisis will be one built out of political agreement (or not). Second, the pre-crisis resilience of the financial system that will minimize the damages inflicted by the next crisis will be built by the institutionalization of regulatory cooperation, which we have discussed earlier.

9.1 DISCRETION IN RESPONSE: THE G20 AND CENTRAL BANKS

The most important cross-border tools of crisis response and minimization feature diplomacy and central-bank-to-central-bank lending. Neither of these response mechanisms are particularly constrained by law or the regulatory alternative to traditional international law, but they are increasingly institutionalized practices.

9.1.1 *The G20*

During the crisis in 2007–2008, aspects of the response were hashed out at G20 summits, at which heads of state and finance ministers worked to create mechanisms that would support each other. At the 2009 London summit, for example, the G20 pledged funds to the IMF and regional development banks to support countries that needed access to funds, and also made the sorts of important-sounding statements meant to reassure markets that leaders were on the job. These actions by the G20, that modern-day Concerts of Europe, are examples of international cooperation untrammeled by law or regulation. Treaties are not negotiated at the G20, and commitments tend to veer towards the immediate rather than the lasting.

The G20 has "begun to take shape as a global 'steering committee,'" and has also settled into a relatively predictable routine for developing and following up on its agenda.[1] G20 meetings begin with an outline, rooted in communiques issued at the conclusion of the previous confab. Within finance ministries, "sherpas" guide the G20 agenda through a series of premeetings and in the time-honored format of international summits, complete a good part of the agenda by the time the heads of state meet. This means that an important part of what leaders do is to put their imprimatur on the process and establish to their own and observers' satisfaction that the meeting was worth having. The meeting concludes with a carefully negotiated and drafted communique, which sets the agenda for future meetings and reports on progress made at the current meeting.

The G20 is not without problems. The prospect of economic governance by a minority of the world's nation-states strikes some as unappealing, though the G20 includes most of largest economies and the most populous countries. Europe is overrepresented while African, and other emerging nations are underrepresented. Some believe that a small number of members wield significant decision-making power, creating even greater representation problems. In fact, the locations of G20 summits are selected by only eight members.

While the G20 has been active in financial-crisis response, most of its members have not practiced close coordination. After both the 1997–1998 Asian financial crisis and the 2007–2008 financial crisis, the G20 met as its members were crafting various individual responses to domestic problems, a dynamic that has been described as "together alone."[2] In the wake of crises, active cooperation began to prove difficult to sustain as the emergency receded.

9.1.2 *Central Bank Swaps*

By the same token, the efforts of finance ministers and central bankers to coordinate their crisis responses are examples of cooperation unconstrained by law. During the last financial crisis, central bankers smoothly extended loans and supplied stable currencies to one another. "Swap lines became mechanisms to outsource the Federal Reserve's bedrock power – its lender-of-last-resort role – to foreign central banks," Colleen Baker has observed.[3] The Fed's credit lines were massive and barely scrutinized. Central banks did $600 billion worth of liquidity swaps during the financial crisis – far more than they had ever done before. In most cases, these swaps exchanged American dollars or other safe currencies for foreign currencies deemed to be less so. The availability of swaps permitted central banks to inject safe currencies into their economies; the swaps locked in the exchange rate at which the initial trade was executed, meaning that central banks could eventually return the stable currencies to initial counterparties at the same rate they got for them in their own currency.

These swap lines proved to be a massive liquidity-disbursing tool, which will likely play an important role in the response to the next crisis. It relies not on network governance (or other forms of international law), but on central-bank-to-central-bank interaction and the willingness of institutions like the Fed to trade dollars for a broad array of other currencies.

These are policy tools deemed to fall within the Fed's discretion as a central bank. Indeed, these macroeconomic actions are thought to be one of the few things central banks can do to stave off a financial collapse. Central banks are supposed to flood a distressed economy with correctly denominated liquidity, encouraging lending and stabilizing the currency. In many countries, the liquidity has to be more reliable than official printed money; hence the extension of lines of credit from central banks with stable currencies to central banks with more volatile currencies.

In general, central banks have managed to act in an unconstrained way because the desire to give them independence, at least for much of what they do in terms of macroeconomic policy, means that they are usually unsupervised by the courts or executive (unless they are controlled by the executive, a frowned upon, but not uncommon, approach in the developing world). Some worry that this leaves them with too much discretion when the global economy is threatened; others wonder if their decisions on whether and how to loan one another money, and to bail out either entire financial sectors, or important firms within them, are ill-suited to the traditional disciplines of administrative law.

What matters is that this form of crisis response differs from cooperation with other regulators. It is transactional and discretionary, and because it has turned into an increasingly important crisis-response tool, one can expect that it will evolve to include increasingly predictable customs. But it is different from an effort to oversee financial institutions. Instead, it is very much about making loans to them.

9.2 REGULATORY COOPERATION

Both diplomacy and central bank lending will likely be important parts of the response to the next financials crisis. Nonetheless, it would be incorrect to say that international governance, at least defined as capaciously as I am inclined to do, will play no role in responding to the next financial crisis.

First, the legal/regulatory institutionalization of crisis response has meant that communication both at the level of banking regulators and at higher political levels of the G20 has been regularized and routinized. Communication from the bottom to the top of each country's organizational chart has now been engaged in an international effort to create standards meant to minimize the risks of a financial crisis.

Second, the constant coordination and international policymaking mechanisms used to set the terms of how regulators should approach the supervision of domestic banks is the focus of that damage-minimization effort. As we have seen, the signature achievement of financial regulators over the past forty years has been the capital adequacy accords concluded in Basel that require banks to hold a significant portion of their assets as either equity or very safe cash-like instruments. The accord now includes alternatives such as the net stable funding ratio and the liquidity coverage ratio, both designed to ensure that banks meet a host of different tests in order to be considered adequately capitalized, and therefore safe to do business with. The idea is that these capital requirements will prevent banks from collapsing in an over-leveraged heap the next time something bad occurs, because the safe assets they are required by regulation to hold will protect them. Regulators and their political superiors are committed to this form of international coordination because financial regulation has a particular cross-border contagion problem. Because of the inter-connected nature of the global financial system, a disaster in one country can easily be exported to another. It means that regulators cannot assume their local banks are safe simply because they have met the domestic requirements of safety and soundness.

An international disruption of the payment system, as happened in 1974, can sweep across even tightly ring-fenced domestic financial institutions. The problem of contagion has led to the institutionalization of lending and cooperation that will mark the response to the crises. And all of this is being done as a matter of regulation enforced domestically but agreed to internationally.

This way, the response to the next crisis will be inflected by regulatory cooperation that differs from traditional international law. The prelude to that crisis – the strengthening of institutions and agencies through regulatory cooperation accomplished through notice and comment, both domestically and internationally, and subject to political supervision and bureaucratic organization – is the very definition of administrative procedure. And the creation of regulatory mechanisms like finance ministry premeetings has resulted in the institutionalization of these practices, making it easier for the next financial crisis summit to act in a meaningful fashion.

These efforts have also become iterative. The enforcement mechanism involves a constant process of peer review to ensure that regulatory harmonization becomes a reality. There are no courts in international financial regulation, but there are constant supervisory committees. In this way, the legal contribution to the response to the next financial crisis is organizational and administrative, but no less real than international law made through the pomp and circumstance of signing a treaty.

9.3 CROSS-BORDER RESOLUTION: A CASE STUDY

During the last financial crisis, the failure of cross-border financial institutions led to often chaotic government responses that made countries more likely to try to bail out their banks, since the alternative – an organized, cross-border resolution – looked unavailable. Because banks that suspect they are covered by a government guarantee are likely to take more risks, because bailouts are politically unpopular, and because without an international process domestic regulators may respond to crises by unproductively ring-fencing whatever assets of troubled banks they can find, there have since been efforts to create a better mechanism for dealing with failing banks. The progress has been slow, but the results have represented a doubling-down on the promise of regulatory cooperation, either because nothing more can be achieved, or because there is consensus that it is the best way to pursue international financial regulation.

During the last crisis, problems created by a lack of cross-border resolution coordination were illustrated again and again. Fortis, a Belgian-Dutch financial conglomerate, was taken over by Belgian and Dutch regulators only to find itself mired in chaotic post-takeover litigation and proxy disputes. Dexia, a French-Belgian bank, fared better when it received a relatively coordinated set of financing guarantees from the French, Belgian, and Luxembourg central banks – although even in that case, the central banks found it difficult to agree on how they should apportion the bailout. Kaupthing, the Icelandic bank that had created branches or subsidiaries in thirteen jurisdictions outside its home nation, was bailed out to the point of diplomatic incident. Icelandic supervisors guaranteed the deposits of Icelandic customers, but were unwilling to bail out those located abroad. Foreign regulators accordingly seized whatever assets of the bank they could find to satisfy their own citizen depositors.

The problem was replicated, although in a substantially magnified way, by the failure of Lehman Brothers in 2008, which as the Basel Committee's Cross-Border Bank Resolution Group put it "consisted of 2,985 legal entities operated in some 50 countries."[4] When the institution failed after the US government refused to bail it out, and the British refused to sanction an emergency purchase by Barclays, a large UK-based multinational bank, various regulators and creditors raced to their courts to find assets that could be used to satisfy the bank obligations; the result was generally thought to be chaotic. Essentially, every creditor and every government scrambled to file claims in their own jurisdictions, trying to seize whatever part of Lehman they could find in the hope that they could beat foreign creditors.

The result was that the recovery rate for unsecured creditors in Lehman was much lower than one would expect in a more conventional resolution of a financial institution; creditors of banks that collapsed during the 1990s did markedly better than Lehman creditors, to say nothing of creditors of nonfinancial firms.

Everybody is supposed to get together and ensure that their domestic agencies have the key attributes of effective resolution regimes, and they are supposed to coordinate with each other. Large financial institutions are meant to be governed by so-called colleges of supervisors, so that, say, Barclays, has supervisors in each jurisdiction in which it operates who communicate with one another. The G20 accordingly urged during its Summit on Financial Markets and the World Economy in 2008 and again at its London Summit in April 2009 that cross-border resolution regimes and bankruptcy laws be strengthened in ways that permitted the orderly resolution of complex institutions.

However, there has been no appetite for creating an international organization that could coordinate these cross-border schemes. Instead, the effort is once again regulatory, with the Basel Committee making a series of recommendations about how resolution regimes ought to be strengthened among member regulators. These recommendations tend to the anodyne: Basel has suggested that "national authorities should consider the development of procedures to facilitate the mutual recognition of crisis management and resolution proceedings and or measures."[5] But not every recommendation is a platitude; Basel has endorsed the power to stay the satisfaction of financial contracts upon resolution, for example.

If anything, the approach has suggested that banking supervisors are particularly comfortable with regulatory cooperation. For the resolution of complex and interconnected cross-border financial intermediaries, Basel has urged the development of colleges of supervisors. Under this scheme, supervisors would "work closely with relevant home and host resolution authorities in order to understand how group structures and their individual components would be resolved in a crisis."[6] More generally, supervisors have been encouraged to simplify and shrink financial institutions that they suspect might be vulnerable in a crisis.

The FSB, which sits above the Basel Committee, has also endorsed the coordination and capacity-building approach. It has identified what it characterizes as key attributes of effective resolution regimes, and encouraged members to ensure that they have regulators with those powers. The FSB has also urged regulators to develop so-called bail-in mechanisms that take debts owed by the banks and turn them into equity held by creditors of the banks. They have also encouraged every authority to obtain the power to temporarily stay early termination rights in financial contracts, and to require financial institutions to follow common practices with financial contracts, including using forms created by the International Swaps and Derivatives Association.

These efforts may not suffice. Already the USA has adopted a relatively unique approach to bailing out financial institutions, the so-called "single point of entry," which would recapitalize financial institutions at the holding-company level. The international networks have indicated their approval of the concept, but implementing it in countries that do not insist that their banks operate through holding companies will be problematic. But because European and other jurisdictions have not structured their financial institutions along a holding-company approach, it's not clear that the single point of entry will really be internationalized. Rumored disagreements on how to handle supervision – how to trust, say, the home country supervisor of a multinational financial institution to take a national champion through resolution – have made the development of a broad regime difficult. The FSB has encouraged its members to honor the decisions of lead supervisors in multinational resolution contexts, but it is not clear that that will be enough.

Although coordinated resolution requires courts in other countries to honor steps taken by regulators leading the resolution, European courts have generally interpreted the EU directive requiring them to honor decisions of regulators leading a resolution narrowly. If coordination has been limited within Europe, one can only imagine that there is even more conflict elsewhere.

Cross-border resolution is the second major way the international regulatory architecture will be used to respond to the next financial crisis. Although cross-border resolution requires coordination, the low-key coordination recommended by international institutions that has developed since the last crisis suggests it will be one of the challenges for financial regulation in the next crisis. If regulatory cooperation can work there, it can work anywhere in finance.

9.4 CONCLUSION

Nobody ever thought the response to a financial crisis would be easy; crises by definition challenge those who must respond to them. Crisis response is particularly difficult for institutions built on informal cooperation and cross-border coordination of domestic regulation. One can see why the welter of agreements to coordinate oversight of financial institutions generally sticks to preparing for crises, trying to make rules for crisis response. Nonetheless, these agreements have influenced how a crisis response will take place, both by creating institutional vehicles through which discretion will be exercised in crisis response, and by serving as the rickety vehicle for the takeover and recapitalization of failing financial institutions.

9.5 POSTSCRIPT: INTERNATIONAL FINANCIAL REGULATION AS A MODEL FOR COOPERATION

We can finally consider the applicability of the kind agencification that has reshaped financial regulation to other areas of international regulatory cooperation. Finance, after all, is just one example of an international phenomenon. Similar regulatory cooperation in antitrust, food and drug regulation, telecommunications, aviation, and other areas has resulted in an epidemic of standardization, or at least efforts along those lines. Joseph Weiler calls this cooperation a "fourth strata" in the geology of international law, a layer in which informal regulatory regimes and self-regulating governance mechanisms – rather than treaties, formal international organizations, or diplomats – predominate.[7]

As a general matter, the turn to informality makes some sense. Informal regulatory cooperation fits well with the international system for two reasons. First, the world is not under the control of a global government that can issue directives with real bite. Accordingly, international governance efforts that rely on suggestion, imitation, and legitimation through claims of expertise, as regulatory governance does, is well suited for fractious times. This in turn may help explain the popularity of soft law among regulators who traffic in hard law at home. Second, while the international system has always been fractious, the need for collaboration across borders has intensified given our globalized world. But collaboration through a formal mechanism, such as a treaty or international organization, is not easy to affect. It makes alternatives to the treaty process particularly tempting.

The question then is whether all regulators should do things as they're done in finance. The globalized governance of finance has proven to be effective. Financial regulation has benefited from being a priority – the political oversight is nothing less than the heads of state of the twenty largest and richest countries in the world. But it remains very much a technocratic and somewhat apolitical process below that level. Finance came to regulatory cooperation cautiously, beginning with agreements on basic principles that every regulator should, and largely could, follow. Its networks then moved on, through white papers, memoranda of understanding, and best practices, to fill out the content of a regulatory regime bounded by those principles. Where possible, especially in banking supervision, it graduated to more specific rules that constrained regulators and regulated industry across borders.

This graduated effort has proven to be successful in a way that more comprehensive and sudden efforts have not, as exemplified by the difficulties involved with agreeing to accept standards of a foreign agency as a substitute for your own, an approach dubbed mutual recognition. Moreover, the architecture now can claim legitimacy in the way that it is overseen, in the procedural predictability of its efforts, and in the legitimate claim its lower-level bureaucrats have for procedural expertise.

International financial regulation's progress has other lessons for would-be regulatory cooperators. Its varied progress suggests that extreme multilateralism can make for unwieldy institutions. The compact Basel Committee has been an important regulator of banks, while the International Association of Insurance Supervisors, which has more members than the world has countries (there are fifty-three participants from the USA alone), has had less success.

Framers of international regulatory efforts in other areas should also consider whether they should mimic some of the substantive values embodied by financial regulation. The common thread of a demand for a "level playing field" – shorthand for national treatment obligations – and a consensus approach to regulation among various financial regulatory networks suggest that these values may be an irreducible minima of any global regulatory process. By the same token, the use of the network, the dependence on the members of the network for implementation, and the exploitation of peer review to enforce the network's values have proven to be flexible mechanisms of organization and enforcement.

This does not mean that derogation from these principles is impossible, or even that the adoption of them will guarantee the success of any international regulatory enterprise. Global governance framers in different areas should expect that any progress in any place will be affected by circumstance. It could be that a regulatory shock or catastrophe will be required before real progress in internationalizing regulation can be made. It could be that other regimes will be affected by the emergence of regulatory entrepreneurs who have particular visions that are persuasive and unpredictable in non-uniform ways. Not every informal effort at regulatory governance will look like the paradigm offered by finance. In fact even financial regulation does not always resemble the financial regulatory paradigm in every particular; although, while outlines of the process of creating global rules in finance are similar across its various subfields, there are real variations in achievements and, to some degree, in organizational form among those subfields.

Financial regulation has had unique advantages that other regulatory endeavors might not share. The globalization of financial institutions and the mobility of capital have been more dramatic than that of trade goods and services. Moreover, financial regulators and financial institutions have been cosmopolitan for some time. Efforts to build communities of regulators who understand one another have probably been easier in finance than in other contexts. Financial regulatory globalization has been eased by the fact that the need has been particularly acute and the conditions facilitating it have been accommodating.

Finally, the effort to improve and elaborate the international financial architecture that existed benefited – unfortunately, of course – from catastrophe. As we have seen, the economic turmoil of the 1970s initiated the development of a global regulatory regime and the global financial crisis in 2008 accelerated efforts to create a regulatory regime that could prevent the next crisis from being so severe. One can only hope that these sorts of crises do not strike other places susceptible to regulation through informal global architecture.

Global financial regulation is a unique accomplishment. It exemplifies an important legal order that does not depend upon traditional understandings of international legal obligation. It is not the case that financial regulation's template is one that policymakers in other contexts would be foolish to ignore. Informal regulatory cooperation does not have to mean the end of regulation through negotiated treaties or the formation of international organizations. Nor does it mean that a regulatory system cannot survive if it does not involve a component of international cooperation.

In the end, informal regulatory cooperation of the sort embodied by the globalization of financial oversight is a particular tool, one of many that can be used to resolve governance problems. The remarkable aspect of the rise of international financial regulation is that it has become such a powerful and elaborate tool very quickly, and that it looks nothing like anything else in the policymakers' toolkit.

Notes

1 Andrew Cooper, *G-20: The Unspoken Issues*, www.cigionline.org/publications/2010/6/g20-membership-and-process-unspoken-issues.
2 Jorge Braga, *Peer Pressure to Meet G20 Commitments: A Promising Innovation?* (2010) www.cigionline.org/publications/2010/6/peer-pressure-meet-g20-commitments-promising-innovation.
3 Colleen Baker, *The Federal Reserve's Use of International Swap Lines*, 55 ARIZ. L. REV. 603, 607 (2013).
4 Report and Recommendation of the Cross-Border Bank Resolution Group at 14 (March, 2010).
5 *Id.* at 4.
6 *Id.* at 5.
7 Joseph Weiler, *Towards a Geology of 20th Century International Law: The Paradox of Law Making and Enforcement*, Speech at Duke Law School (Feb. 12, 2001), *quoted in* Don Suh, Note, *Situating Liberalism in Transnational Legal Space*, 12 DUKE J. COMP & INTL L. 605, 612 (2002).

Index

Advantages of international financial governance, 160
African Development Bank, 106
"Agencification" of international financial governance, 6, 15, 158–9
Aggression, crime of, 131–2
Agricultural Bank of China, 144
AIG Financial Products, 84
Alibaba, 145–6
Alternatives to international financial governance, 8–9
American Insurance Group (AIG), 27, 84
Andrews, Paul, 66
Ant Financial, 145–6
Argentina
- Basel Committee and, 15
- IOSCO and, 66

Argumentative nature of international law, 129, 130, 131, 133
Asia Pacific Economic Cooperation, 103
Australia
- Basel Committee and, 57
- IASB and, 109
- IFRS and, 109

Baker, Colleen, 58, 153
Banco Espirito Santo, 152
Bank for Credit and Commerce International (BCCI), 108, 152
Bank for International Settlements (BIS), 48, 61, 88, 111
Banking
- Basel Committee (*See* Basel Committee on Banking Supervision)
- in China, 144–5
- shadow banking, 145–6

Bank of America, 27
Bank of China, 144
Bank of New York Mellon, 27, 57
Barclays, 57, 156, 157
Basel Committee on Banking Supervision. *See also specific Accord*
- generally, 9, 15, 40–1, 48, 99, 113
- banks in multiple jurisdictions, 14
- capital adequacy rules, 46–7, 51–2, 68–9, 143
- China and, 15, 33, 142, 143, 145, 148
- Concordat, 51–2
- consensus in, 50
- Core Principles for Effective Banking Supervision, 52
- CPMI and, 111, 112
- creation of, 46, 48
- Cross-Border Bank Resolution Group, 156
- cross-border resolution and, 156, 157
- currency swaps and, 58
- deposit insurance and, 99–100
- exclusivity of, 15
- FSB supervision, 48, 49, 51, 57–8
- globally systemically important banks, 144
- "governance without law" in, 51
- Group of Governors and Heads of Supervision (GHOS), 49
- G20 and, 48, 51, 57–8
- IAIS compared, 83, 84–5, 86
- IMF and, 48
- institutional form of, 48–51
- IOSCO compared, 62, 63–5, 67–8, 70, 75
- lack of supervisory authority, 50–1
- as member of FSB, 18, 20–1
- membership in, 33
- MFN treatment and, 23–4, 47
- national treatment and, 21–2, 47, 56
- notice and comment process, 56–7
- objectives of, 49
- offshoots of, 101
- peer review and, 29, 30, 47, 50, 56

as policy source, 15
post-crisis financial regulation and, 58
Principles for the Supervision of Banks' Foreign Establishments, 51
purpose of, 49
Regulatory Consistency Assessment Program (RCAP), 30, 56
as regulatory network, 58–9, 101 (*See also* Regulatory networks)
"ring fencing" and, 56
rulemaking and, 25, 47
secrecy in, 50
selective exit and, 37
subsidiarity and, 28–9
successes of, 51–9, 159
swap lines and, 58
transparency in, 50, 56–7
Basel I Accord, 47, 52–3, 56, 71, 143
Basel II Accord, 29, 47, 53–5, 59, 143, 145
Basel III Accord, 22, 24, 30, 47, 55, 56–8, 145
Bear Stearns, 54, 71
Born, Brooksley, 138
Brazil
Basel Committee and, 15
IOSCO and, 67
regulatory networks and, 143
swap lines and, 58
Breeden, William, 68–9
Brexit, 36
Brummer, Chris, 9, 14, 38, 41, 71
Buthe, Tim, 99

Canada
Basel Committee and, 57
IASB and, 109
Carney, Mark, 23
Casey, Kathleen, 1
Central banks, crisis response and, 153–4
CGFS. *See* Committee on the Global Financial System (CGFS)
China
generally, 10, 142
adoption of international financial governance, 144, 149
Basel Committee and, 15, 33, 142, 143, 145, 148
Basel I Accord and, 143
Basel II Accord and, 143, 145
Basel III Accord and, 145
China Bank Regulatory Commission (CBRC), 144, 145
China Insurance Regulatory Commission (CIRC), 144, 147, 148
China Risk Oriented Solvency System (C-ROSS), 147
China Securities Regulatory Commission (CSRC), 144
discontent regarding international financial governance, 142–3
financial sector, 144–5
financial stability in, 143–4
FSB and, 33
G20 and, 16, 142, 143, 149
in IADI, 145
IAIS and, 142, 143
IMF and, 40–1, 148
insurance sector, 146–7
IOSCO and, 67, 142, 143, 148–9
limited voice in international financial governance, 143
neocolonialism and, 149–50
securities markets, 147–9
shadow banking system, 145–6
UK compared, 148
US compared, 148
World Bank and, 40–1, 148
in WTO, 145
Yihang Sanhui, 144
China Life, 147
Chinese Taipei, Financial Supervisory Commission, 88
Citigroup, 27
Cohen, Rodgin, 8
Colombia, IOSCO and, 66
Committee on Payments and Market Infrastructure (CPMI), 111–12
generally, 72, 73, 101, 107
Basel Committee and, 111, 112
CGFS compared, 112
creation of, 111
FSB and, 112
IOSCO and, 112
membership in, 111
Principles for Financial Market Infrastructures (PFMIs), 112
Red Books, 111
regulatory cooperation and, 112
Committee on the Global Financial System (CGFS), 101, 107, 112–13
Comparison of international financial governance with other institutions
advantages of international financial governance, 160
EU, 34–7
final settlement and, 36
GATT, 36
IMF, 40–1
institutionalist camp, 38, 39
international law and, 40–1

Comparison of international financial (cont.)
law and, 38–9
political science and, 39–40
quiet integration and, 36, 37
realist camp, 38–40
selective exit and, 35, 36–7
voice and, 35–6
World Bank, 40–1
WTO, 34–7
Construction Bank of China, 144
Constructivism, 130–1
Cooke, Peter, 8, 50
Cooperation. *See* Regulatory cooperation
Coordinative role of international law, 127, 128, 129–30
Cox, Christopher, 8, 111
Cox, James D., 119
CPMI. *See* Committee on Payments and Market Infrastructure (CPMI)
Credit Suisse, 57
Crisis response
generally, 10, 151–2, 158
case study, 156–8
central banks and, 153–4
communication in, 154–5
coordination in, 151, 155
cross-border resolution, 156–8
damage minimization in, 152, 155
domestic versus international response, 151
G20 and, 152–3, 154–5
importance to international financial governance, 160
international financial governance and, 152
peer review in, 155
regulatory cooperation in, 154–5
swap lines and, 153–4
Criticism of international financial governance, 4
Cross-border resolution, 156–8
Currency pools, 72
Currency swaps, 58, 72
Customary international law, 122–3

Deposit insurance, 99–100, 102
Deviation from principles of international financial governance, 160
Dexia, 156
Dimon, Jamie, 4
Doha Round, 94
Domestic component of international financial governance, 6, 124–7
Dorf, Michael, 33–4, 44
Drezner, Daniel, 40
Dualist view of international law, 124–5
Dudley, William C., 112

European Central Bank, 61
European Commission, 101, 106
European Union
cross-border resolution and, 158
IAIS and, 93
international financial governance compared, 34–7
MFN treatment and, 32–3
national treatment and, 21, 32–3
regulatory networks and, 32, 143
rulemaking and, 24
Solvency II, 93
subsidiarity and, 28, 32–3
Treaty of the European Union (Maastricht Treaty), 28, 36
UK and, 36
US-EU Covered Agreement, 83–4, 94–6

Feibelman, Adam, 40
Financial Accounting Standards Board (FASB), 110
Financial Action Task Force (FATF), 106–7
generally, 20, 41, 101–2, 108
associates, 106
black list, 107
creation of, 106
40+9 Recommendations, 106
gray list, 107
G20 and, 107
International Co-Operation Review Group, 107
IOSCO compared, 107
membership in, 106
monitoring, 107
observers, 106
standards, 106
terrorism and, 113
Financial institutions
Basel Committee (*See* Basel Committee on Banking Supervision)
in China, 144–5
shadow banking, 145–6
Financial Sector Assessment Program (FSAP), 29, 30, 105
Financial Stability Board (FSB)
generally, 14–15, 16
Basel Committee on Banking Supervision (*See* Basel Committee on Banking Supervision)
China and, 33
Compendium of Standards, 89, 99, 101, 103, 112–13, 114
CPMI and, 112

cross-border resolution and, 157, 158
IADI and, 103
IAIS (*See* International Association of Insurance Supervisors (IAIS))
IMF and, 18
initiatives of, 19
international financial governance and, 18–20
IOSCO (*See* International Organization of Securities Commissions (IOSCO))
membership in, 33, 99
MFN treatment and, 23
national treatment and, 21–2
objectives of, 18–19
peer review and, 19, 131, 139
plenaries, 19–20
regulatory networks and, 101
rulemaking and, 25, 27
shadow banking and, 146
standard setters and, 107–8
subsidiarity and, 28–9
systemically important financial institutions (SIFIs) and, 84
"too big to fail" list, 27
World Bank and, 18
Financial Stability Forum, 103
Foreign exchange trading (forex), 3–4
Fortis, 156
France
Basel Committee and, 57
IAIS and, 85
IASB and, 109
Franklin National Bank, 4, 46, 48
Freeland, Charles, 48, 51
Free Zones case (PCIJ 1932), 125

Gadinis, Stavros, 38
General Agreement on Tariffs and Trade (GATT). *See also* World Trade Organization (WTO)
generally, 76
creation of, 5
"governance without law" in, 3
international financial governance compared, 36
MFN treatment and, 23
national treatment and, 21, 22
peer review and, 30
subsidiarity and, 28
Generally Accepted Accounting Principles (GAAP), 63, 73, 74–5, 109–10
Germany
Basel Committee and, 57
IAIS and, 85
IASB and, 109
Giancarlo, Christopher, 2–3
Globally systemically important banks, 144
Global systemically important insurers (G-SIIs), 91–2
Goldman Sachs, 27
Goldsmith, Jack, 127, 137
Goodhart, Charles, 22
"Governance without law"
generally, 10
in Basel Committee, 51
informality of international financial governance, 159, 160–1
"legalish" system of international financial governance, 5
in WTO, 3
Graduated approach to international financial governance, 159
Greece
Basel I and, 53
Basel II and, 55
EU and, 35
Greenberg, Evan, 91
Grotius, Hugo, 128–9
Group of Banking Supervisors in Arab Countries, 50
G20
generally, 14
Basel Committee and, 48, 51, 57–8
China and, 16, 142, 143, 149
communiqués, 16–18
consensus in, 17
crisis response and, 152–3, 154–5
cross-border resolution and, 157
FATF and, 107
historical background, 15–16
international financial governance and, 15–18
London Summit (2009), 157
meetings, 16–18
MFN treatment and, 23, 24
national treatment and, 22
peer review and, 29–30
post-crisis financial regulation and, 16
quiet integration and, 37
regulatory networks and, 101
Seoul Development Consensus, 24
Summit on Financial Markets and the World Economy (2008), 157
Gulf Co-Operation Council, 106

Herstatt Bank, 4, 46, 48
Herstatt risk, 4, 108
Higgins, Rosalyn, 134, 141
High-frequency trading, 72
Hirschman, Albert O., 35–6, 44
HNA, 147

Hong Kong
  Basel Committee and, 57
  Chinese securities firms relocating to, 147
  IFRS and, 109
Horizontal nature of international law, 129
Human rights, 125–6

IAASB. *See* International Auditing and Assurance Standards Board (IAASB)
IADI. *See* International Association of Deposit Insurers (IADI)
IAIS. *See* International Association of Insurance Supervisors (IAIS)
IASB. *See* International Accounting Standards Board (IASB)
IFRS. *See* International Financial Reporting Standards (IFRS)
IMF. *See* International Monetary Fund (IMF)
India
  Basel Committee and, 15
  IAIS and, 90
  regulatory networks and, 143
Indonesia, Basel Committee and, 15
Industrial and Commercial Bank of China, 144
Informality of international financial governance, 159, 160–1
Institutions of international financial governance. *See also specific institution*
  generally, 9
  Basel Committee on Banking Supervision (*See* Basel Committee on Banking Supervision)
  exclusivity of, 15
  FSB (*See* Financial Stability Board (FSB))
  G20 (*See* G20)
  historical background, 13–14
  IAIS (*See* International Association of Insurance Supervisors (IAIS))
  IOSCO (*See* International Organization of Securities Commissions (IOSCO))
  as policy sources, 15
  post-crisis financial regulation, 14
Insurance
  bilateral agreement between EU and US, 83–4, 94–6
  in China, 146–7
  deposit insurance, 99–100, 102
  effect of financial crisis on, 84
  global systemically important insurers (G-SIIs), 91–2
  IAIS (*See* International Association of Insurance Supervisors (IAIS))
  internationally active insurance groups (IAIGs), 91
  low level of coordination in, 83–4
  siloing and, 14
  systemically important financial institutions (SIFIs), 84
Interamerican Association of Securities Commissions and Similar Agencies, 64
International Accounting Standards Board (IASB), 108–11
  generally, 101, 108, 113
  creation of, 109
  funding of, 110
  governance, 110
  IFRS and, 71, 75, 107, 109–11
  IOSCO compared, 108, 109, 110–11
  regulatory cooperation and, 68
  rulemaking and, 25
  standards, 108, 109
International Accounting Standards Committee (IASC), 68
International Association of Deposit Insurers (IADI), 102–4
  generally, 101–2, 115
  budget, 116
  China in, 145
  core principles, 102–4
  creation of, 102–3
  Enhanced Guidance, 103
  FSB and, 103
  governance of, 103
  as regulatory network, 101
International Association of Insurance Supervisors (IAIS)
  generally, 9–10, 15, 83–5, 96, 99
  Basel Committee compared, 83, 84–5, 86
  bilateral agreement as alternative, 83–4, 94–6
  budget, 87
  bylaws, 87
  capital standard, 92–3
  China and, 142, 143
  committees, 87
  Common Framework for the Supervision of Internationally Active Insurance Groups (ComFrame), 91–2, 93, 147
  decentralization in, 87–8
  deposit insurance and, 99–100
  effective insurance supervision, 89
  exclusivity of, 15
  executive committee, 86–7
  general meeting, 86
  general secretariat, 87
  global systemically important insurers (G-SIIs) and, 91–2
  Group-wide Supervision Framework, 89
  guidance papers, 89
  incorporation of, 85

information exchange, 89–90
institutional form of, 85–8
Insurance Core Principles (ICPs), 88–9, 90–1
internationally active insurance groups (IAIGs) and, 91
IOSCO compared, 83, 85
low level of coordination in, 83–4
Macroprudential Policy and Surveillance Working Group, 88
as member of FSB, 18, 20–1
membership in, 85–6
MFN treatment and, 23
mission of, 86
Multilateral Memorandum of Understanding (MMoU), 30, 90, 96
observers, 86
peer review and, 30
as policy source, 15
Principles on Group-wide Supervision, 89
Recommendation Concerning Mutual Assistance, Cooperation, and Sharing of Information, 90
regulatory cooperation and, 83–4, 88
as regulatory network (*See* Regulatory networks)
rulemaking and, 25
siloing and, 14
successes of, 88–93, 159
UK and, 93
US-EU Covered Agreement as alternative, 83–4, 94–6
voting, 86
International Auditing and Assurance Standards Board (IAASB), 104–6
generally, 101–2
Clarity Project, 104, 105
as ethics regulator, 104
notice and comment process, 105
oversight, 104–5, 106
standards, 104, 105
International Auditing Practices Committee (IAPC), 104
International component of international financial governance, 6
International Court of Justice, 8, 11–12, 130
International Covenant on Civil and Political Rights (ICCPR), 126
International Covenant on Economic, Social, and Cultural Rights (ICESCR), 125–6, 136
International Criminal Court (ICC), 25, 131–3
International criminal law, 131–3
International Criminal Tribunal for Rwanda (ICTR), 132–3
International Criminal Tribunal for Yugoslavia (ICTY), 132–3
International Electrochemical Commission, 99
International financial governance. *See specific topic*
International Financial Organization (proposed), 5
International Financial Reporting Standards (IFRS), 71, 73, 74–5, 107, 109–11
International law, international financial governance and
generally, 10, 122
aggression, crime of, 131–2
argumentative nature of, 129, 130, 131, 133
breach of obligations, 130
comparison of international financial governance with other institutions, 40–1
consensus and, 133
constructivism and, 130–1
coordinative role of, 127, 128, 129–30
customary international law, 122–3
dualist versus monist views of, 124–5
horizontal nature of, 129
human rights and, 125–6
international criminal law, 131–3
jus cogens, 123–4
legal process approach, 126–7
legitimation of, 122
peremptory norms of, 123–4
realism and, 127–8
revisitation and, 129, 133
similarities between, 133–4
skepticism toward, 127–8
state interest and, 133
treaties and, 123
written rules, 128–9
International Law Commission, 123–4, 128
Internationally active insurance groups (IAIGs), 91
International Maritime Exchange, 74
International Monetary Fund (IMF)
generally, 2
Basel Committee and, 48
China and, 40–1, 148
creation of, 5
developing countries and, 149
FSB and, 18
international financial governance compared, 40–1
peer review and, 29, 30, 32–3
regulatory networks and, 33, 101
WTO and, 144
International Organization of Securities Commissions (IOSCO)
generally, 9, 15, 62–3, 99
Affiliate Members Consultative Group, 64
African-Middle East Regional Committee, 66–7

IOSCO (cont.)
Asia-Pacific Regional Committee, 66–7
Basel Committee compared, 62, 63–5, 67–8, 70, 75
best practices, 71–2
board, 66
budget, 66
bylaws, 64, 65–6, 77
China and, 67, 142, 143, 148–9
consensus in, 63, 68
consultative committees, 67
Core Principles, 73, 81
CPMI and, 112
cross-border enforcement and, 14
currency pools and, 72
currency swaps and, 72
European Regional Committee, 66–7
exclusivity of, 15
failure to promulgate standards, 71, 74–5
FATF compared, 107
flexibility of, 67, 70
FSB supervision, 63, 68
general secretariat, 66, 77–8
harmonization and, 68–74
high-frequency trading and, 72
historical background, 64
IAIS compared, 83, 85
IASB compared, 108, 109, 110–11
incorporation of, 65
informal "club" structure, 64–5
institutional form of, 63–8
Interamerican Regional Committee, 66–7
International Disclosure Standards, 73, 81
joint reports, 70–1
London Interbank Offered Rate (Libor) and, 72
as member of FSB, 18, 20–1
membership, 64
Memorandum of Understanding on Enforcement (MOU), 63, 69–70
MFN treatment and, 23, 24
money laundering and, 70
national treatment and, 22
notice and comment process, 63
Objectives and Principles of Securities Regulation, 70, 74, 148
peer review and, 63, 75–6
as policy source, 15, 72
Presidents Committee, 65–6
Principles for Financial Market Infrastructures (PFMIs), 22, 112
quiet integration and, 37
regional committees, 66–7
regulatory cooperation and, 68
as regulatory network, 101 (*See also Regulatory networks*)
Resolution Concerning Mutual Assistance, 69
rulemaking and, 25, 26–7
short sales and, 69
successes of, 68–74
UN compared, 66
WTO compared, 66, 76
International Standards on Auditing (ISAs), 104
International Swaps and Derivatives Association, 157
Interpol, 106
IOSCO. *See* International Organization of Securities Commissions (IOSCO)
Iran, FATF and, 107
Ireland, IASB and, 109
Italy, Basel Committee and, 57

Jackson, John, 25
Japan
Basel Committee and, 33, 57
Financial Services Agency, 88
FSAP and, 30
FSB and, 33
IASB and, 109
IMF and, 40–1
regulatory networks and, 143
World Bank and, 40–1
Jessup, Phillip, 126
JPMorgan Chase, 27
Jus cogens, 123–4

Kapstein, Ethan, 99
Karmel, Roberta, 109
Kaupthing, 156
Keohane, Robert, 39
Klieman, Gary, 67
Kokott, Julianne, 43

Lasswell, Harold, 133–4
Lefort, Daniel, 124
Legitimation
of international financial governance, 122, 124
of international law, 122
Lehman Brothers, 54, 71, 156
"Level playing field," 21–2, 159–60
Libya, US air strikes in, 130
London Charter, 131
London Interbank Offered Rate (Libor), 72

Maastricht Treaty, 28, 36
Malanczuk, Peter, 124, 129
Mattli, Walter, 99
McDougal, Myres, 133–4

MetLife, 27
Mexico
  Basel Committee and, 15
  IASB and, 109
  swap lines and, 58
MFN treatment. *See* Most favored nation (MFN) treatment
Mitrany, David, 33–4, 43–4
Money laundering, 70. *See also* Financial Action Task Force (FATF)
Monist view of international law, 124–5
Moody's, 54
Morgan Stanley, 27
Morgenthau, Hans, 39–40, 127
Most favored nation (MFN) treatment
  generally, 6
  Basel Committee and, 23–4, 47
  EU and, 32–3
  FSB and, 23
  GATT and, 23
  G20 and, 23, 24
  IAIS and, 23
  IOSCO and, 23, 24
  as rule of international financial governance, 23–4
  trade versus international financial governance, 24
  WTO and, 23, 32–3
Muller, Huib J., 1, 50
Multilateralism, 159
Musca, Xavier, 4

National Association of Insurance Commissioners (NAIC), 85, 86, 87–8
National treatment
  generally, 6
  Basel Committee and, 21–2, 47, 56
  EU and, 21, 32–3
  FSB and, 21–2
  GATT and, 21, 22
  G20 and, 22
  IOSCO and, 22
  "level playing field" and, 21–2
  "ring fencing" and, 22–3
  as rule of international financial governance, 21–3
  WTO and, 21, 32–3
Neocolonialism, 149–50
Netherlands, IASB and, 109
New Haven School, 133–4, 141
Newman, Abraham, 39, 99, 131
Nicaragua Harbors case (ICJ 1986), 130
Nomura, 57
Nordic Supervisory Group, 50
North Korea, FATF and, 107
Nuremberg Trials, 131

Obama, Barack, 94
Organisation for Economic Cooperation and Development (OECD), 53, 101

Pakistan, FATF and, 107
The Paquete Habana (US 1900), 122–3
Paraguay, IOSCO and, 66
Pauwelyn, Joost, 34–7, 44
Peer review
  generally, 6–7
  Basel Committee and, 29, 30, 47, 50, 56
  in crisis response, 155
  FSB and, 19, 131, 139
  GATT and, 30
  G20 and, 29–30
  IAIS and, 30
  IMF and, 29, 30, 32–3
  IOSCO and, 63, 75–6
  as rule of international financial governance, 29–31
  World Bank and, 29, 30, 32–3
  WTO and, 30
Permanent Court of International Justice (PCIJ), 125
Ping An, 147
Porter, Tony, 67, 99
Portugal, Basel I and, 53
Posner, Elliot A., 39, 99, 127, 137
Post-crisis financial regulation
  generally, 6
  Basel Committee and, 58
  G20 and, 16
  institutions of international financial governance and, 14
  regulatory networks and, 31
Powell, Jerome, 2, 47
Principles for Financial Market Infrastructures (PFMIs), 112
Prudential, 27
Public Interest Oversight Board (PIOB), 104–5

Quarles, Randal, 2

Raustiala, Kal, 8, 9, 38
Regulatory cooperation
  CPMI and, 112
  in crisis response, 154–5
  IAIS and, 83–4, 88
  IASB and, 68
  IOSCO and, 68
  "sticky" nature of, 3

Regulatory networks. *See also specific network*
generally, 4–6, 7
bylaws, 32
decentralization in, 32
deposit insurance and, 99–100
flexibility of, 31–2
FSB and, 101
G20 and, 101
IMF and, 33, 101
informal creation of, 31
legal authority of, 32
as main vehicle for international financial governance, 31–2
OECD and, 101
other networks, 10, 99–100, 113
post-crisis financial regulation and, 31
quiet standard setters, 101–2
UN and, 32
World Bank and, 33, 101
WTO and, 32
Restatement (Third) of Foreign Relations Law, 8, 33, 123
Revisitation, 129, 133
"Ring fencing," 22–3, 56
Romano, Roberta, 39
Rome Statute (ICC), 131–3
Rulemaking
generally, 6
adjudication versus, 25
Basel Committee and, 25, 47
best practices, 26–7
EU compared, 24
FSB and, 25, 27
"hard" rules, 25–6
harmonization, 25–6
IAIS and, 25
IASB and, 25
IOSCO and, 25, 26–7
as rule of international financial governance, 24–8
WTO compared, 24
Rules of international financial governance
generally, 9
contextualizing, 32–4
MFN treatment (*See* Most favored nation (MFN) treatment)
national treatment (*See* National treatment)
peer review (*See* Peer review)
regulatory networks (*See* Regulatory networks)
rulemaking (*See* Rulemaking)
subsidiarity (*See* Subsidiarity)
Russia
Basel Committee and, 15
G20 and, 16
regulatory networks and, 143

Sabel, Charles, 33–4, 44
Saudi Arabia
Basel Committee and, 15
G20 and, 16
Schwarcz, Stephen, 145
Securities
"building block" approach, 79
in China, 147–9
IOSCO (*See* International Organization of Securities Commissions (IOSCO))
short sales, 69
Securities and Exchange Commission (US) (SEC)
cross-border enforcement and, 14, 62
financial crisis and, 54
GAAP and, 75
IASB and, 109, 110–11
International Disclosure Standards and, 80–1
IOSCO and, 64, 66, 72–3, 74
regulatory networks and, 32
Seidenstein, Thomas R., 118–19
Shadow banking, 145–6
Short sales, 69
Siloing, 14
Simmons, Beth, 73
Sindona, Michele, 4
Singapore
Chinese securities firms relocating to, 147
swap lines and, 58
Singer, David, 39, 99, 131
Slaughter, Anne-Marie, 7, 31, 38, 40, 127
Soft law, 7–8
South Africa
Basel Committee and, 15
FSAP and, 29–30
IFRS and, 109
South Korea
Financial Supervisory Service, 88
swap lines and, 58
Sri Lanka, FATF and, 107
Standard & Poor's, 54
Stanford, R. Allen, 62
Stanford International Bank, 62
Stark, Barbara, 136
State Street, 27
Statute of the International Court of Justice, 8, 11–12
Steiner, Henry, 126–7
Subsidiarity
generally, 6
Basel Committee and, 28–9
EU and, 28, 32–3

FSB and, 28–9
GATT and, 28
as rule of international financial governance, 28–9
WTO and, 28
Sullivan, Thomas, 93
Suzuki, Eisuke, 134
Swap lines, 58, 153–4
Syria, FATF and, 107
Systemically important financial institutions (SIFIs), 84

Taiwan, Financial Supervisory Commission, 88
Tanzer, Greg, 66
Terrorism. *See* Financial Action Task Force (FATF)
Trans-Pacific Partnership, 94
Transplants, 144, 149–50
Treasury Department, 2
Treaties, 123
Treaty of the European Union (Maastricht Treaty), 28, 36
Trichet, Jean-Claude, 4
Trump, Donald, 2–3
Turkey, Basel Committee and, 15
Tweedie, David, 118–19

Uniqueness of international financial governance, 160
United Kingdom
Basel Committee and, 57
Basel I and, 52, 56
Brexit, 36
China compared, 148
EU and, 36
FSAP and, 30
IASB and, 109
IOSCO and, 71
regulatory networks and, 143
state interest regarding international financial governance, 133
United Nations
Charter, 3, 33
crime of aggression and, 131–2
Economic and Social Council, 125–6
Human Rights Committee, 126, 137
IOSCO compared, 66
regulatory networks and, 32
United States
Administrative Procedure Act (APA), 67, 73
Basel Committee and, 33, 47, 48
Basel I Accord and, 52, 53, 56
Basel II Accord and, 59
Board of Immigration Appeals (BIA), 25
China compared, 148
Commodity Futures Trading Commission (CFTC), 64, 72, 73–4, 81–2
cross-border resolution and, 157–8
Dodd-Frank Wall Street Reform Act, 13, 94–5
Federal Deposit Insurance Corporation (FDIC), 4, 48, 102, 145
Federal Insurance Office, 83, 94
Federal Reserve, 4, 48, 58, 83, 153–4
Form 20-F, 73
FSAP and, 30
FSB and, 33
General Accounting Office (GAO), 60
IAIS and, 86, 89
IASB and, 109, 110–11
ICC and, 133
IMF and, 40–1
international law and, 122–3, 125
IOSCO and, 63, 71, 72–4
Libya, air strikes in, 130
National Association of Insurance Commissioners (NAIC), 85, 86, 87–8
National Labor Relations Board (NLRB), 25
Office of the Comptroller of the Currency (OCC), 48
regulatory networks and, 143
Sarbanes-Oxley Act, 71, 72
Securities and Exchange Commission (SEC) (*See* Securities and Exchange Commission (US) (SEC))
"single point of entry," 157–8
state interest regarding international financial governance, 133
systemically important financial institutions (SIFIs), 84
United States Trade Representative (USTR), 94, 95
US-EU Covered Agreement, 83–4, 94–6
World Bank and, 40–1
University of Reading, 57

Vagts, Detlev, 126–7
Verdier, Pierre-Hugues, 38–9
Vermeule, Adrian, 127
Vienna Convention on the Law of Treaties, 123, 125, 136
von Rosen, Ruediger, 68

Walsh, David, 89–90
Weber, Max, 138
Weiler, Joseph, 34–7, 44, 158–9
Wells Fargo, 27
White, John, 109–10

World Bank
generally, 2
China and, 40–1, 148
creation of, 5
developing countries and, 149
FSB and, 18
international financial governance compared, 40–1
peer review and, 29, 30, 32–3
regulatory networks and, 33, 101
WTO and, 144
World Trade Organization (WTO). *See also* General Agreement on Tariffs and Trade (GATT)
China in, 145
"governance without law" in, 3
IMF and, 144
international financial governance compared, 34–7
IOSCO compared, 66, 76
MFN treatment and, 23, 32–3
national treatment and, 21, 32–3
negotiations regarding joining, 144
peer review and, 30
regulatory networks and, 32
rulemaking and, 24
subsidiarity and, 28
Treaty, 36
World Bank and, 144
Wright, David, 66, 75–6

Yemen, FATF and, 107

For EU product safety concerns, contact us at Calle de José Abascal, 56–1°, 28003 Madrid, Spain or eugpsr@cambridge.org.

www.ingramcontent.com/pod-product-compliance
Lightning Source LLC
LaVergne TN
LVHW022218200926
848481LV00006B/2016
9781108468596